Ghosts Have Warm Hands

A Memoir of The Great War
1916-1919

by

Will R. Bird, MM

The 42nd Battalion, The Black Watch of Canada

CEF BOOKS

Canadian Cataloging in Publication Data
Bird, William R. (Will Richard), 1891-1984
Ghosts have warm hands: a memoir of the Great War, 1916-1919
ISBN 1-896979-00-9
1.Bird, Will R. (Will Richard), 1891-1984. 2. Canada. Canadian Army. Battalion, 42nd--Biography. 3. World War, 1914-1918--Personal narratives, Canadian. I. Title.
D640.B52 1997 940.4'8171 C99-017909-5

Published by: **CEF BOOKS**
P.O. Box 40083
Ottawa, Ontario, K1V 0W8
613-823-7000

This publication has been supported by the Canadian War Museum.

Originally published by Clark, Irwin & Company 1968.

Second printing October 2002

Also by CEF BOOKS

Access To History; The Canadian History Series

Number 1: **Gas Attack! The Canadians at Ypres, 1915**
Number 2: **Futility & Sacrifice: The Canadians on the Somme, 1916**
Number 3: **Winning The Ridge: The Canadians at Vimy, 1917**
Number 4: **Slaughter in the Mud: The Canadians at Passchendaele, 1917**
Number 5: **The Suicide Raid: The Canadians at Dieppe, August 19th, 1942**
Number 6: **D-Day! The Canadians And The Normandy Landings, June 1944**
Number 7: **Deadly Mission: Canadian Bombers Over Nuremberg, March 1944**
Number 8: **Hard-Won Victory: The Canadians at Ortona, December 1943**
Number 9: **The Battle For The Atlantic: The Royal Canadian Navy In The Second World War, 1939-1945**

CEF CLASSICS

The Letters of Agar Adamson edited by N. Christie
Only This by J.H.Pedley
The Great War as I Saw It by F.G. Scott
For Freedom And Honour? by A.B. Godefroy
The Journal of Private Fraser edited by R.H. Roy

Preface

"Ghosts Have Warm Hands" is one of the most powerful memoirs ever written about the First World War.

It's original incarnation was published in 1930 under the title "And We Go On". The author, a soldier in the 42nd Canadian Infantry Battalion, The Black Watch of Canada, experienced 2 years of Hell on the Western Front. It is remarkable how Will Bird has recorded his war in such exceptional detail, and how the character of his comrades shines. His story reflects the power of the camaraderie felt by the soldiers of the First World War, specifically their loyalty to each other and their pride of being "in the trenches". "Ghosts Have Warm Hands" also shows the humour these men used to protect themselves and to survive in circumstances beyond our comprehension. To read about the humorous experiences and the practical jokes against such a deadly backdrop is an insight -a step into another time.

What is also unique about "Ghosts Have Warm Hands" is that the events and the people are completely verifiable. I have researched the men mentioned in the text and have been able to identify almost all of them. They are listed alphabetically in a "Glossary of Names" at the back of the book. Of the 120 or so soldiers mentioned in the book, half did not survive the war. Many of those were recruited from the same region of Nova Scotia as Will Bird and enlisted in the same Battalion, the 193rd Nova Scotia Highlanders.

Will's experiences were not only physical but also ethereal. Within his exceptional detail is also a rarely discussed event "the psychic side of war". In fact the author, Will Bird, wrote in his preface to "And We Go On" that the book was an effort to reveal the psychic or supernatural effects war had on its participants. He wrote " Every human emotion ran its full gamut in that land of topsy-turvy, and prolonged tensity of feeling wrought strange psychological changes which warped the soul itself....Unconsciously there were born faiths that carried over through critical moments, and tortured minds gripped fantasies that served in place of more solid creeds.".

There can be no doubt that the death of his younger brother, Stephen, in 1915 profoundly affected Will in his attitudes towards the war, the Authorities that conducted it and the Germans. His strong personal connection with his beloved brother seemed to enable him to connect with him in the hereafter. Stephen's parting comments to Will were " if there is anything I can do for you, just let me know, and if I don't come back maybe I'll find a way to come and whisper in your ear".

Even in the post-war period when Spiritualism was an important vehicle to the hundreds of thousands bereaved families, Will knew his own experiences would be difficult to grasp so he recorded each of them in his diary. "Every case of premonition I have described is actual fact; each of my psychic experiences were exactly as recorded". Supernatural experiences are not new in War memoirs, but to mix it in with the accuracy of Will Bird's story enhances the credibility of Will and Stephen's encounters.

Will Bird was a front-line soldier and an exceptional observer of the character of men. And never has the character of men been tried like it was in the First World War.

"Ghosts Have Warm Hands" records those observations, those characters, the agony felt by those men from so long ago. It captures events of 80 years ago for a new generation, to whom the name of Passchendaele has long passed out of meaning.

Will Bird's personal agony remained with him until his death in 1984. The nightmares caused by the horrors haunted him until his death. The brutality of war refused to leave him alone, and in 1944 at Buron, Normandy Captain Stephen Stanley Bird, the son Will Bird had named after his beloved brother, was killed. He was 24.

I respectfully dedicate the reprint of this Classic memoir to the Memory of Stephen Carmen Bird (1886-1915) and Stephen Stanley Bird (1920-1944).

Norm Christie

Contents

Maps

Map 1: The Western Front

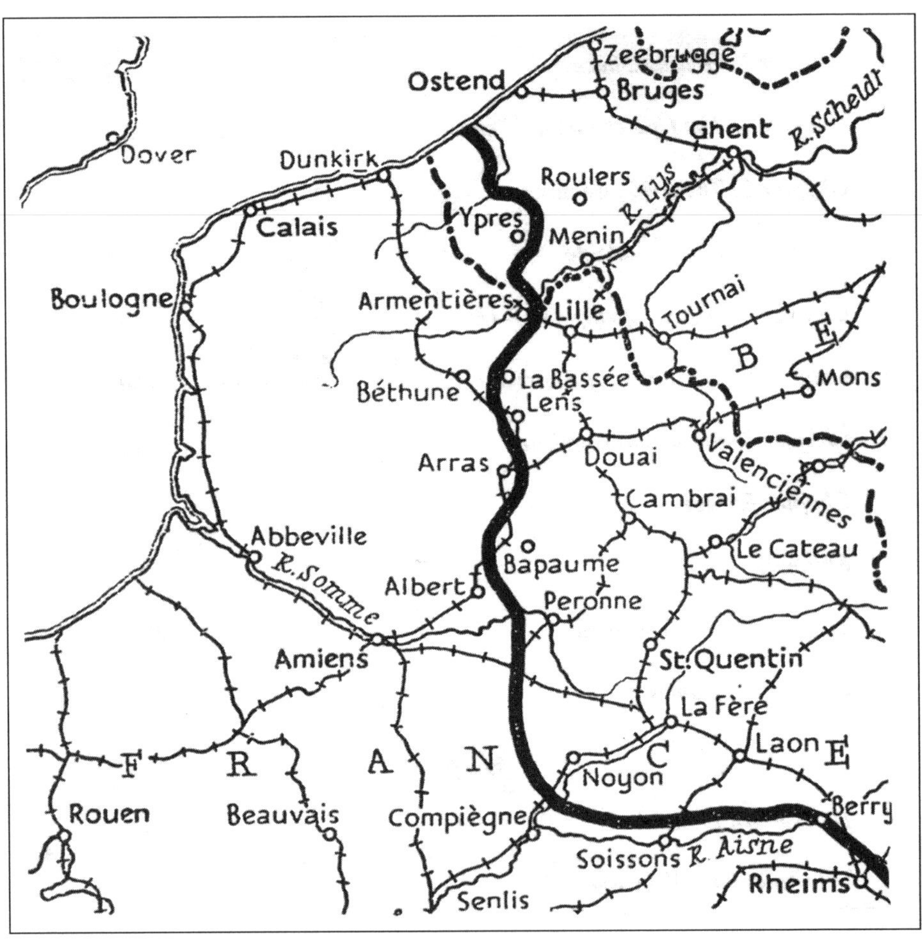

When recruiting for World War 1 began in my home town of Amherst, Nova Scotia, I was twenty-four years old. I had been in Western Canada on a harvest excursion and had serious thought of settling there, but I returned home to enlist at the outbreak of war. Nevertheless, twice as many men tried to enlist as were needed and any excuse was used to turn a man down. In my case it was bad teeth. Disgusted, I went back to the West and was there when my youngest brother, Steve, was killed. I immediately returned and tried again to enlist, was accepted, reached France in December 1916 and served until the war ended with the 42nd Battalion, Royal Highlanders of Canada (Black Watch), composed largely of men from Ontario and the Maritimes.

It was a wonderful experience, in the sense that life in the trenches forced men to know each other in a manner that is impossible in civilian life. One got to realize that courage is a quality which comes to the fore unexpectedly and is often greatest where least expected.

Fictitious names have been used frequently in order not to cause any curiosity on the part of readers. The events related in this book, however, are all true; their telling is based on diaries that I kept during the period.

Chapter 1: Getting There

It was a warm July day at Aldershot Camp in Nova Scotia, and "B" Company of the 193rd Battalion of the Nova Scotia Highlanders Brigade had fallen in and was standing at attention while orders were read. The last one startled me: "Lance-Corporal W. R. Bird will take a six-weeks' course at the Royal School of Instruction, beginning today. During the period he will be exempt from all battalion duties."

An hour later I was listening to a lecture on night marching. It was the summer of 1916. I had no thought of being accepted for overseas after three failures due to bad teeth, but when I heard old Doctor Baird was the recruiting medical officer in our town, reportedly getting two dollars per man, I headed for his office. In ten minutes I was "in." He did nothing save fill out papers. I had known him for years and had guessed what he would do.

Through the spring we had drilled at Amherst. My younger brother, Steve, had enlisted in the 25th Battalion in 1914 and had been killed in action in France in 1915. The last time I saw him we had a long talk and he held my hand in his warm grasp as we said goodbye. "If I don't come back," he said, "I'll try to find some way to keep an eye on you."

Knowing him as I did, I felt a queer thrill go over me. Later his letters from England tried to induce me to stay home. All the army brass, he wrote, were incredibly stupid, the weather in England was horrible and it rained half the time. When he reached France he emphasized the fact that army life was far from ideal.

The second morning at classes in the training school we were lined up and given boxing gloves-odd numbers taking on the even. My first opponent was from the Cape Breton Highlanders. Fortunately for me, he was as slow as he was big and I survived. The next morning I faced a chap my own size and ability from our "A" Company and no harm was done. But the third morning I was out of luck. My odd number was from the 97th American Legion and grinned as he told me he had been in the ring in Boston for many bouts. "Don't be scared," he said. "I won't hit you. Just you try and hit me. It will be a workout."

I did my best but could not land a blow, and suddenly an officer from Brigade was standing beside us, watching. "Move!" he snapped at me. "Use some footwork. Change your style."

He became sarcastic as he watched my efforts, and suddenly the Boston lad suggested gently that the officer put on the gloves and show me. No sooner had he spoken than the officer shed his tunic and took my gloves. He was a well-built man and at least twenty pounds heavier than the boxer.

It was all over so quickly. In less than a minute the officer was lying on his back listening to the birdies, a whistle had blown calling us to the dug trenches, and I was hurrying away as fast as feet would take me.

The course became increasingly tougher. We were at the halfway mark when I returned to camp one night at five to find it deserted and our sergeant-major roaring at me to get on my equipment and fall in for guard. He had been seven years in the British Army, had a bull voice, and long acquaintance with the second-in-command, another Englishman.

Are you crazy?" I asked. "Read the orders by the colonel's tent." They stated I was exempt from all battalion duties while on the course.

"Don't talk back to me," he roared. "Get on your equipment. What had happened was that the battalion was out on field work and had not returned, and he had suddenly realized it was our turn for guard, a point which he had completely forgotten. Had he so explained it to me and asked me to do him a favour, I would have responded gladly, though I was very tired and hungry.

As it was, I told him I had nothing to do with the battalion and walked off to town. When I returned late I was placed in a prisoners' tent and in the morning was marched before Major Fordley. Our commanding officer, Colonel Stanfield, a fine man, was often absent. When I was marched in I was asked what I had to say.

"One question," I returned. "Are the orders posted in front of this tent true or false?"

"You are impertinent," snapped the major. "Seven days." The seven days were to be spent at our "Fox Farm" on the hill. There all were kept under close guard like criminals, given bread without butter and slim rations, made to march back and forth each day wearing full pack. The man in charge was from the American Legion, a rough-tongued, red-faced bully called Simms, whose continual shout was "You broke your mother's heart but you can't break mine."

We had one respite. When Sergeant W. A. Fox of our own unit was in charge, he marched us from sight into a grove of trees and there we rested a full hour. The worst punishment was the lack of food. Old bully Simms had his tent at the entrance to the Farm, and each night at six a cook delivered an entire roasted chicken with all the accompaniments to his table. The prisoners had been reduced to three and we slept in the first tent inside the Farm. So I concocted a plan. At a few minutes to six we would take our water pails and apply to the guard to be taken to the pump, which was within ten feet of Simms' tent. We watched. The chicken arrived but Simms was not in sight. The guard was a nervous type and when we came with our pails he told us to hurry. I filled mine, while the other two bumped against each other. There were hot words and they came to blows. The guard tried to break it up and was twisted about so that his back was to me. The chicken was dropped in my pail of water. Then I begged the chaps to ease up. They did, and a thankful guard got us back into the Farm.

There were six tents in a row reaching back from the entrance. I went through them to the last one, unrolled the tent flap, put the chicken in it and rolled it up again. I was just back in our tent when Simms arrived, had a quick look around and began shouting.

The guard was grilled without mercy. Simms yelled at him until he scarcely knew what he was saying. A sergeant was called. Soon he and Simms came into our tent and searched where we slept, looked around to see if we had dug a hole anywhere to bury the lost one. No luck. They searched the other tents. Dire threats were made and after an hour another chicken arrived. We had no light of any sort and had to turn in at dark. At ten Simms sneaked in the gate and came to our tent with a flashlight, but we were lying there and looking hungry. He tried it twice later, so we made no move until two a.m. Nothing ever tasted sweeter than that chicken.

That turn in the Fox Farm changed me from a soldier proud to be in uniform to one knowing there was no justice whatever in the army. I was determined to buck every Simms and Fordley I met, to outwit all their type if possible.

We were marched on board the *Olympic* at dusk and sailed for England on Friday, October 13, which date made some of the lads miserable. Being last on the boat we were consigned to the smelly depths of "F" deck, where the hammocks were strung so closely it was necessary to crawl under them on hands and knees. The odours were terrible. I went up on deck at once and watched some Lascars emerge from a ladder way. A moment's chat with them informed me that one could use the ladder to go to any deck, even the upper boat deck which was out of bounds to us. So around ten that night two figures went up the ladder to the forbidden territory, quickly untied the covers of a life boat and got into it. There we slept in clean fresh air, and in the morning were down below as our fellows were astir, swearing about the foul air that had more than twenty of them sick.

The next night was equally pleasant, but then the sergeant-major spotted me and Bill Brown together. We were both in his bad books. Brown had outwitted him by making an appeal to the company commander when he was placed on guard duty out of turn. The sergeant-major took us down a deck to a ship's officer and said we were to scrub decks. Then he left. The officer pointed to mops and buckets, and he left also. We had no instructions so we went toward a door facing us, opening it with care and ready to duck away if it led to an occupied room. But no one was there. The place had cupboards on both sides, and tables. We took our mops and bucket with us, waited a moment, listening, then opened one of the cupboards. It was filled with pies!

We selected a cherry, used a knife from the table drawer to cut it in half, and had a real feast. There was a door at the other end of the place but it was locked. The pie having vanished, we explored further. We seemed to be in a food storage. In one cupboard were roasted chickens, still slightly warm. It was about eleven so we figured the noon meal for officers would include chicken, and as our breakfast left much to be desired we hastily divided one of the birds, placed it in our empty pail, and retreated. Across the way from where we had met the ship's officer were three doors. One was locked but the second opened into cases of canned goods, piled high. Most of them bore Australian labels and it was easy to realize they contained canned rabbit.

The nearest cases made good seats and there we sat and ate our chicken, a long and very satisfactory ritual. What to do with the bones became something of a problem but was solved by dropping them back of the farther row of cases, which were about four inches from the wall. We reached Liverpool in five days and during that period digested seven pies, three of them cherry, and five chickens. We went to our table at mealtime to get tea but ate little, and were kidded as really being seasick. Each day we went at the same time to do our shopping for food, and each day we left our mops and bucket in a corner of the first room. No one moved them.

We arrived at Witley Camp in Surrey on a miserable day, wet and chilly. Our hut had a stove at one end. The "beds" were boards on blocks that kept us about ten inches from the floor. Brown was for taking a place near the stove, but most of the boys had hurried out to find beer, and I could visualize the results. So I took a place at the cold far end of the hut. Brown refused to join me. About half an hour after "lights out," the sergeant of Five Platoon and six others arrived, all tanked with beer. They fell around their beds, arguing loudly as others came in. The sergeant insisted on a quick lights out, and most of them simply took off their boots and that was their undressing. The stove was stoked to redness and those nearest it complained bitterly. An hour later the parade to the door began. It was left open much of the time, letting in a chilly fog, while a pair would stand in sock feet and urinate just outside. The climax came when one lad staggered from his repose to let loose against the stove. Rough hands propelled him to the door and he sprayed all the way.

We were inoculated. The food was horrible. The weather was clammy and no one seemed to know what we were to do. But Brown and I found that Godalming was a nice little village near our camp, and there we went as much as possible. Leave was given and all of us went to London for six days as our turn came around. I went with my older brother, Hubert. We found the city an enormous place, crowded with Australians. Getting overnight accommodation was a problem. By late afternoon we were near Westminster Abbey and saw a place run by the Catholic Women's League. We went in and had tea to take off the chill, asked about a room for the night and were told by two of the ladies to return if we had no luck. We had no luck and slept that night in the little pool room of the place, on a bed made up on the floor. It was warm and we were happy there, making the place our headquarters. The main feature of our leave was going to "Chu Chin Chow," one of the finest shows I have ever seen.

Arrived back at camp, I was harshly told by the sergeant-major I was to go on a three weeks' "wiring course." The vehicle taking us would pick us up in an hour's time. There were two men from the 134th Battalion, myself and a man from the 219th in the truck, and we went no more than ten or twelve miles before arriving at a dismal-looking wartime building. In a field nearby were three lengths of barbed wire fences. They were different in design, and at the far end of the fences were four or five rolls of wire and a maul! This was to be our "course."

We saw a pub in the distance, and a small shop. There was a farm across the road with carts in the yard and hens wandering around. The truck drove away and left us there, so we dumped our equipment in the building and went to the pub. Two sergeants from a British unit, a Bedfordshire regiment, sat like stewed owls by the stove. Four privates from Canadian units were in a cluster nursing beer mugs. They grinned greetings, and within ten minutes we learned they had been at the place four days and had not so much as touched the barbed wire. The head lad was an English officer and he had vanished, probably on a big bust, and the two sergeants had been drinking steadily. They slept at night in the "ice box" and returned to the pub when it opened. The quartet slept in the haymow of the barn. It was decently warm, as there were cattle just below.

This place was our first big eye-opener as to what went on under the heading of "military training." We stayed our allotted time. An elderly corporal who nested in the rear part of the "ice box" prepared our meals. We had enough money, however, to buy good bread and pastry from the farm kitchen. We slept in the haymow and it was warm. The officer never returned while we were there. We took long walks when the weather was decent, and when it wasn't we sat in the pub. We never had one hour's instruction and, as far as we could tell, the two sergeants were never sober.

There was little drilling going on when I returned to the company. There had been a great row over the food, a small riot when the cooks had things thrown at them. A hundred and one rumours were circulating. We heard there was a pay day near, and the next day a notice was posted saying men were wanted to go to France to reinforce the Black Watch. In ten minutes I was before the major asking permission to go. He agreed but the medical officer turned me from the draft on account of my bad teeth. I asked if he could not have the dental officer put them in order, and he said there was not time. I went out and saw across the road a draft of the 134th Battalion on dental parade. Going to one chap who was my build, I offered him two shillings to let me take his place. He quickly agreed. We exchanged tunics and caps and I took his pay book. Their dental officer looked at my teeth and said three were in bad shape, should be pulled. I told him to go ahead. He seized his pliers. Twenty minutes later I was before the company commander again, requesting to be placed on the draft. He looked at my mouth and agreed.

Brown had got on the draft without trouble. We went that last evening to Godalming and had a decent meal, a good bath and an hour's enjoyment of fine music, then were seized at camp for being out of bounds and went to France under open arrest.

Chapter 2: The Crater line at Vimy

It was a wild December night when the boat left Southampton, terrific wind and rain. Rumour said we would not sail, but a rough sea meant trouble for the submarines, and after being filled with pies and rolls supplied by women who came to the dock, we filed on board. As soon as we were out in the Channel all went below and the deck was battened down. The sea often washed right over the craft. We had to strap all our equipment to anything solid we could find and lie down, as the wild tossing would throw you violently. In an hour nearly everyone was sick and casting up all that had been eaten before getting on board. The passageway to the boiler room below had a ledge about twenty inches wide on the right of the stair, with an iron rail running three inches high. I lay on the ledge and gripped the rail. The fumes from below were as nothing compared with those around me. At midnight I was sick for five minutes, taking care to be well away from my ledge. Then I returned and slept till morning.

When we docked in Le Havre the deck was a fearsome sight, the men trying to clean their uniforms. The stench was deadly. I got my equipment and edged close to the exit. Then we were allowed up. The gangplank was already down. I raced to the wharf and never stopped. There were some buildings beyond and I shot into the first alleyway. The others yelled laughingly after me, but an officer halted them. Then he and another came and picked out twenty of the men looking fittest and took them back to clean the boat with mops and buckets. The task took an hour. The rest of us stayed in the sunshine while they laboured.

As soon as we marched away from the dock, French women and kids were alongside trying to sell "Apoo, Choc'lay, Orange."

We gave them no heed and after quite a march arrived at a camp that was three inches of mud no matter where you turned. We were shown tents on a slope. The floor boards had the same list as the hill, and the unfortunate who slept on the downward side might slide out in the night. At mealtime we waded through the slime to the door of a long dirty hut. Inside the entrance, a trio of unwashed characters broke up loaves of bread and tossed a chunk to each man, the size of your chunk depending on your luck. Another pair poured each man a tin of cold, greasy tea and you received a piece of stringy meat in your messtin top. You went to long tables and ate your food from your fingers. Everything was dirty. Presently an officer and sergeant entered the front of the hut and walked rapidly between the tables, not looking right or left. At the rear door they paused just long enough to shout: "Any complaints?" They vanished before anyone could reply.

The next day we were marched up steep hills and winding, greasy paths, with full packs, to the "Bull Ring," where we made the rounds of specialists in bomb throwing, trench building and bayonet fighting. The mud and the inane chatter of the instructors were enough to make anyone desperate, and after four days of it I saw in the grey light of dawn a large draft of men being sent from tents farther up the hill. They went without breakfast in chilling mist. I spoke quiet words to Brown, Belliveau and another. We got out early to the "dining room" and back before the rest, seized our belongings and hustled up to the vacated tents. They were piled with abandoned blankets. We selected one tent, settled in it, listened to the sergeants haranguing the men in the muddy lanes below, and saw the column march away, slipping and sliding as usual then lay back in the blankets and slept the morning away.

In the afternoon I started my diary. Tommy sat up and began writing in his. "I can hear them `canaries'[1] at the Bull Ring," he said. "That Welsh sergeant is yapping like a fox terrier. Over at the bags the bayonet lad is spitting blood and yelling that the only good German is a dead one. He said if he had fifty in a row he would go along and cut the throats of every one. Did you ever hear such rot?

No one came near us. We got meals and were never questioned. Some men were detailed each morning to remain behind to "clean" the camp. Probably it was felt we had clicked for such duty. We went to the town one evening, a long walk, and found it organized to separate the soldier from his money with the least possible effort.

The main places open were two lousy movies and red-light centres. We were glad when our train pulled out of Le Havre. In mud and slush and a snowstorm we had been paraded through an open hut, stripped naked save for boots that the muck tugged from our feet, to be examined by a doctor who sat in the gloom beside a table and checked off names. He did not even look up as I went, in full vocal condemnation of the whole setup, to dress again in the mud.

"This programme is arranged," Tommy shouted, "to make us glad to go up the line."

The train moved slowly, and as it went we heaved from the windows the body belts that had been issued, odd tins of bully and enough ammunition to reduce our loads to reasonable weight. The track was littered with material as each man dumped his lot.

All the time we had been at Le Havre we had no mail, but when we left the train and started marching toward Mount St. Eloi a sergeant brought a cartload of parcels. There were no letters, however. We stopped at a miserable farm overnight and there divided our treats. Several of the men had not received anything but we made it up to them. I had three parcels, and our supper was fruitcake and fudge. Since all we had for the day was tea and bully, we ate plenty.

In the morning a dull thudding noise woke us. We sat up, shivering, and looked at each other, conscious of a queer tightening inside. Part of it was caused by too much fruitcake, but the rest was caused by the thunder of the guns. Our parcels lost their importance. We drank the hot tea a surly army cook served us and went to the farm house, carrying all the cakes and candy that were left over. Three skinny women and a swarm of kids fought over us as we gave out the lot.

We began marching and with each mile the thudding of the guns increased. As we passed the twin towers of the old abbey of Mont St. Eloi, a sergeant of the 42nd Royal Highlanders of Canada joined us. He led us to their transport lines and there we were lined up for an inspection. We were very hungry, had marched fast in a drizzle and were ready to collapse. A brick-hued, bulging officer inspected us. He looked as if he had been bred in the purple hielands o' bonnie Scotland, and he talked as if he considered himself the repository of the regimental honour. He told us we must realize what great privilege was ours to join the ranks of the Royal Highlanders. He hoped, he said, that we would do our best-and his tone implied that he thought our best would be pitiful enough and that implicit obedience to all orders would be much to our advantage.

[1] Military Instructors

At dusk another sergeant came and led us to Neuville St. Vaast to join the battalion. It was January 3, 1917. We were told the place had once been a town built on chalk, but shell fire had reduced it to rubble. Soldiers occupied the cellars. We were divided into groups and eleven of us were shunted into a cellar, in which were timbers holding shreds of wires. They had been bunks once. Rats ran into holes as we lit candles and then came boldly back and stared at us. It was a cold and wet-smelling place. We sat on our packs and wondered. There was Arthur Burke, Herman Black, Laurie Bacon, Mel Baillie, Belliveau, Roy Baxter, Earle Black, Ira Black, Brown, Mickey and myself. Our guide had gone. Not an order had been given us, we knew nothing about the lines, where we drew rations, or what platoons we were supposed to be with.

"Let the Royal gents do the worrying," said Brown. "They know where to find us."

We could hear voices, so I looked into the next cellar. It was the same as the ane we were in. Hugh MacKinnon was there, Charlie Jenkins, Glenn Lunn, Howard Gordon, Christensen, Legge and Joe McPherson. Tommy came in behind me and looked around.

"Next door," he said, "they have dandy bunks, hooks for the equipment and braziers heating the place. I said `hi' to them but they never answered. We're stuck in these holes because we're new."

"Sure," I agreed. "And in six months' time we'll do the same with other new ones."

We went out together and around a corner to see a man dragging a pack out of a low entrance. "Are you looking for a billet?" he asked.

"You bet," said Tommy."Get right in there, then," said the man. "There's bunks and a stove and extra blankets. We're moving out."

Ten minutes later Laurie and Tommy and Baxter and I were in that cellar. Our equipment was hung in place and we each had a good bunk. No one came to disturb us. We had a comfortable night. Next day Tommy and I went outside and looked around. We saw signs, "Keep low. Use trench in daytime," and went along to find a Y.M.C.A. canteen. We bought tinned goods and chocolate and went back to our little home and stayed all day. At night we went out again and found the sergeant-major's place. He was Scottish and dour but a very decent sort. He piled out sixty letters for our group, told us we were in "D" Company and that his name was Kennedy. We could ask him anything we wanted to know.

On our way back we went by the cellar we had first entered and saw Mickey. "How did you like it?" he asked.

"Like what?" blurted Tommy.

"The working parties." Mickey told us that all the draft but our four had gone to a trench in front and filled and emptied sandbags until nearly morning. It had rained and been beastly cold.

We grinned and went back to our cellar. For three days we stayed there and drew rations. Then, through Tommy's being anxious to see what the front was like, we ventured out after dark and fell in with the crowd. The sergeant in charge was a small man with a caustic tongue-Joe Waite. He put three of us under a Corporal Stevenson, who told us within ten minutes he was a veteran of the South African War, that the 42nd was the best unit in the 3rd Division, and we were "damn lucky" to be with it.

He led us down a long trench, and at last we were really at the front. We had become used to the slamming roar of gunfire and now we also heard the barking of machine-guns. Bullets came singing overhead, to go swishing into the darkness. Some struck on wire and we heard the sibilant whine of ricochets. We had sandbags to fill. One man held them and the other shovelled in gruel-like mud. When twenty were filled a man jumped on top and emptied the bags as they were handed up to him. It was ticklish work, as the one emptying had to jump down when machine-guns opened on that section.

We got soaked to the skin. The cold slime ran down our wrists as we lifted the bags, and our boots sunk in the mire until our feet were numbed, sodden things. All the next day we growled at Tommy for causing us such a night. Then, at dusk, Stevenson found us. Three of us were to go at once to an emplacement used by a big mortar they called a "flying pig."

When we got there we noticed a peculiar odour. All the shapeless ruin of Neuville St. Vaast stank of decay and slime, but this new smell halted us. "Here's bags," said Stevenson. "Go in there and gather up all you can find, then we'll bury it back of the trench. Get a move on."

A "flying pig" had exploded as it left the gun and three men had been shredded to fragments. We were to pick up legs and bits of flesh from underfoot, place all in the bags and then bury them. It was a harsh breaking-in. We did not speak a word as we worked. When we were done Stevenson told us we could go, but Tommy and I lingered in a trench bay and stared over the dark, flickering, silhouetted landscape.

Over the tangle of wire in front lay the no man's land about which we had heard. Not two hundred yards away were the Germans in their trenches. A thin stalk of silver shot up as we looked, curved over in a graceful parabola and flowered into a luminous glow, pulsating and wavering, flooding the earth below with a weird, whiteness. It was a Verey light. We craned our necks and stared. Jumbled earth and debris, jagged wreckage: it looked as if a gigantic upheaval had destroyed all the surface and left only a festering wound. Everything was shapeless, ugly and distorted.

We went on doing working parties and gradually got acquainted with the rest of the company. There were only a few "originals," the rest were reinforcements like ourselves, mostly from the 92nd of Toronto. Back we went to Mont St. Eloi and were billeted in huts on the hillside. It was wet and freezing cold at night. After the first day of sleeping and resting the men grew garrulous, and we listened to all they said about different craters such as Patricia, Birken, Common and Vernon. Across from where we slept was a Scot who was always singing "Maggie frae Dundee" or quarrelling with Stevenson, who had charge of the hut. Next to him was a tall, clean-built man, Roy MacMillan, from the 92nd. He and I became friends and he told me his experiences on the Somme.

When we went back for a second trip in the line, the wind was raw with driving rain. Once more we were on working parties. All this time we had not got to know an officer, and when we asked who commanded the company all they grunted was "Dugout Ray." One night Tommy and I were detained by Stevenson, who had us repair a place that had caved in. We were wet and cold and hungry. Rations were very slim, six men to one loaf of bread, and only bully and hardtack to help out. The hot tea kept up the morale. We got our messtins from our bunks and went over to a corner, where a sullen-faced man dished out the dinner. He stayed in the dugout and heated tea and mulligan and though he avoided shell fire we did not envy him his lot. There was no tea for us, he announced, but at that moment Stevenson came and got his messtin full.

We stepped forward and looked in the dixie. There was plenty more and I said so. The cook snarled back that we had better be in France more than five minutes before trying to run things. Tommy took charge. He was well built and fast with his hands. He gave the fellow one short minute to fill his tin or else. The tin was filled. Later, when we were supposed to be sleeping, I heard the "old-timers" discussing us. They agreed it would be bad policy to try to run us, and the cook received no sympathy.

It was another six-day trip, but when we went back to Mont St. Eloi we felt old soldiers, and "Maggie frae Dundee" rang out merrily. This time there was a parade. Our company commander was a genial-looking gentleman. Our platoon officer was a MacDonald and seemed a good sort. We were taken to the "baths." In an old building through which the winter wind whistled, we undressed on a floor covered with slime and in turn crouched under an icy trickle from overhead pipes, the water always failing when one had soaped himself. When we went to get dressed we found our shirts were gone and a bleary-eyed character tossed over any size garment he happened to pick up, with unmatched socks.

When we went back to the line, Stevenson told me I would be one for Vernon Crater, and from the way he said it I judged it would be something unusual. Roy MacMillan joined me and said that he was to team up with me, that Vernon was a three-sentry post, had not been held in daytime before, and was not more than sixty yards from German posts. We were to hold the place for four days.

The weather turned the coldest France had known in thirty years. All the ground was frozen like iron. We wore leather jerkins over our greatcoats, had Balaclavas under our steel helmets, and socks on our hands. The supply of gloves was only enough for the oldtimers. It was very clear weather and every sound carried, so that we moved with utmost caution and very slowly. The main trench was a long, black-shrouded ditch full of dark figures muttering to each other, and there were hissed curses when a steel helmet clanged against a rifle barrel.

We turned from the main trench and went up a low-walled reach to the post, a wide affair in three sections. The right-hand corner was like an enlarged well with a fire step. Two men were placed there. On the left was a similar post and in it were Laurie and old Dundee. MacMillan and I were in the centre, a cup-like hollow. Behind us was a roofed space about six feet square in which Corporal Sellars, in charge, stayed. He had a seat there, a flare pistol and flares, and extra bombs. A blanket was hung over the rear entrance.

MacMillan explained everything about sentry duty, and I did not duck when the first flares went up. We could hear the Germans walking in their trenches, hear them coughing, hear them turning a creaking windlass that would be hauling up chalk from a dugout under construction. At daylight we put up small periscopes on slivers stuck in the sandbagged parapet and watched through them until dark.

The next night I saw my first uncaptured German. He was only a boy, as young-looking as Mickey, and he was standing waist-high above his trench wall as one of our flares burst directly above him and placed him in dazzling light.

He did not move at first-both sides had strict orders against any movement when a flare burst-but I knew he had seen me because I was as high on our side. He waved, and some wild impulse caused me to wave back to him as I jumped down. MacMillan cursed me soundly. After midnight I stepped back to talk with Sellars and, as it was bright moonlight, pushed aside the blanket at the rear and looked toward our trench. Ping! A bullet embedded itself in the wooden post beside me. I ducked back, very frightened. There were hurried steps outside and a corporal from the trench wanted to know if anyone was hit. A new draft of men, the 132nd from New Brunswick, had come into the line and one of them had watched our post all the time, thinking it was the German front.

A light snow fell the next day and whitened the jagged wilderness between the lines. There was a wrecked cart near the German wire, and as I peered at it, it blotted out, then appeared again. A whisper alerted MacMillan, and we detected two of the enemy crawling outside their post. "If we can catch them it's leave for us," hissed MacMillan. "Strip off your gear."

We shed jerkins and greatcoats and steel helmets, and examined our rifles. Unluckily mine stood at the back of the post and water from melted snow had frozen over the muzzle. MacMillan's had the breech uncovered and it was a lump of mud and ice. We jumped for our bombs and found them blocks of frozen mud, then looked over and saw the Germans re-entering their post. With first light we cleaned our rifles and bombs and made sure they would remain in good order.

Each morning a sergeant brought a rum issue just before light. I did not take mine and Laurie did not take his. A dozen or more of us in the draft never drank or smoked. This morning an officer was with the sergeant. He came in and stood beside me as MacMillan had his turn off and asked many questions while the sergeant was at the post on the right. He told me his name was Larson, that he was from Bear River, Nova Scotia, and thrilled with the front line. He wanted to know how near the Germans were.

I told him and he said it sounded unreal to him. It had become light as he talked, and when I put up the periscope it was shot away by a German sniper. "That fellow must be very near," said Larson.

"I'll take a quick look."

"Don't!" I yelled and grabbed at his coat. He stretched up in spite of my protest. The bullet entered his forehead and went out the back, breaking the strap of his helmet and carrying it to the rear of the post. I lowered the body to the trench floor and covered the face with a clean sandbag.

MacMillan was shocked. "Too much rum!" he said. The sergeant came from the other post and he was stunned. He said he would report what had happened and was hardly away when we heard a shot on the left post. The sergeant had given old Dundee two extra rum rations, mine and Laurie's, and the Scot had seized his rifle and started to clean it, saying he was going to get the sniper. The weapon went off in his hands and the bullet struck the frozen side of the post, chipping bits from it. One struck Laurie on the foot and stung badly.

MacMillan tried to calm Dundee but he refused to listen. The rum had him wild. He raised up to aim his rifle, and the German shot. Dundee's head was turned so that the bullet took both eyes out. He tumbled down, clawing at his face and groaning.

Something had to be done and quickly. Sellars would not go for help. So I shed my equipment and crouched low as the sergeant had done. It was hard to keep that way, but when I raised ever so little a bullet burned the back of my neck like a hot iron. I reached the trench and got a stretcher bearer and stretcher. We were careful going in and arrived safely. But Dundee was in a bad state. We had to tie him on the stretcher, as he would not listen to anyone. Getting the stretcher and its load to the trench took almost half an hour. The stretcher bearer was ahead, pulling the stretcher, and I pushed from the rear. Finally it was done. Then I crawled back and sat all day beside the dead officer.

At dark we were relieved by the Princess Patricias. We went to Neuville St. Vaast again and into the cellars. Before morning a few of us were called out to form a ration party and we saw how easily a man could get a "blighty." We passed an old ruin with a long wall extending beyond it, light flickering through a small opening as flares went up. As we passed by there was a snapping of machine bullets overhead but they were disregarded, since the wall protected us. Then a man behind us yelled. A chance bullet had come through that brick-sized opening and hit him in the leg. He was bandaged and went cheerfully down the line.

When we returned with the rations I slept several hours, then was wakened and told to put on my pack and go with three other men to Mont St. Eloi. There we would meet a sergeant who would take us to a bombing school. The three of us met, had no conversation, but trudged out of the line and in due course arrived at long huts, where we found ourselves with men of the other battalions of the brigade. We were to be instructed in shooting rifle grenades and throwing Mills bombs. Our practice would be with live ones.

It was very pleasant. The hours were short and the rations plentiful. The next day at noon as we lolled in our bunks, there was a sudden shrill tearing sound and a terrific explosion just outside. Pieces of shrapnel came through the side of the hut. We leaped to the floor and raced from the building. A second shell came and there were loud cries for stretcher bearers. Four men were killed and seven wounded, but there was not a third shell.

To my delight I quickly learned the proper elevation for shooting rifle grenades, made top marks and also did well with the throwing. The battalion came to the huts at Mont St. Eloi and had it easy. When our six-day course was over I reported back to the platoon and was told I had been transferred to the battalion bombers. Tommy declared I had pulled strings to get such a shift. The weather became colder than ever, and we went into the line again and relieved the Pats.

The bombers were a grand lot, and I teamed with Sammy Sedgewick, a real gentleman. Chiefly we had to patrol the trenches. We had a good dugout and plenty of rations, and our hours were much easier than in the company, where a man did six hours on and six hours off with monotonous regularity all the time he was in the line. There you came down from your post, chilled through, dazed from lack of sleep, and pushed your way into the crowded underground to your chicken-wire bunk. You could lie and eat your rations, and consider yourself lucky if there was any lukewarm tea. The warmth of the men thawed the earth and chalk walls enough to make them ooze dampness. Rats were everywhere, podgy brutes with ghoulish eyes. They crawled over you as you lay under a blanket and tried to shiver yourself warm.

Twice in one night Sammy and I had a bomb target. A sentry stopped us and whispered as he pointed to dark blurs working at the German wire. We sent two rifle grenades among them and a Lewis gun helped to complete the job. Later another sentry said the Germans were working at something opposite his post; he could hear thumping sounds, as if they were driving posts. We listened and heard the noise, set our rifles carefully and fired. There was the red flash of explosion and then a long-drawn yell that ended in a screaming heard all along the line. The enemy sent over "darts" in reply, but none fell near us.

It was cold as ever the next night and no working parties were about. The ground was like rock. Sammy and I found a Lewis gun crew asleep, every man, and removed the gun, threw chalk and wakened them. They had a bad minute and didn't likely doze again that night. Sometimes I stopped with Mel Baillie or Mickey or Jenkins and talked with them of the home town.

The war changed men mightily. Down in dugouts where there was hardly room to breathe, men who had come from comfortable homes moved without complaint. All grousing was reserved for the "brass hats," who were supposed to be responsible for all that went wrong. The men were unselfish, each with a balance and discipline of his own. We endured much. Dugouts reeked with odours of stale perspiration and the sour, alkaline smell of clothing. There was never enough water to permit frequent washing and when we could get warm the lice tormented us. The vermin were in every dugout, millions of descendants of the originals of 1915. We seared the seams of our shirts with candles, fought them constantly but never conquered them.

The third afternoon the sergeant sent me on an errand up La Salle Avenue, a trench often strafed. Another man was walking ahead of me, and as we hurried along I heard the familiar *phew-phew-phew* in the air and yelled. The fellow sprinted like mad and I tried to follow suit, but my world crashed in a bang. A million bells rang in my ears. Lights danced and sparkled and I could not get my breath. Hands tugged at me. Eventually I got up, to stare at a smoking crater not ten feet from where I had fallen. The big "rum jar" had fallen between us, though the other man was twice as far from it. He was shell-shocked and taken from the line. I was sick for an hour and my head throbbed half the night but I stayed in the trenches.

The next night I stopped to talk with Fernley, a quiet fellow of the 42nd who was a real friend. He stood his rifle against the side of the trench and was pacing up and down and beating his chest with his arms in an effort to get warm. We chatted a time and then I moved on and was about ten yards from him when a German "dart" burst on the parapet several feet from where Fernley was walking. He sank to the duckboards like a wet sack. I hurried back to him and spoke but he did not answer. He was dead.

There was not a mark on him. I got the sergeant and he examined Fernley, but he was mystified too. We carried him to the dressing station and they stripped him and could not find a mark of injury. I went back to the trench and looked around. Suddenly I noticed Fernley's rifle still standing there-and the top part of the bayonet gone! The mystery was soon solved. The piece had entered an armpit and pierced his heart. Not a drop of blood had issued from the wound.

We were in supports again, then back in the front trench. Seven men went out with sickness, two with foot trouble, and I found myself on a crater post doing a regular turn of six hours on. It was very cold and I was about fifteen yards from the main trench. One night I saw someone coming up the sap with no rifle. That meant he was an officer, and when he stood with me in the post and asked questions I was careful, for a time, about what I said. He asked me where I was from, what I had done before the war. I told him of taking up a homestead in Alberta, the big money I had made for a time working for an eccentric American who used the name Smith. Smith had imported four wolf hounds from Russia and purchased a pair of half-broken broncos and a buckboard. He built a large box on the back of the buckboard and put the hounds in it. The box had a door attached to a wire. When he saw a coyote we drove past it, and at the second of passing the door was flipped up and out shot the hounds, who would run the coyote down. There was a bounty of fifty cents per coyote snout. I told the officer about our hunts, about the hard work on the harvest field, and about the sugar maple trees in the hills where I was born. He stayed and stayed and brought the talk around to the battalion. How did I like the infantry? I was careful, and he knew it. He laughed at some of my answers and finally asked me if I knew who he was. I said I had no idea. He asked who commanded the 3rd Division.

"Major-General Lipsett,"[2] I said.

"Does he ever come to the front line?" was the next question. I said I did not know. We were standing shoulder to shoulder in the narrow post and he nudged me. "You're an interesting fellow, Bird," he said. "I am Lipsett!"

The information was so surprising I became tongue-tied and he nudged me again. "I don't blame you in the least if you don't believe me," he said, "so I'm going to give you a snapshot I had taken in 1913. All I ask is that you will not tell your mates I did so."

He tugged the postcard-size snapshot from an inner pocket and gave it to me, shook my hand warmly and left. I still have that picture.

The sergeant came and said I was for a reconnaissance with him. We crawled out under our wire at a place where it had been raised, and moved away by inches as we wormed between Durrand and Duffield Craters. After each yard we listened, so that it was an hour before we were in a position to examine the enemy wire. When we got back to our trench we were nearly frozen. The other bombers said a raid was to be made from both our craters and from the Patricia posts. The next day the Stokes mortars pounded the German line.

The raid was on February 13 and zero hour was 9:15 a.m. The German trench was to be given a baptism of rifle grenades, so each bomber was given ten grenades. We had exactly two minutes to shoot them. It was easy to make a mistake and cause a premature burst, but no accident occurred and we got our barrage away on time. Then we went into a tunnel entrance and awaited the raiders' return. Two officers and six men were wounded. Two prisoners were taken.

That night we relieved the "Van Doos" and it was my job to guide their bombers to our dugout. There were only six of them and they had me nervous before my chore ended. They had had too much rum, they lagged all the way, talked loudly, and one man played a mouth organ. The 42nd bombers took a chance overland and we got out ahead of the company. Shortly after they took over, the Germans gave the Van Doos a housewarming in the shape of a "Minnie" bombardment. We were told they had thirty casualties in the hour.

[2] Major General Louis J. Lipsett (1874-1918). Commander of the 3rd Canadian Division, 1916-18. Killed in action October 14, 1918.

The next day we marched and marched and marched, going through several towns, and at last arrived at Divion. After the long session in the crater line with little exercise, it was a hard grind. Three fellows dropped out. My legs were very tired but I lasted the route. We moved into a billet and a runner arrived to tell us the bombers were no more. A re-organization was taking place and we were to return to our respective platoons.

When I woke in the morning I was very stiff and sore. Someone reported me, and the battalion medical sergeant, a prince of a fellow, came and asked me about my experience with the "rum jar." He said I had undoubtedly suffered a concussion, that I was to remain in billets and go on sick parade in the morning. Our billet was a French cottage, a miner's home. Downstairs was a fair-sized room with a tall, pot-bellied stove, table and chairs. Two small bedrooms opened from it. Upstairs was one large space. There was no window and we slept on the first floor, four of us.

I was glad to go on sick parade in the morning, as the battalion was to be reviewed by General Nivelle[3]. Captain Hale, the gruff medical officer, asked a few questions, then gave me a paper and told me to report to a medical hut in Bruay for a heart examination.

Three others were going to the same hut and we sat in the chilly outside room for two hours before an orderly came and asked our errands. The man next me had sore feet and said he had been there since nine o'clock. There were twelve of us in all and we sat there, shivering, until one o'clock. Then a doctor appeared and snatched our papers from me and from the man with the sore feet, since we were seated nearest the inside door. Then he reappeared and yanked me into the inner room, where four medical officers were sitting and a stove gave lovely heat. I was ordered to remove my boots. I protested, tried to tell them it was my heart that was to be examined. I was sternly told to keep quiet. One doctor scanned my feet briefly, ordered me to put my boots on again. Then I was thrust out and they yanked in the fellow who had the bad feet.

Back at billets I found the medical sergeant and told him what had happened. He advised I see Captain Hale and get another paper from him. I declined, then was at once notified I was up for guard. We had by all odds the finest regimental sergeant-major in the 3rd Division-Percy MacFarlane. He had talked with me several times, telling me he was from Nova Scotia and proud of it. Now he came and told me not to worry over shining brass or the like.

We were marched to an old brick barn and reached our quarters overhead by a shaky ladder on the outside of the building. It was terribly cold. The barn had a hundred vents for the wind. We lay on bare boards and it was impossible to keep warm. The sergeant went away, returning after a long time with a jug of rum. Earle was on guard with me and neither he nor I took the regular rum rations, but we were shaking with cold and the sergeant gave each of us a cigarette tin of rum. It warmed us to a certain extent but we were soon cold again. The sergeant went away, the jug with him, saying it was a foolish stunt to have a guard there on such a night. So we simply moved into the *estaminet* and stayed there until midnight when it closed.

The sergeant did not return and after another half hour of waiting we went to our billets. There was nothing whatever to guard.

Christensen, the Dane, got in wrong with the officers on Sunday. He suddenly decided not to go on church parade, saying he had no religion, was an infidel. They

[3] General Robert Nivelle (1856-1924). Commander of the French Army, 1917

crimed him for his refusal.

The sergeant did not return and after another half hour of waiting we went to our billets. There was nothing whatever to guard.

Christensen, the Dane, got in wrong with the officers on Sunday. He suddenly decided not to go on church parade, saying he had no religion, was an infidel. They crimed him for his refusal.

Some mail reached us the next day, and, as I had only candles for light in the cottage loft, I asked Madame if I could write some letters on her table. She could speak some English and was most friendly. She said I was to come down any time I was not sleeping. So I brought my paper, and had just begun to write when she filled a tin washtub with water that had been heating on the stove and without ceasing to ask me questions about Canada, in which she was intensely interested, began stripping off her clothes. Soon she was naked and standing in the tub, but the conversation went on. It was a startling experience and was redoubled when the daughter, who worked in the coal mines, came in. She calmly undressed and got into the tub after adding some hot water. She was as slim as her mother was fat and I made a lot of mistakes in my writing. Before I had finished Father arrived, stood in the tub and was scrubbed by Madame.

One of the chaps in the loft with me was Flynn, an Irishman who had false teeth. They were army issue and did not fit properly, so he took them out for sleeping. He came in late that night after having many beers in the *estaminet.* So he only took off his boots and put his teeth on the floor before dropping into slumber. Soon we were wakened by wild yelling. A rat had come up through the wall and seized Flynn's false teeth, and was dragging them to the hole in the wall when Flynn wakened. He was not quick enough. Down the wall went rat and teeth. The shouting was enormous and Flynn stormed downstairs where Madame and Monsieur were lighting a lamp. There was nothing they could do, as there was no opening in the wall. The argument and commotion lasted an hour and next day Flynn went on sick parade to get new teeth.

That night the sergeant-major called me to his billet and asked if I would like to be promoted. He said papers received showed I had been an N.C.O. in my old unit. He was very kind despite his gruff appearance, and I told him I wanted to have much more experience before thinking of such a move. He said I was probably right but they were very short of corporals.

Some of our men were sleeping in a barn on straw. Three of them had heavy colds. One was Hillary from our unit, a college graduate from a good home. He was very sick that night, and Christensen went to the medical officer and said it was necessary to get an ambulance at once to take Hillary to hospital. He was told the patient would be examined the next day, but the ambulance did not come until late afternoon. It was altogether too late. Hillary died the next morning. Christensen was so angry that he wrote a letter to Hillary's parents telling exactly what had happened. The letter was stopped by the censor, and Christensen was given fourteen days' punishment.

New platoons were formed and all were shifted into new billets. I found myself at the other end of the village, teamed with Charlie MacDonald, an "original" who had been in the transport lines and had come to grief through some infraction of the rules. He was a fine type and we were good friends at once. Burke was with us, a clean lad who spoke French fluently, along with Tommy and a chap named Jasper.

Map 2: The Crater line at Vimy

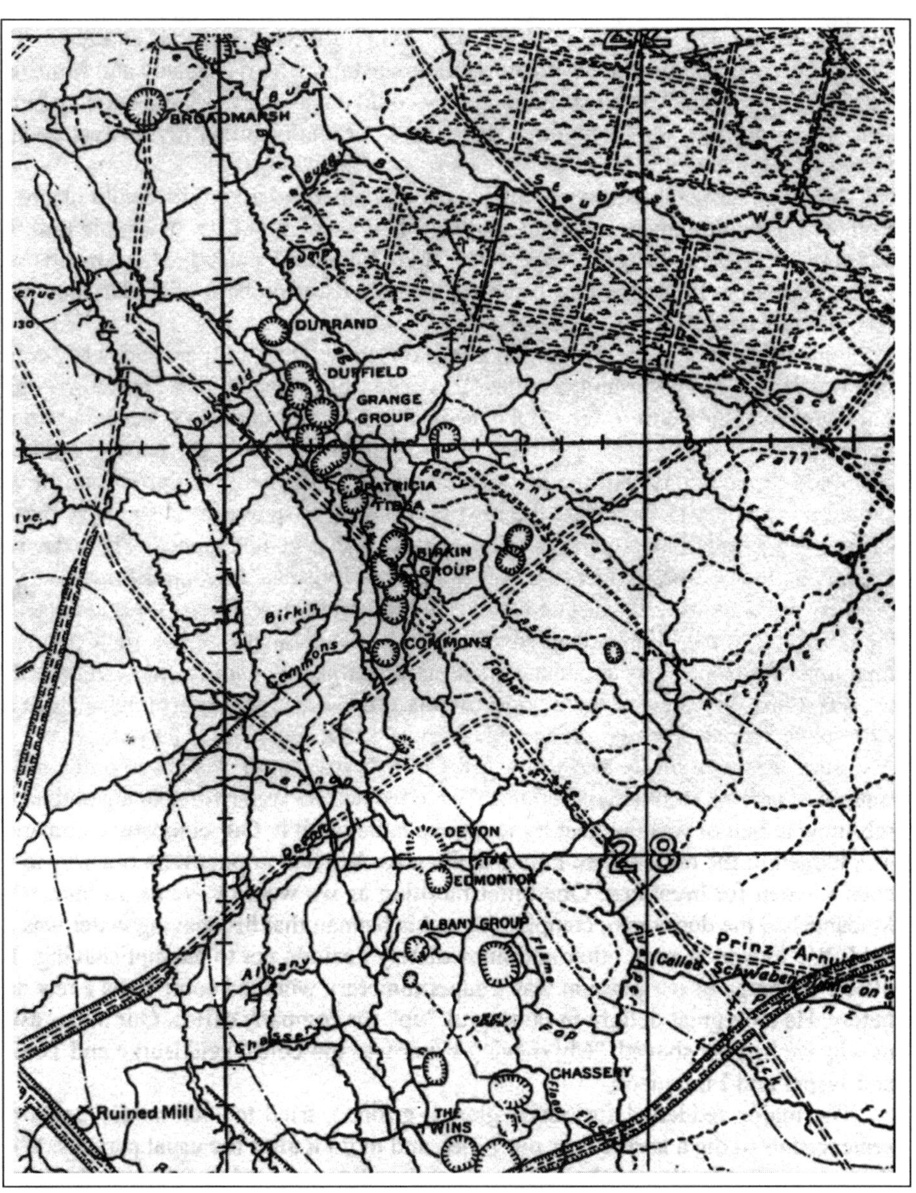

New platoons were formed and all were shifted into new billets. I found myself at the other end of the village, teamed with Charlie MacDonald, an "original" who had been in the transport lines and had come to grief through some infraction of the rules. He was a fine type and we were good friends at once. Burke was with us, a clean lad who spoke French fluently, along with Tommy and a chap named Jasper.

Water was very scarce at my new billet. The house pump was out of order and all water was carried from a neighbour's. Twice we had no water for shaving and had to rub snow in lieu of washing and try to force a lather with it. Our company commander was lodged in the only decent house in the area. We had to pass it on our way to the cook kitchen for breakfast. One bitter morning as we went by we heard him, when Madame had the door open, complaining to his batman that his shaving water was too cold. We looked at each other and immediately decided not to attempt shaving. The officer in charge of our platoon was a supernumerary who had come to us a few days before. He took great delight in putting us "up" for company office. Our major asked us why we had not shaved. "My shaving water was too cold," said Burke and Tommy and Jasper and I in unison.

The major reddened furiously, glared, grinned, tried to look severe again and sentenced us to dig a latrine near our billet, and to do it after the usual parades. When the time came, a burly member of the military police escorted us to the garden of one of the French houses and ordered us to go to work. The owner of the place happened to be home. He emerged and asked, in French, what we were doing. Burke at once explained we were going to bury some doubtful bombs there. They might not explode but we had decided they were not safe to have at our billets. The Frenchman went wild. He tore the shovels from our hands and threw them away, then rushed at our escort as if he would claw him. That gallant hastily told us to stand by for further orders. We went back to our billets and there the matter ended.

The 42nd had a good football team and it defeated the Shino Boys (Royal Canadian Regiment), then the 49th, and we were marched to Marle-les-Mines to watch them play. They won the divisional championship. Sir Robert Borden[4] came and reviewed us, then General Lipsett and finally General Byng[5]. The old hands said we were in for a bloody slaughter after so many inspections, and the next day we began to train over tapes representing the German trench system at Vimy Ridge.

One day I was given just enough fatigue duty to clear me from parade and was going back to my billet when I was approached by Sergeant Jim Cave of the battalion scouts. I knew him by sight, and everyone who mentioned him said he was one of the very best. He told me he was going to arrange some targets to shoot at and asked me if I cared to come along. In Canada I had taken great delight in shooting and had made high scores in training, so I went eagerly. I found the targets were simply tin cans stuck on a hillside. I surprised Cave. There were four of his snipers and myself and we began shooting. In ten shots I never missed, and seven hits were the best his snipers made. Cave took a can and placed it at 150 yards, telling me I could

4 Sir Robert Laird Borden (1854-1937). Prime Minister of Canada, 1911-1920.

5 Sir Julian Byng (1862-1935). Commander of the Canadian Corps, 1916-1917. overnor-General of Canada, 1921-1926.

use a rest. I punctured the can on my first try. Then he asked what platoon I was in and where I had learned to shoot. I told him how much I had handled hunting rifles, that my father, an officer of the old 93rd Regiment, had been an expert marksman.

The battalion moved to Dumbell Camp, a miserable swamp in the wood near Villers-au-Bois. We bagged slimy mud and made walls three feet high, four feet apart, then covered them with corrugated iron, anything we could salvage, and camouflaged the whole with broken branches from the wood. It was wet and very cold and rations were scarce. The round French loaves we had bought in Divion soon vanished and we were seven on a loaf. Even bully was scarce. Never again was I as hungry as during that period. If we saw a bit of hardtack tramped in the mud, we would seize it, rub off what mud we could and eat it.

From that mess and in a half-starved condition we were rushed to the front line. The Germans had blown a mine north and adjoining Durrand Crater, and a party of them had been repulsed by our "A" Company, which was in the line. Thirty yards of front line had been destroyed and it was important that a new trench be made, with saps leading to new posts. This was to be our job. The Germans shelled the Quarry Line and all the back areas as we marched in, and the slippery mud made the going hard.

More new men had joined us at Divion. Among them were a pair generally avoided. Slim was a tall, thin, bony lad, not over seventeen, uneducated, who had lived like a gipsy until the war. An illegitimate from a New Brunswick village, he did not know who his parents were and could not read or write. Joe, his mate, was a French Canadian, uneducated, who had no dependents. They did not get any mail, were slovenly in drill, would not wash or shave unless compelled to do so.

As we entered the communication trench Slim fell in at my heels. Burke was next to him, then Laurie. An officer named Stewart took charge of us, and we filed from the cover of the trench to open ground. Sharp orders were hissed at us. A brigade wirer led the way. We had to dig in along tapes and were exposed, in easy range of enemy snipers and machine-guns. The mud was deep and we did not know our location. Each man worked feverishly. All around us in the dark was a deafening clamour of shell fire and rattling of machine-guns. Flares were soaring in quick succession, illuminating the area where we dug.

Slim stuck so close to me I had to push him back in his position. We dug and dug. I struck barbed wire in tangles, and the brigade man came with his cutters and helped me clear the lot. He was not twenty feet away when he groaned loudly and sank to earth, shot through the body. Bullets were snapping all around us. Slim crouched down on his knees and huddled close to earth, yet never slackened his shovelling.

Suddenly there was another call for stretcher bearers. Lieutenant Stewart had been shot through the stomach. He died that night. Finally Slim and I had our portions dug as deeply as required and were out of the rifle fire. We sat there while the others finished, and when all were done, word came for us to go back. We had not gone a dozen yards when Burke dropped, shot through the head.

It was daylight when we reached camp. We had left at seven in the evening. No rations had come up so we simply scraped mud from our legs and crawled into our swamp shelters. About two in the afternoon rations arrived. We sat up and ate our sixth of a loaf there and then, made a messtin of hot tea and ate a precious tin of bully, then lay down again. At seven orders came and we marched out again, chilled to the bone, still hungry and very tired. Once more we worked under machine-gun fire, but we were mostly deepening shallow trenches and making posts with fire steps, and none of our party was hit. We stumbled back to camp at daylight, so exhausted we scarce knew what we were doing, each man moving automatically, trying to follow the fellow in front, shaking with cold, heavy-eyed in the grey light, every muscle clamouring for rest, for the torpor of sleep. Once more there were no rations. We made a tin of tea, drank it and wormed, mud and all, under the corrugated iron.

A third night we went, forcing ourselves into action. We had eaten all our rations when they arrived and had two tins of hot tea. The Hun was shelling more fiercely. As we entered the sunken Quarry Line we came in contact with a line of mules going up with rations and ammunition. Our party took the near side of the embankment and suddenly Hun "whizz-bangs" began to erupt all along and we crouched to cover. Twice we narrowly escaped a salvo and then, just before reaching the head of our trench, more shells came. I jumped ahead and squeezed between a mule and the bank. The brute knew as well as I the safety of the earth wall and thrust solidly against me, pinning me so I could not move.

Wham! Wham! Wham! Three explosions so near I could feel the "lift" of their concussion. Then wild yells: "Stretcher bearer! Stretcher bearer! On the double!" Men were down on the rails behind us and those in front were running for the trench mouth. Tommy found me when I called to him, and he came to the rear of the mule and pulled it by the tail. It tipped over, sagged in a heap, dead, and I discovered my legs were soggy with its blood. It had saved my life.

Up in the trenches the men were so dead beat the non-coms could not make them work, no matter how they threatened. Every man was desperately hungry. We went back an hour earlier than previously, but were an hour later getting out. Some of the men simply sagged down, indifferent to everything, completely exhausted. Those of us who kept going soon were away from the officer and non-coms, who were finding it difficult to get the party back. At the camp there was no sign of Laurie. He had fallen in some distance behind me on the way up and I had not seen him. I waded through the slime until I found the stretcher bearer.

"Who was hit at the Quarry Line?" I asked.

"Four," he said. "Laurie was badly hit, a hole by his spine. We sent him back but he'll never make it. Cockburn was hit in the legs and it was he who did the yelling. That small shrapnel is like fire. The other two were from Thirteen Platoon."

With Laurie gone, I had the shelter to myself. When the rations came I did not tell them he was not with us, but took his ration and ate it as well as my own. That night we went in and took over the front line.

No sooner were we established than a sergeant came and told me I was to report to Cave-I had been transferred to the snipers. For a moment I was tempted to refuse no matter what trouble resulted, for Sellars had just arranged that I would be on his post with MacMillan, and I was to have the next six hours off duty.

However, I swallowed all retorts and went with the sergeant. Cave and the snipers were in a snug dugout. They had plenty of rations and I was immediately given my share. Cave told me I would work with Pearce, an English chap who was a very reliable sniper. In the next bunk were Gordon Sedgewick, a brother to Sammy but entirely different, and Farmer. Lance-Corporal K. K. McLeod was in the corner and he was one of the finest men in the whole battalion.

That night the Germans bombarded our trenches but no one was hurt. "Rum jars" put our candles out and brought down showers of chalky earth, but the roof held. In the morning Pearce and I went out, as soon as it was light, to a sniping post on the crater line. After a really fine dinner with the snipers, and an excellent breakfast, I felt more like myself. A steel plate was placed on a high point and camouflaged on the enemy side with wire and rubbish. We lay on dry strips of brick and blocks that never held any rain, and there was a depression dug out by shovel like an armchair for the man not watching at the plate. Pearce swung back the small plate that covered the observing slit and told me to use his glass and scan the German lines.

It was most interesting, as the powerful lens brought everything to you with startling clearness. The various colours of the German sandbags were clear, spades lying on the parados, tiny curls of smoke issuing from a dugout flue, and the occasional glimpse of the tops of big pot helmets as their wearers stepped over some small barriers. For two hours I lay there until my legs were cramped and chilled from the unusual position, then Pearce led the way back to the dugout-to get a pot of hot tea. What a change! We simply went out to the sniping post when we felt like it, came in when we felt like it, had a bite to eat when we felt like it, and had more food than I had seen in months.

In the afternoon we went again as a faint drizzle ended and there was some indifferent sunshine. While studying a tangle of wire and stakes away over on the left I had a momentary view of a grey figure flitting to cover, but that was all. "Don't be discouraged," advised Pearce. "We got two of them this week and they'll be very careful, but a fresh battalion will soon relieve them and one unit never seems to warn the other about danger spots."

Sedgewick and Farmer were scouts and did their work at night. I heard them reporting a prowl they had made to Cave and was thrilled as I listened. After they were in their bunks I awaited a chance and talked with Cave, told him I would like to be a scout. He eyed me as if doubtful of my ability and explained that it was a grim game, requiring special qualities of character and training, strong nerves, keen hearing and a sense of direction in the darkness. A man was often required to play a lone hand in a tight situation, and had to be always prepared for the unexpected. I told him I was sure I could learn patrolling and would like to have the chance.

Pearce led the way out the next day. We watched all the morning and much of the afternoon and saw nothing. There was no need to be impatient, he said. He had eighteen kills to his credit and had taken months to get such a bag. It was dull and chilly but the next morning there was sunshine and we were out early. I was no more than in position than a German in full pack rose almost waist-high at a place in their trench. The sight was so amazing it took me a moment to discover that during the night our guns had knocked down some of the German parapet. The German was evidently a new man in the sector and unaware of the nearness of our lines. He was looking around as I scored my first hit. It was not a great shot, the distance was not more than one hundred yards and I had cross-hair sights-but I had really killed a Hun.

"Good stuff," praised Pearce. He rubbed his hands gleefully and noted down the facts in his record book, but had not finished when a second German, also in pack, rose in the same place. I shot him as soon as he appeared, as my finger was taut on the trigger. Hardly had he fallen than a soldier without any pack and a rifle in his hands stepped up on the piled earth. I could count his tunic buttons through the telescopic sights and shot him through the left breast. As he pitched down from view two more Germans suddenly appeared at a spot to the left. They did not have packs and neither wore a helmet. One had an immense head, almost round, and he glared and pointed a finger. His mate was dark and his hair close cropped. He had binoculars in his hand. I shot him and as he went down the binoculars were flung in a high loop over his head.

The fellow with him was aiming a rifle in our general direction. Pearce gripped my shoulder. He had been watching with the glasses outside the plate. "Shoot!" he rasped. "You won't get a chance like this all day." .

I drew back and handed him the rifle. A queer sensation had spread over me like nausea. "Go ahead yourself," I said. "I've had enough."

He seized the rifle and took quick aim. I saw the dark flush that spurted over the face of the big-headed man as he sank from view, one hand clawing at the sandbags. Then, over on the left, a German got up and walked overland carrying a big dixie. He was clearly a cook and his actions indicated that a new battalion was in the line. Pearce shot him and the dixie was flung away, spilling some liquid. Then an officer stepped into view at a blown-in part and waved to someone. He sank down as Pearce shot him, and pitched forward. No other Germans appeared but we could see their shovels as they cleared the damage our shelling had done. Pearce shot at a helmet twice and twice a spade waved a miss. Then we went back to the dugout and Pearce said I would have to explain myself to Sergeant Cave.

Cave looked at me oddly as I told him I had all I wanted of sniping. He said I had too big a kill for the first time, that if I had only shot one German I would have been all right. Then he informed me there was to be a raid the next day, April 1, between Durrand and Duffield Craters, and that I was one of the snipers who must get on top of the parapet as the raid started and shoot any German who tried to get away overland. After the raid he would talk to me again.

That night I could not eat. Pearce asked if the shooting had upset me. I said I did not think so but that I had no appetite. It was a long time before I could get to sleep and then I soon woke. I was so hot I threw off my blankets and tossed and turned. I could not eat any breakfast and Pearce was worried. "I can get you off the raid if you like," he said.

I told him the raid had nothing to do with the way I felt, got ready and went out. The barrage started and filled the morning with uproar. Our Stokes battery put over its quota and, as per usual, most of their shells fell short. Six of us climbed from the trench as soon as the raiding parties went over. I watched carefully but no German tried to get away overland. There were two prisoners, one a little short man, and they came on their own to us, stumbling and running with hands up. The raiders started back on the run and an officer shouted for us to get down.

The others jumped at once, but I was dizzy and got down very carefully. The company officer came towards me. "That fellow acted as if he were drunk," I heard him saying to Captain Hale, our medical officer, who was seated near the stretcher bearers who had waited in the trench.

I sat down on a fire step and Hale came over to me. He stared at me, then put fingers under my ears. "Why don't you report when you're sick?" he demanded. "Do you want to spread the stuff all around?"

"What stuff?" I managed.

"Mumps, man!" he roared. "Come along."

He took my rifle and laid it on the fire step, yanked off my equipment and slung it there, took me by the arm and started me out to the Quarry Line. When I reached his post I was all in. The medical sergeant got me a drink and was very kind, putting me on a trolley that ran back to Mont St. Eloi. Away I went, with a man sitting beside me. We stopped and I saw an ambulance. The man put a tag on my tunic and took me to the ambulance, and I crawled in at the back. There was no other passenger.

After a time we stopped and the driver told me to get out, as this was the clearing station. I got out and an orderly came and read my tag, then took me by the arm. We went to the rear of a big building where there was a brick shed with a locked door and small windows. He unlocked the door and pushed me in, then snapped the lock in place.

Feeling rotten, I looked for some place to sit or lie and found I had company. A soldier with several days' growth of beard and trousers stained black at the knees was going around and around in circles on a stone floor that oozed slime, and all the time he was muttering: "I'm a lion! I'm a lion!"

In a second I forgot my weakness. I got to the door, which had an open grating, and yelled to a man who was at a cook wagon attending some kettles. He came over and I offered him five francs for a messtin full of stew, showing him I had the money. He went at once and filled a messtin, returned with a key in his hand and unlocked the door. As he opened it, extending the messtin, I kicked it so that the hot mixture went over his head and shoulders. He yelled in distress and I ran for the road. Another ambulance was near where the other had been, and I dove in the back of it as it started. There was a man on the rack above me but he was unconscious. We swayed and rocked along the rough road as a snowstorm began. It was quite some time before we stopped and I climbed out at once, walked across a yard to a tent and was confronted by an orderly.

He read my ticket and asked who had sent me there. I shrugged, and he said Canadians were for some other hospital. Another orderly came and had a look at my ticket. "It makes no difference," he said. "Take him in."

The orderly led me into a marquee that served as the "mumps ward." Four men were huddled around a brazier. There were a dozen cots consisting of stretchers resting on high hurdles or benches, and seven were occupied. The orderly told me to get into one of the free ones. Boards were laid on footways and beneath them were two inches of water. Drifting snow came in the open tent entrance and melted on the boards.

One of the men by the stove pointed to the cot farthest from the door and helped me get my balance on it. Any lurch would topple the whole thing into the water. It was quite a feat to sit on the stretcher and undress, but I managed it. "Hide your clothes " advised the man by the brazier. "Else they'll take them to the !delouser and they'll stay a tight wrinkle long as you have to wear them."

So I hid everything under my blankets and was just settled back on the pillow when an orderly came and asked for my uniform.

"Another chap just got it," I murmured, and he went away. The men by the stove yawned and departed, and the fellow next to me snored a deep refrain. Not a doctor or nurse or orderly came during the next two hours and finally I went to sleep. When I woke it was morning and snow had blown through a rip in the tent. Some of it had reached my cot and melted, so that one shoulder was damp. Two of the men in the other cots were cursing violently. They had received a load of the snow and their cots were soaked. A fellow who had been by the stove brought me a mug of tea and some bread and jam.

It was noon before a medical officer came. He was as poor a type as one could imagine. He asked a few questions, put a hand on my forehead, said I'd be all right in a day or so and passed on. The nurse was looking outside all the while. The other lads had even less attention. They told me I was in the most slipshod hospital in France, an Imperial outfit at St. Pol, and the doctor would not be back for two days at least, perhaps longer.

Three of the men who had been in bed got up and dressed and brought us something to eat. They said they had been well for two weeks and had simply stayed in the marquee, slipping out any time the doctor made his rounds. No one bothered them and they were having an easy time. An English orderly they called "Spike" came and told me I had better move into the next ward. He was a fine young man, had been two years at medical college, and was very bitter against all those in authority at the hospital.

I moved to the bigger tent. It had no leaks. In the six days I was there the doctor never looked in at me again. The only nurse who came was a Canadian girl from Ontario. When she found I was from Nova Scotia she came often to talk with me, as she was on night duty. She told me things were worse than I could realize and her only hope was to get away from the place. Spike came in often and he told me I need not fear any bad results as I was on the mend, had really been sickest the morning I left the front. He advised me to move to a third tent, because the one I was in was to be made ready for casualties after the great attack on Vimy Ridge.

There were only four of us in the third tent. Soon I felt so much better that I got up and dressed, then inquired about the routine for getting our meals. I was told all tents had numbers and ours was sixteen. All they asked was "How many in your tent?"

That night at supper hour I took the big tray and went boldly to the cook tent. "What number?" yelled a Cockney with a moustache.

"Sixteen!"

"How many?"

"Eight!"

The food was placed on the tray and back I went. The others stared, and I explained. They shook their heads. They would not dare try such a trick, as someone might come from the cook tent and check. From what I had observed there seemed little chance of any such investigation, and I went each mealtime and drew enough for eight men, which made no more than a decent meal for four.

Easter morning we were surprised to see an officer and orderlies come into the tent and start placing oranges and cigarettes on the tables. "Don't touch them," said the officer. "There's to be an inspection first. After it is over we will come and tell you and you can help yourselves."

Something made me mistrust him. Presently a retinue of red tape and high-blown officials passed through the tent, pointing at the exhibits and nodding. No sooner had they gone than in came the officer who had brought the treats, with the same orderlies. They snatched away everything from the first two tables. But I had put the oranges and smokes on my table under the bedding, and the man next me grabbed his cigarettes and would not yield them, although the officer threatened to use force. Soon afterwards Spike came and told us the same trick had been pulled at several tents, but word had spread and the last ones took care of the treats in time. The rumour was that the officers and nurses were to have a big party in their quarters that night.

We had great talks in the tent. One man was a Newfoundlander. Another was from Sussex, the third from Kent. The Kentish man had been a sergeant but had been reduced to ranks for not saluting an officer in the dark. He was not bitter about it but laughed at the episode. He said patriotism was not a password in his unit, that loyalty was a word they sneered at; discipline, with the death penalty behind it, was a canker we could not cure. He said he admired the Canadians and Australians, as they were free and easy with their officers. But some of the English officers were as bad as the Germans. "One thing there has never been," he said, "and that is an ounce of common horse sense in the way a war is run and men handled."

He was bitter about some of the discipline handed out, so I told him about the day we had seen "Old Sunshine," the regimental sergeant-major of the R.C.R.'s, have a man spreadeagled to the wheel of a cart. We went up the hill and cut the fellow loose, and along came Old Sunshine roaring threats. None of us ran. We simply stayed and defied him. He was told that if the man, or any other, were tied to another wheel we would get him, sooner or later, tie him to a cartwheel and send the cart downhill. We were not drunkards or rowdies. He grew hoarse and went away, but all of us saw the fear in his eyes and never again did we see an R.C.R. on a cartwheel.

When we were astir in the morning we heard guttural voices in the big tent. I went over and it was filled with German wounded. They stared at me, mostly indifferent but some friendly. One with a turban-like bandage on his head was stolidly eating bully as though it were an occupation instead of a meal. A very pale young fellow repeated some word over and over and made motions of drinking. I got a mug and water bottle, filled both and took them to him. He smiled and patted my hand. Spike came and asked me if I minded giving him some aid. It took us until after ten to give all of them their breakfast.

We fed them the next three days and then they were taken elsewhere. I asked Spike where I would get my pay book fixed up regarding the stay in hospital. He said the officer I should see was away for a few days and advised I await his return. I waited one day, then had a bath at the bath house, drew a new tunic from a quartermaster, walked away from the place and boarded a train. As I left, a bandy-legged Scot who had been hanging around the place for six weeks, dodging doctors, looked at my balmoral and said anxiously, "Ye'll no disgrace the tartan, wull ye, lad?"

By devious ways and both kinds of luck I finally reached Mont St. Eloi, and there to my astonishment and joy found Mel Baillie. He had gone down the line with mumps the same day I had, had also taken French leave from his hospital and was anxious to get with the boys. One of our lads, Gerald Gard, had been back of the lines with some ailment, had acquired mumps and given them to six different members of the 42nd.

We went over Vimy Ridge just at dusk. The Canadian attack of April 9 and 10 had left it a jungle of old wire and powdered brick, muddy burrows and remnants of trenches. The barrage had been the biggest of its kind to date. Much traffic was going along one main track, so we walked a way and sat in a crater to rest. I had walked at least ten miles and Baillie had done the same. Suddenly he spoke and pointed. To one side of us, in a sort of alcove to the crater, three dead men were reclining, gazing incuriously before them, their faces almost black. We rose at once and climbed from the place, and almost fell over another dead man crouched in a shell hole, rifle still in hand, as if ready to spring.

In the twilight just before darkness, we stood and looked down over the Ridge on the enemy side. The first flares were rising in scattered places. We could not distinguish the lines. The air was damp and chilling, causing an unearthly feeling to predominate. The dead men, the solitary flares, the captured ground, gave us a sense of ghosts about, and hurried us over to a semblance of a trench leading down the slope.

Two hours later we found Fourteen Platoon, hardly recognizing it. The sergeant was there, and MacDonald, but most of the others were strangers. They were from the 73rd Royal Highlanders, a unit of the 4th Division so decimated during the attack on Vimy Ridge that they had been replaced by the 85th Nova Scotia Highlanders. MacDonald told us our company had gone straight through to the objective in spite of sleety snow and mud and confusion, but a flanking fire from the left, where the 4th Division had been held up, had taken a heavy toll. Belliveau and Jenkins and Joe McPherson had been killed in one area. One shell had wiped out Stevenson and two others. MacMillan had been shot in the stomach and had died after waiting hours in the trench. Gilroy and Westcott and Legge had been killed by machine-gun fire. Herman Black had run amuck. They found him almost at the bottom of the Ridge, near a battery position, with eight dead Germans about him, four of them killed by bayonet.

We hunted up Mickey and Ira Black and Eddie Cuvilier, Glenn Lunn and Tommy. They were sitting in the dugout after a hard day of rebuilding roads, each man suffering from bodily fatigue, crawling vermin and the clammy chill of mud-caked clothing, their faces brooding, enigmatic, even Mickey looking curiously old. Months before we had marched eagerly to Mont St. Eloi, our tin hats askew and with a cheeky retort for every comment, hiding whatever secret apprehensions we had. Now we had changed.

Two things I would remember about Vimy. The first was my experience in a working party. They sent Tommy and me one night to a place where they lowered us down, by a ladder that was quite vertical, to a chalk tunnel. It was cold outside, but when we got down there all sound stilled and it was warm. We had to shed our greatcoats and equipment at once. We tied sandbags over our boots and went, crouched on all fours, along a tunnel in solid chalk just four feet high and hardly three feet wide. At the face of it we worked in turns, and fast. The chalk face was sprayed with vinegar. Then one man cut it with a knife as it softened and passed back large chunks to his helper, who in turn placed them in the hands of another man near him. Thus the chalk removed was handed back and finally reached a small trolley drawn on tracks which took it to the hoist. There the stuff was raised and dumped, a sure sign to Fritz of underground operations. The air was dank and close and we sweated a great deal. It was amazing how far we proceeded in that one night. The man in charge forbade anyone speaking. At any moment it was possible the removal of a newly cut chunk might reveal a German dugout filled with men! For weeks afterwards my whole body would tense when I thought of that night.

The second episode I would remember was the issuing of whale oil to rub on our feet. It came in jugs and was colder than ice. It would prevent trench feet. Orders were that every man should rub it on his feet once in twenty-four hours while we were in those winter trenches. I did so religiously and never had the least trouble. But we had a big chap who had blustered much until we were within sound of the guns. Then he had tried in every way to get from the front, going on sick parade, complaining of blindness, even trying to wound himself slightly. He had been caught in the act and warned of what his punishment would be, so he never used the whale oil, although the sergeant who made the nightly check was told he did. The result was that after two days his feet started to swell. It was learned later he had purposely walked through wet places and the cold had penetrated. His feet became so bad he could not walk and finally he had to be taken out on a stretcher. The last we heard of him was from a lad who had been to see him in a hospital in England. Both feet were huge blobs of mis-shapen flesh. He could only move around on crutches and his feet would never be normal again.

We left the Ridge and went to Vimy village, relieving C.M.R.'s (Canadian Mounted Rifles) there, and doing working parties, digging trenches, putting up wire near the front line. During the first night I was sent out with two men as a covering party for the men working with the barbed wire. It was cold and miserable. We were made to inspect the area through binoculars so we would recognize the various landmarks and not put the wire in a wrong place. We were out soon after it was dark but did not take nearly enough wire the first time and had to return for more. So it was midnight before we were finished. Luckily the Hun did not hear anything, but it was very chilling to stay crouched in position for hours, and the night seemed endless. All I could think of was the fact I had no place to go when we were through. Getting our party ready had taken so long that I had no chance to prepare any sort of shelter.

As we went back and drew near the railway embankment someone called in a low voice. I went over and found two of the men from the 73rd had dug a neat bivvy into the embankment. They were very decent chaps and insisted they had made the place wide enough to accommodate the three of us. We snuggled in, and with a ground sheet pegged to hold over our heads we were really comfortable. In seconds I was dead to the world.

The ground sheet pegged over our heads was pulled free and fell on my face, rousing me. Then a firm warm hand seized one of mine and pulled me up to a sitting position. It was very early, as first sunshine was glittering on the dew-wet grass. I was annoyed that I should have to do some chore after being out so late. I tried to pull free. But the grip held, and as I came to a sitting-up position my other hand was seized and I had a look at my visitor.

In an instant I was out of the bivvy, so surprised I could not speak. I was face to face with my brother, Steve, who had been killed in 1915! The first notice from the War Office had said: "Missing, believed dead." After a time one of his mates wrote to say a boot had been found with his name on it. The Germans had mined the Canadian trench and blown it up.

Steve grinned as he released my hands, then put his warm hand over my mouth as I started to shout my happiness. He pointed to the sleepers in the bivvy and to my rifle and equipment. "Get your gear," he said softly.

As I grabbed it he turned and started walking away rapidly. It was hard to keep up with him. We passed make-shift shelters filled with sleeping men of my platoon. No one was awake. Now and then a gun fired off toward the Somme or a machine-gun chattered, but on the whole it was a quiet morning. As soon as we were past the shelters I hurried to get close to Steve. "Why didn't you write Mother?" I asked.

He turned and the grin was still on his face. "Wait," he said.

"Don't talk yet."

Then I noticed he had a soft cap on and no gas mask or equipment. Somehow he had learned where the 42nd was, and our "D" Company, but how in the world did he know where I was sleeping?

We left the company area and headed directly into a collection of ruins that had been Petit Vimy. "There's no one around here," I said. "How did you know where to find me?"

At that moment my equipment, slung hurriedly over one shoulder, slipped off and fell to the ground before I could catch it. As I stooped and retrieved it Steve went into a passageway in the ruins and I ran to catch him. Arrived there, I saw one way went right and the other left. Which way had he gone? "Steve!" I called. There was no answer, so I dropped my rifle and gear and ran to the right. It only took minutes-two or three-to get to the far side, but there was no sign of my brother. I ran back and called again, took the way to the left, searched and searched again, called repeatedly, but could not find him. Finally I sat down on my equipment and leaned back against a bit of wall. I was tired and sweating and excited. A great desire to find our officer and get the day off took hold of me, but I realized I did not know where the officer or sergeant-major were, and if I left the immediate area and Steve returned he would not know where I had gone. Probably he had no pass and did not want to be seen. If only I had not bothered with my equipment I could have kept up with him!

Minutes went by. I got up and made another search of the

ruins. The sun began to glisten on the tops of the broken walls. I settled back more comfortably on my equipment and heard the usual morning stir of guns firing registering shots. The sun got warmer. I dozed.

Suddenly I was shaken awake. Tommy had me by the arm and was yelling. "He's here! Bill's here!"

I stumbled up, dazed, looked at my watch. It was nine o'clock.

"What's made you come here?" Tommy was asking. "What happened?"

"What's all the row about?" I countered.

"You should know. They're digging around that bivvy you were in. All they've found is Jim's helmet and one of Bob's legs."

"Legs!" I echoed stupidly. "What do you mean?"

"Don't you know a big shell landed in that bivvy? They've been trying to find something of you."

It seemed utterly incredible. I put on my gear and followed Tommy. There was a great cavity in the embankment and debris was scattered over the whole area. Mickey came running to shake hands with me. Then the sergeant was calling and I saw he was talking with an officer.

When we got nearer I saw it was an artillery officer of high rank and saluted him.

"What made you leave the bivvy?" the sergeant asked. "The boys say you got in there with Jim and Bob."

"I did," I said. "I was there till daylight."

"What made you leave then?"

It was the artillery officer who asked the question, and I hesitated, felt it would sound foolish if I told them exactly what had happened.

"Don't be afraid," he said. "We're all friends."

He looked a real gentleman, so I told him my story in detail. He made notes in a book he carried, asking my name, where I was from, and all about Steve. Then he shook my hand. "You have had a wonderful experience," he said.

The sergeant looked as if he did not know whether to believe me or not, but a runner came with orders for another move and I hustled to get something to eat. Neither Tommy nor Mickey mentioned the matter to me through the day, and that night we were over to the left doing working parties again until late. I slept in a bivvy MacDonald and I had made but it was past midnight before I could doze off.

I had seen Steve as clearly as I saw Mickey. His warm hands had pulled me from the bivvy. His voice had been perfectly natural. He had the old half-grin I knew so well. He had saved my life.

I had joined the Methodist Church when I was fourteen and had been as decent as the average. At evenings in the Y.M.C.A. I loved the singing of hymns. I did not like the compulsory church service and the officers singing "O God, Our Help in Ages Past." But now I knew beyond all argument or theory, by any man learned or otherwise, that there was a hereafter, and there would never again be the slightest doubt in my mind about it.

For a few days I sensed that the sergeant had not believed my story but it did not worry me in the least. Then a batman let me know the officers had talked about the incident and regarded my story as the result of too much rum. This was rather amusing as I never took the ration and everyone in our company, except the officers who were new, was aware of the fact. However, in a few days the matter was forgotten by the men. And it was only as I lay ready for sleep that I thought of it.

Chapter 3: The Avion Sector

After two more days of working parties we were told to fall in at dark to march back over the Ridge. Our regular sergeant was gone on leave and we had Ormandy, a sergeant from the 73rd Royal Highlanders. A major had just come to us that trip, a supernumerary, one of the type that was the bane of platoons, sent up front to get some experience. I had to go twice over the Ridge with him, acting as a sort of guide and N.C.O. Then Ormandy came and told me I was to guide the party to one of the Vimy tunnels on our old front.

When the time came to fall in, the Germans began throwing over long gas shells that exploded on contact with the ground. They looked like pencils seen against the sky. We put on our respirators and waited in some ruins until there was a lull. "All right," called the major. "We'll go now."

We were just on the path and away from the place when the shelling was resumed. The first salvo came very near us and I shouted for all to hurry and follow me. There was a level spot just ahead over which we would make good time and beyond a sort of shelter of old stubs.

But the major was bellowing "Halt!" at the top of his voice, and we stopped. The shells were dropping very near but that stupid major made us line up, number and actually form fours and right turn-when not twenty feet away, two stubs made it impossible for more than a single file to go through. He led the way through, seemingly deaf to the shouted comments, then what we all expected happened. Two shells fell on our immediate right. The third just missed the major-worse luck-and struck MacDonald, who was following him, full on the chest. The blow killed him instantly. The shell exploded and the contents went over a leg of the major.

Baillie was back of MacDonald, then Tommy, then myself. All three of us were knocked down as MacDonald was driven back against Baillie. It took not a minute to see that MacDonald was past help and we all ran as we should have when I shouted. It was hard to see with gas masks on. Harry Hayward fell into the one water hole near the path. He was a very short fellow and went in completely, rearing up without his gas mask. I dragged him out. He started to shout he had lost his mask, and rather than hold things up I took off mine and gave it to him.

Meanwhile Ormandy had rushed to the major, who was writhing in agony. He shouted for men to stop and help the stretcher bearer, but all knew the major was entirely responsible for what had happened. Ormandy had to overtake four men and forcibly stop them and threaten them with full punishment before he could get them back. The major was rolled on a stretcher and carried up the path. One minute later another salvo of gas shells dropped where he had been. Then we were away from the area and at last reached Grange Tunnel. There a lad from the 73rd, Lorne Kennedy, introduced himself and had me share his tin of beans heated over a tommy cooker. They were delicious. He told me he was from Arnprior, Ontario, and we were good friends thereafter.

Next day we got out in the sunlight. It was perfect weather, clear and warm, and the grass had yellowed with dandelions. Larks sang overhead and in that same blue air planes wheeled like great hawks, the early sunlight glinting on white wings, as many deadly duels were fought. The sergeant-major hunted me out and said I was to go to Cave as a scout as soon as all reorganization had taken place. Then we went back in the line, relieving the 5th C.M.R.s and doing several working parties.

The first night in I went out in charge of a covering party of three. It was dark and the Hun kept sending up flares, which made things bad for the boys trying to put up wire. They were old hands at the game, however, and remained as still as the earth itself while the flares lit up the scene. By three a.m. the job was finished and the night so mild that we slept on the grass.

We had it easy through the day, but at night Sergeant Ormandy came and said I was to go out with him on a patrol. My only experience of patrolling had been crawling out between the craters on the Ridge. However, I was glad of the opportunity. Ormandy said an officer using binoculars had spotted something on the right of our company front and about thirty yards from the German front line. We were to learn whether or not it was being used as a machine-gun post at night.

The flares were plentiful for an hour and then stopped, which meant that Fritz had a patrol or working parties out. It was quite dark and we crawled slowly, the grass making no sound. There was occasional shelling and the machine-guns were never still for long, but it was quiet out in no man's land. Not a sound came from the German line in front of us. There was an old stub between their first and second lines. It had been shot away until the top had a splintered section extended from it like the thumb of a hitchhiker. I had taken particular notice of it but said nothing to Ormandy, as he told me he would take the lead. We went very slowly and listened for long intervals. The dew began falling and the weeds and grass became wet. The guns stopped firing. Every tiny sound we made seemed magnified by the gloom. As we waited, listening, I put my head down to earth and was able to see the top of the stub. Its location told me we had kept much too far to the right and that we were nearer to the German trench than Ormandy thought. I whispered the fact to him. He resented my comment at first but had not crawled his length before he turned and told me to take the lead.

Immediately I swung sharply left, and soon we encountered ground torn up by shell bursts. This was encouraging, as when looking through binoculars in the afternoon I had noticed a distance of almost a hundred yards in front of the German trench torn by shelling. The rough ground made it harder going but to his credit Ormandy made no objection. Then the company on our left sent up flares, and by their light I made out an oblong shape within feet of us.

Inches at a time we edged toward it, hearing nothing. We squirmed on and my hands touched charred wood. The something the officer had spotted was the foundation of a shed of some sort that had been destroyed by fire. No one was near it. But as we lay there we heard voices coming from our right and knew we were quite near an outpost. We began crawling more quickly, our mission over, and finally wire loomed across our path and a very Canadian challenge was given.

We were soon in our trench and Ormandy was kind in his praise.

"I've been out twice before on patrols," he said, "but I have to admit I was lost when you took over. You must have some sort of instinct about direction?"

Some perverse whim restrained me from explaining about the old stub and its thumb. Then we were meeting the new officer who had taken over the platoon. He was from Montreal and current rumour lined him up as a former taxi driver. He was not at all interested in our report, and his only concern seemed to be getting himself a better batman than the one he had inherited. The batman's name was French and hard to remember, and for some reason or no reason at all everyone called him "Giger." He was very nearly a dimwit, had just enough intelligence to be allowed to enlist. Twice he had discharged his rifle in a dugout, narrowly escaping killing someone, and an irate sergeant had decreed that he should be a batman.

Ormandy assured the newcomer that we were short-handed, that Giger would have to be his man until we had more manpower.

It was cloudy the next day. Orders came from company headquarters that we were to put up wire in front of a "jump-off" trench some yards ahead of our main line. It seemed that some visitor from Brigade had ventured up during the afternoon lull in shelling and had reported that we were quite vulnerable to sudden attack. To us it seemed that night that old Heinie knew what was going on. Twice our party of twelve men was led out into no man's land and we had the wire and screw stakes ready when flares went up and machine-gun fire flattened us on the grass. Each time we were taken back into the trench and told we had made too much noise, that we were to wait an hour. Some of the new men had made more noise than necessary, but it was most annoying wren a drizzling rain began.

Tommy and Baillie got to talking and then asked Mickey and me if we would go out with them and put up the wire without a covering party. We agreed at once. The officer shrugged and told us to go ahead. In less than an hour the job was done and we were not disturbed. The rain became heavier then and our relief was a long time coming.

When it did arrive, our new officer ordered us to climb out over the back of the trench to let the relieving party file in. As we stood there in the rain, flares went up and our wet ground sheets glistened. The Hun saw us, so we had to flop on the wet grass and mud with all our equipment of haversacks and messtins. We were soaked and mud-plastered when we got up and then the officer led us out by an overland route. He got mixed up, would not take any advice from Ormandy, would not wait for a guide, and took us on and on in pitch darkness while the rain poured in torrents.

There had been casualties among the Lewis gunners, and extra pans of ammunition were passed back among the platoons. Each of us carried the pans in turn. Just in front of me was Bill Childs, the sanitary man of the company, ten years older than any of us, night-blind, and crusty of temper. He was handed a pair of the drums of machine-gun ammunition connected by a strap and grumbled loudly as he slung the contraption over a shoulder. We came to a wide, shallow trench crossed by a plank. The far end of the plank had sunk down into the opposite bank until it was sloping downward, and muddied feet had made it slippery. Old Bill's feet shot from under him. His kilt flew up. He sat down hard on the greasy plank and skidded to the far end, bringing up heavily with the drums of ammunition crossed so that the strap was strangling him. As soon as he got air he denounced all wars, the Great War in particular, all battalions, the 42nd especially, all officers and present company not excepted.

We were convulsed at first by Bill's harangue, then afraid he would get himself in wrong. Tommy tried to subdue him. But old Bill never quieted until we were over by another trench, half full of water and with no crossing.

"These damn maps are no good," said the officer as we stood awaiting instructions. "Wait here till I find where we are." He vanished into the night, and Ormandy told us we should look around and find some way to a road.

Baillie and I explored and found a sap running from the main trench. It was quite narrow and we pulled the sides in with our entrenching tools until we had soft earth heaped high above the water. We spread a ground sheet on it and lay down. It was a tight squeeze but we lay there lengthwise to the sap with the other groundsheet over our heads, while the rain poured down.

We slept in spite of everything, as we were utterly worn out. At daylight an icy touch roused me. I woke to find that one shoulder was under water and that I could not move. The sides of the sap, loosened by our work, had slid in more, had almost buried us, while the water, dammed by our block, had risen until it was ready to drown us.

Throughout the entire war I was never as scared as I was during the next ten minutes. We could not move an arm or leg, were absolutely helpless, and the rubber sheet over our heads smothered our calls. But we yelled and yelled and yelled and at last, just as my ear filled with water and my nose was blowing bubbles, Tommy found us. He yanked up the sheet and dragged us out, and for a time we could not speak. We had been entirely too near to a hideous ending.

We looked around and saw Old Bill sitting on the ground, beneath a stake on which his ground sheet was fixed so as to shed the rain from his head. The others were in comparable positions. Ormandy was gone, as were three or four others. We moved off and in daylight could see the road we should have taken. Back near the Ridge we met the officer coming to find us. He was as drenched as if he had sat out under a water spout and he walked along without a word.

In an hour we had billets of a sort. In an old cellar our group built a fire from wood found in an overturned cart, and there we stripped and dried our kilts, fervently hoping every louse had drowned. The sun came out and by afternoon the horrible night had passed into history. We went back to Villers-au-Bois, where our section was billeted in a barn. The weather repented and we had three days of glorious sunshine. A draft of new men came to the platoon, but before I got to know them Ormandy came and told me to report to Sergeant Cave as a scout.

The scouts had been reorganized and five new men, of whom I was one, were joining them. I knew Bulmer, a husky from our old unit, Brown, a mild-mannered "original," Jimmy, a tall, observant, quick-tempered young man, and Wilson, who was very capable.

K. K. McLeod was most friendly and I had long talks with him. Before we could make a trip with the scouts, Bulmer had some leg disease that crippled him and sent him back to Canada. The rest of us, we four, were initiated into the mysteries of night work, shown how to crawl around without making a noise, how to read a compass and a map, how to make a report. I teamed with Wilson and found him a grand fellow.

There was a day's delay in going back to the trenches. I mustered nerve enough to ask for a day's leave, and it was granted without question. I had extraordinary luck; as I left my billet a big car slowed down and the driver asked me for a light. He was an officer's chauffeur, he said, and his "boss" was stationed in Houdain, in conference for the day. He asked me where I was going. I explained I had the day off, and so he drove me to Ferfay, where the divisional school was in progress, and then to

Olhain Chateau, surrounded by a moat of 15th-century construction. It was a wonderful treat for me. The sky was summer-blue, and sunshine made whiter the cottages with their red-tiled roofs. The hedges were in bloom and fruit trees were white with blossom. We had a real dinner at Houdain, after which the chauffeur drove me back to my billet.

We went back over the Ridge and relieved the C.M.R.'s at the railway dugouts. Everyone was excited about a Brigade raid to be staged on the night of June 8. The Hun front line and second lines were to be taken, held for a time and then vacated. Wilson and I visualized some important action, but to our surprise Cave told us there would be nothing for us to do. We would move up in case we were needed but would remain at the first trench taken.

At dark we left the embankment and as we moved along the trench I saw our platoon ahead of us. Suddenly the Hun fired a salvo of shells overhead. Everyone began to hurry, but it was minutes before another came, and one shell hit the trench about fifty yards in front of us. When we reached the spot, there lay Slim and his pal, Joe. They had been lagging at the rear of the platoon and both had been killed instantly.

Tapes were laid to the front line, white lines that led to first aid stations, and guides for bringing back prisoners overland. In the dark they looked like pathways for ghosts. The barrage was heavy. After a time it lifted and the battalion attacked. A runner came to me and said I was to report to the signals officer. It was likely he was in the captured German front line so I went there. Several dead Germans were sprawled about and much damage had been done to their front line posts. One Heinie lay huddled in a corner and as I arrived I heard one of the new men in our "D" Company saying: "I'm going to try my bayonet in that chap. It can't hurt a dead man to stick him and I want to know what it feels like."

He posed his steel, ready to make the thrust in spite of several protesting voices, when the German yelled and jumped to his feet. In a moment our men were testing all the other bodies lying about but no other "live corpse" was found. The Germans were sending up orange sprays, red rockets, green flares, golden chains, seemingly all the varieties they had, but their artillery made small response. Word circulated that all objectives had been taken and there were thirty prisoners. Then I found the signals officer.

"We have laid a wire over to a place in front," he said. "It is hidden in the grass and leads to a hole that looks as if someone once started to dig a well. It is just what we wanted. We will lower a man with a phone, and you, into it before we leave. I want you to do the observing as the Germans come back in their lines and the signaller will phone us. The hole is bordered with tall grass and weeds. At dark you can get out easily and gather up the wire as you come in. The Hun will be too busy repairing his front lines to send out any patrols."

It sounded a hare-brained idea but I was in no position to argue. I met the signaller, a short, swarthy fellow who plainly did not relish his job, and we were led to the place. A pole had been salvaged from somewhere, and as the word to retreat came the signaller dropped an arm over the pole, holding his phone in one hand. Men at either end of the pole raised it, until he was lifted clear of the ground, and carried him directly over the hole. He let go and dropped down. The place was little more than five feet deep, and dry. Then it was my turn. They took my rifle and gave me a revolver and binoculars, the best I had ever used.

The Germans had begun a desultory shelling of their front and it was evident that they thought the captured trenches were being held. The shooting kept on until about five o'clock and then I heard the Germans moving in the outskirts of Avion, a village just back of their front line. The signaller had dug a place for his feet in the bottom of the hole, using the earth removed by his entrenching tool as a seat. He had complained bitterly about the chore until I had to tell him he was wasting his breath. From time to time he tested the wire and made contact with headquarters.

As it got light I carefully made little channels through the weeds and grass, cutting them off at the root with my knife, until I had nine of them that gave me a clear range of vision in all directions. The first thing I saw was a dead man to our right, a member of the 49th Battalion, according to his colour patches. Presently I could hear voices in the German trenches. Soon, to my amazement, we heard other voices calling for help. Apparently there were a dozen or more wounded lying just back of their trench or wherever they had crawled, and not one had made a sound previously.

Suddenly a head shot up in the trench in front of our hole, about thirty feet away. The face was broad and the nose blunt. The German stared for minutes and then climbed over the parapet. I slipped the safety off my revolver and told the signaller we might have to beat it. He was so jittery at once that I regretted speaking. But the German had not noticed our hiding place. He crawled out to the dead man and took his boots, socks and puttees, went through his pockets, got nothing, and went back.

Soon I could see Germans coming from Avion. There was a broken brick wall over on our left and I saw it concealed the entrance to a dugout. An officer appeared in the trench to our left, and there were loud words and orders. He was speaking to an elderly-looking Hun with a thin neck, who was carrying a pole with a white flag tied to it. The fellow came along to the spot where the boot-stealer had climbed out and in a moment, after more shouting from someone, he appeared, holding the pole as high as he could reach. No shot was fired at him and presently stretcher bearers came out. They carried in eleven bodies from the area along the front. And in the meantime other stretcher bearers were taking in wounded from between the trenches, the ones who had been shouting for help. These fellows carried the wounded in ground sheets tied to poles, and some of them were groaning, piteously.

Another officer appeared and talked with the first one in very loud tones. Many soldiers were now in the lines and I made out three different communication trenches. Watching carefully, I found two more dugout entrances. Over twenty wounded were carried toward Avion but some of them were taken from one of the dugouts. By night the parapet along our area had all been repaired, all the wounded and dead were gone and there was a strong garrison in the front trench. Everything had been phoned back to our headquarters but the signaller had become very uneasy. We had nothing to drink all day, as we had not thought to fill our water bottles, and all there had been to eat was one tin of bully.

As it became dusk there was much loud talking in the trench and then three or four Germans climbed out. They were arguing, and the signaller was frantic with fear. He was sure we would be found. But they were only taking the body of the 49th man for burial. Then our guns began to open up and after the long quiet of the day the shelling seemed louder than usual. Gradually it grew darker, and when the Germans sent up a first lot of flares, we made ready to quit our post. As the last flare died out I boosted the signaller out and followed him. We caught up the wire and lost no time, were out two hundred yards at least before more flares rose. I headed for our scout dugout and was more than pleased to find that Wilson had my rations and had got some candy bars from the canteen.

There was no call for me to go and report what I had observed. It seemed that the reports by phone were all that was needed, or else they did not think it an important matter. None of the "old men" in the section mentioned my work or asked a question. They had nothing to do with the newcomers. None of them spoke to us except McLeod and Farmer. Sergeant Cave was careful to be neutral. The actions of Sedgewick and his mates did not bother me in the least, but Jimmy was resentful and spoke his mind in their hearing. Brown stayed in his corner with his beloved pipe. As long as he had a bag of Old Chum and matches he cared nothing about the war.

Cave said I could have the day and night off, but I became restless. It was a lovely afternoon and after a long attack on my "seam squirrels"[6] I went out to have a look around. Soon I had got to where our platoon was holding trench posts. After a chat with Tommy I noticed an old sap that ran from his particular bay. Some wire was strewn across it and evidently no one had used it in months. I wondered how far it went, and as it was very quiet along the front, told Tommy I was going to crawl out a distance and see what was there. He yawned and nodded agreement and out I went as he held the loose wire up.

The sap was no more than three feet deep. I moved along it leisurely and was out a good hundred yards from our trench before realizing it. Then I found an enlarged place with a badly rusted trip wire around it. Lying there, wondering who had arranged the trap, as it was now filled with weeds, I saw tall grass further along become agitated. Instantly I got down into the enlarged place, ignoring the trip wire. I kept to one side and released the safety on my Lee Enfield.

After a wait the head and then the shoulders of a young German officer appeared. He had even features and a small brown moustache. There was more of the trip wire in his path, and he put down his Luger pistol and carefully removed the strands. At that moment I raised up, my rifle ready.

The look on his face cannot be described. He seemed utterly paralysed, incapable of action. A long minute passed, and another. Neither of us moved. I had my finger crooked on the trigger, ready, and he saw that I had. He paled and his eyes seemed to dilate. Then he smiled!

I had fully intended taking him prisoner or shooting him if he tried to get away, and yet as he backed off quickly I did not do a thing. Back he went, foot by foot, still smiling, not hurrying too fast, but always moving, and I started toward him. He did not hurry faster and had another grin as I picked up the Luger. Then he was gone around a turn and as he vanished he gave a little half-wave, half-salute.

I hurried back after first hiding the Luger in my gas-mask carrier. I called myself names and yet did not say a thing to Tommy, beyond telling him there had been an old post out there with trip wire. In the dugout I could not bring myself to tell Wilson since the others would hear. I went to sleep, alternately sorry and thankful that I had not shot the German, and next day we were relieved by the 58th Battalion.

We went back in the line July 2 and were practically in Avion. The scouts were established in a cellar. As we looked through our binoculars in the morning, we saw roses just in front of the German wire. Slightly to the right was the ruin of a house

6 Lice.

that was nearer the German lines than ours, and we heard Cave say another battalion had used it as an observation post. Some of the battalion were in excellent dugouts with carpets on the floor, real beds, clocks, stoves and mirrors, furnishings looted from abandoned French homes.

No orders were given Wilson or myself, and Cave went somewhere to attend some conference. It grew dark. I got out of the trench, crawled toward the German line using the house ruin as cover, and saw the roses were much further out in no man's land than I had thought. To the right was another lot, even nearer, and though it was a foolhardy thing to do I kept going, selected a beautiful red rose and got back with it. Not a shot was fired. It was a nice night and I was not in any hurry to go in. The Germans did not seem much interested in us, only putting up the occasional flare. When I did go to the dugout again a royal row was in progress. The "old-timers," after a long and careful reconnaissance, had reached the house ruin. They had ventured in and had been badly scared by hearing Jimmy's voice, a few feet away, ask them if they thought it was all right. He was seated by the opening where a window had been, watching the Hun lines. He had gone there as soon as it was dark, and had also gone where I had been and picked a rose.

Sedgewick and his mate claimed that the Germans had heard Jimmy talking. There had been considerable machine-gun fire shortly after he spoke, but as it was not concentrated on the ruin it was extremely doubtful he had been heard. McLeod made both parties close the argument. Hostility remained in the air, however, while Jimmy and I wore roses.

Cave returned and sent me with a message to our company headquarters. The Germans had begun pitching "Minnies"[7] into our lines, keg-shaped shells that rose in high trajectory and dropped to explode on contact. Our cellar opened onto a street along which one could walk in safety from machine-gun bullets, and as I went I saw the red trail of a "Minnie" soaring over. I stopped and watched. Two men were coming along the street behind me. The "Minnie" began dropping and I yelled a warning and ran around the house I was near.

My decision was correct. The "Minnie" dropped in front of the building and there was a tremendous explosion as it hit the cobbles. Stones and bricks flew in all directions. I ran around to where the two men had been. They were officers of the Princess Pats[8]. One was dead. The other had his leg blown off and was sitting holding the stump trying to stanch the bleeding. I ran back and got a stretcher bearer who bound up the stump. Strangely, the officer did not lose consciousness. He told me the other officer was a Captain Molson and asked if I would get word to the Pats to come for the body. One of our runners came along and he knew where a company of Pats was close by. I stayed by the body until the stretcher bearers came. The first thing they did was search the captain's pockets. They got about five hundred francs.

Then I went on to company headquarters and delivered Cave's message. I didn't know what the message was about, but next day Cave told Wilson and me to go over to the right of "D" Company's front, where an old ruin occupied part of no man's land. He told us to get into the place, if possible in daylight, and observe. We found the place rather exposed, but reached it and made our way up the stairs, where we found enough roof remained to give us a hiding place. Just beyond where we lay was

[7] Type of German Trench mortar shell.

[8] The officers killed were Captain Percival Molson, of the Montreal beer-brewing family and Lieutenant Donald McLean of Burnaby, British Columbia.

an opening large enough for a man to step through. We were not in the ruin five minutes before we knew we had the finest observation post in that sector.

In ten minutes we counted over forty Germans in view. Apparently they were not veterans of the front, as they had no sentries posted. We watched a carrying party going across a field, sheltered by an embankment, and a group of twenty who were building what we supposed would be a "Minnie" emplacement. They were mixing concrete and a big non-com was directing operations. Using our binoculars, we could see he had a long dark scar down one cheek. Out of sight of the boss, a fat Heinie was trying to light his pipe, and we had to laugh at the anxious look on his face.

I wiggled back to the stairs, went down them and crawled through the grass and weeds again to report our find. Within the hour an artillery officer arrived, and after making him aware of the need of careful movements, I took him out to the ruin. He had a phone with him and we threaded the wire along the ground. Wilson and I were tingling with excitement mixed with apprehension. The workers were busy as ants around the construction when the first shell dropped among them. The officer had his battery fire a first shell far over into a field, a second to the right, a third a little nearer, then had made his calculations and scored a direct hit.

When the smoke cleared we saw four Germans lying inert and two wounded ones crawling away on hands and knees. No others were in sight. The officer had that one gun remain registered, then began sniping at other targets. He sent a carrying party diving into a dugout entrance we had not noticed and made two more kills, one a chance hit on a lone runner, blowing the fellow into the air, the other on a party of three who emerged from a latrine and stared our way.

Two Germans showed their heads near the emplacement and both had binoculars. We knew they were getting suspicious, so the officer stopped his guns, told them not to fire again until he gave orders. At that moment we heard quick steps on the rickety stairs behind us and a loud voice. Lieutenant Crood was an impetuous officer of our "A" Company. He had heard about our observation post, had run out to it and up the stairs, and before we could stop him he had stepped full length into the opening beside us and was surveying the German lines.

One scoop gathered our tunics and binoculars. Wilson and I ran a dead heat to the nearest houses and the artilleryman was not far behind us. He had not even bothered with the phone. Crood shouted after us, then started down, no doubt bewildered by our conduct.

Crash! A shell went through the top of the ruin, blasting out the entire corner where we had been and covering Crood with a shower of debris as he ran. It was a miracle he was not killed. We saw him dash wildly into company headquarters and we kept on, far along the side of an old railway track, until we were back at our cellar. The Hun smashed the ruin to powdered brick and kindling, then kept right on and levelled the houses where the "A" Company officers had been. We heard they were trapped in the cellars for two or three hours, and that Lieutenant Crood received the colonel's compliments. The battalion was relieved, and we went back to Chateau de la Haie.

When I visited my Fourteen Platoon, I met a short bow-legged fellow they called Bunty and heard a story about him. He had made himself a bivvy under a parados, as it was easier digging there, and had so constructed it that he could sit like a Hindu statue and go to sleep. He was a heavy sleeper and was very scared of shells. Tommy found him asleep there one morning and got a dud shell that was lying back of the trench. He made a cleft in the parapet directly in front, scooped out earth between Bunty's legs without waking him and put the dud into the cavity. Then he threw a Mills bomb into the grass back of the parados. The explosion wakened the little man rudely, but there was no outcry. Tommy, hiding around the bay, had to emerge to see what had happened. Bunty was rigid, unable to move or speak. Tommy dashed to him, seized the dud and hurled it over the parapet. Bunty rallied, and got up and shook Tommy's hand so fervently that Tommy swore he would never play another trick on anyone. He was a fine boy and was truly penitent.

Mel Baillie had got into trouble. A German airman had the habit of coming over each morning when it was light, flying very low over the trench and shooting at our men. On the third morning Baillie was ready for him. He had two loaded rifles beside his own and he pumped lead like a machine-gun. The airman swerved violently, and every man in the platoon declared Mel had hit him. He never returned but an officer new to the unit had Baillie on the carpet. Orders were that no man was even to look up while an enemy airman was overhead, and never to shoot at them under any conditions.

Sergeant Cave was kind. He let me have three days off during our stay at Chateau de la Haie, and I picked up rides all over the country, visiting the 85th in the 4th Division and taking some souvenirs to the miner's home in Divion. He had said I could leave anything there I wished, and I left the Luger and a sawtooth bayonet I had bought from one of the engineers for ten francs.

We moved to Berthonaval Wood, where a scout specialist came to give us some pointers. We had a meeting in a small glade that seemed remote from war. Dashes of blue cornflower, scarlet poppy and yellow mustard added a vivid touch to the sun-drenched grass. All around was a wall of trees. We did not hear anything new and the instructor was not by any stretch of imagination a fluent speaker. The next morning the long-expected happened. Jimmy clashed with the "old-timers" and chased the pair of them from our quarters. Cave was angry when he returned and heard the story. He told Jimmy to leave the scouts and get back to the company, and I went along with him. Brown and Wilson stayed. They were not turbulent "Bluenoses." Brown would never be troublesome. He would make a good billet orderly. Wilson was a better man than any of them save McLeod.

It was good to be back with Fourteen Platoon. We had a new company commander and he seemed a very decent sort. I had to report to him. He informed me he would use me for all patrols or listening posts and would like it very much if I would accept stripes. I did not want to offend him, but I did not want to be a non-com, so I asked him to give me plenty of time to think it over.

The 42nd was a grand battalion. There were some excellent officers and men. Sergeant Jimmy Davies in our "D" Company was one of the best. The company-sergeant-major, Kennedy, had no equal. Regimental Sergeant-Major Percy MacFarlane was a prince. Captain MacLeod, the Adjutant, was a very fine officer and man, and Major Ralph Willcock was by far the best leader of raids in the brigade. We had quite a day back at Chateau de la Haie when Brigadier A. C. Macdonell[9] came to say good-bye, as he was taking command of the lst Division. Everyone had a good word for him and stories of his decisions and actions were legion. All hands and the cook were

[9] Sir Archibald Cameron Macdonell (1864-1941). Commander of the 7th Infantry Brigade, 1915-1917.

shined up to say farewell when the brigade presented arms, but the old fire-eater seemed overcome with emotion. He put his horse to the gallop and left without saying a word.

The battalion moved to Lozinghem and our platoon was billeted in a barn. A new officer took command of us, McIntyre, one of the "originals," who had been a sergeant. He was a rough and ready Scot, perfectly frank with everybody, and we all liked him. We had an ideal vacation. Rations were good and we were paid. The weather was glorious summer, quite warm during the day, cool and starlit at night. There was an aerodrome at Auchel, just above us, and at all hours the planes were roaring overhead.

At the coal mines they used pumps Saturday nights to get clear of water accumulated during the week. The water filled an oval below the pit head to about three feet. It was soon warmed by the sun and there on Sunday afternoon the female population bathed, with an audience from the 42nd lying on the banks and exchanging banter with the ladies, aged from seven to seventy-five. As bathing in the home was carried on in the fashion I had witnessed at Divion, and urinals were beside church doors and, at farms, beneath the kitchen window, there was no false modesty whatever. Most of the bathers were a scrawny type, over-worked and lacking a proper diet. There were no more than four or five in the forty-odd bathers one would look at a second time. They chatted with us, as the majority could speak English, and the main entertainment was the performance of a very skinny grey-haired grandmother, who proudly showed us she could lay her extremely long breasts over her shoulders and they would stay there.

The people of Lozinghem were unusually friendly. We were welcome in any home to buy eggs and chips. Each place had the big pot of stew on the stove, and as the fat decreased more was added. We were sure the pots had been filled when the first soldiers reached the area and since that time had simply received additional fat, never being emptied and filled with new. One miner was a barber; after he was scrubbed and had his evening meal he would cut hair for a couple of hours. As there were inspections, and few in the company who could cut hair, everyone made fullest use of him. It was impossible, of course, for the miner to look after all who wanted his services, so his wife assisted. She had a small infant and sometimes carried it on one arm while she used her scissors on the hair. Two or three brash lads thought they would avoid morning shaving and demanded service. The miner would not bother with them-the hair-cutting rate was higher-but his wife was quite expert with the razor. They were very low on shaving soap, however, and when she quietly squeezed warm milk on bristly chins the customers did not return.

We were intrigued by the people's acceptance of the conduct of their priests. The first free day in the village some of us were having eggs and chips at noon when a rather pretty girl ambled by. Two of the lads whistled sharply and waved. Madame smiled and shook her head. "You waste your time," she said. "That is the priest's girl."

"He can't have a girl," one chap said. "They have no children. They are not allowed to marry."

"Stupid!" chided Madame. "She is his girl, she sleep with him. It is a great honour for her. And she has been with him since January."

"Is that long?" we asked.

"Better than most," came the answer. "He change every two or three months for a new one."

We never forgot an exhibition of their blind acceptance of priest rule. It was at the harvest time. The crop was tremendous and of utmost importance. The only handicap was the lack of harvesters. The United States had word of the situation and shipped over several hundred up-to-date binders as gifts to the French farmers. One arrived at a farm where some of us were billeted. The farmer hitched his horses to it the following morning and started out, then stopped. The sheaves had not been tied.

As we went out to the field to see what was wrong, we saw the farmer's boy returning with a priest who had been summoned and who carried a censer. The priest walked around the binder three times, chanting something and swinging the censer. Then he told the farmer all was well. The binder started, but out spilled the grain as before. One of our lads ran forward. "Wait!" he said. "The twine isn't threaded in place." He made some quick adjustments.

"Now go," he said.

Away went the binder and out tumbled properly tied sheaves. The farmer waved his whip and shouted thanks. But the priest, his face working in utmost fury, ran in front and screamed at the farmer, who stopped. The priest made him unhitch the horses and take them to the barn. He forbade him to use the binder, and there it was when we passed by in the winter, rusting to junk. And the biggest part of a bountiful crop of grain rotted in the field.

Those days at Lozinghem were long remembered. With plenty of good food, all were in the pink of health. There were ten of us in the barn, Baillie, Mickey, Tommy, Cuvilier, Bill Brown, Lugar, Hayward, Johnson, a western boy with a good voice, Orr, an "original" who had a job in London until June, and myself. The boys were better singers than any of the canteen choirs we heard, and the farm ladies brought us cups of coffee and buttered dark bread after an evening of hearty singing. The coffee was ground chicory but it was hot and we were not fussy.

Orders were suddenly issued that we were to have "physical jerks" before breakfast. It was an idiotic arrangement but persisted for a short time. The bugler roused us and we were to hurry to the training field for snappy workouts. No one would move quickly, however, as everyone wanted breakfast before trying any running. The first morning McIntyre raced into the field away ahead of us, and when we arrived called us cripples and babies and all kinds of soft pets. Baillie casually reminded him we were not officers, that we had not come from ten months of good living in England, and that even now we did not have four-course meals awaiting us, with batmen to serve us.

McIntyre took it all in good part and did not rush us in any way. When we started to return, he offered five francs to anyone who could get back to our billet before him. Three of us did and he paid without a murmur. Soon afterwards the before-breakfast foolishness was eliminated.

Then it was announced that a prize would be given for the best drilled platoon in the brigade, and at once McIntyre set to work. He did not trust any non-com drilling and took sole charge himself. In a short time we were performing like guardsmen, as we really took a pleasure in the work and we wanted to please the officer. Any good soldier liked being in a smart unit. One by one we met Thirteen, Fifteen and Sixteen Platoons and defeated them.

Then came competition with winners of the other companies. We won our first go and at noon talked with a runner who informed us the losers were getting a day's leave as compensation, and the rest of our company was being taken to a good show in Auchel.

That decided the issue. We purposely made a few mistakes as the afternoon contest began, and lost our chance. We expected a verbal explosion but McIntyre only grinned. "You blighters let me down," he said. "But I'm glad you did. I want to have a good time myself." No officer ever met a difficult situation more diplomatically, and we loved him. He had come up from the ranks and knew the score.

Two more "originals" came to the company-Captain Arthur who took command, and Nobby Clark, a sergeant. Jimmy Davies acted as C.S.M. most of the time, though Kennedy was still with the battalion. Arthur was a perfect gentleman, one of the finest men I have met anywhere, and one of the best soldiers in the 3rd Division. We marched to Cite St. Pierre and did a short trip in the vicinity of Hill 70, where there had been some hard fighting. Beyond enduring a terrible stench from unburied bodies exposed to August heat, and considerable shelling, there was little to record. A second trip at Fosse 10 was but a routine tour. The sector was a zigzag warren of old trenches and enormous slag heaps, rusting wire and rotting sandbags. The slag heaps dominated everything, grim, shell-pounded hillocks, sombre sentries in a sombre landscape.

Our next move was to trenches in front of Mericourt. No man's land was three times as wide as any we had seen before. The Hun line was a thousand yards or more away, and the open space was mostly grassy field with a few trees and several old stubs that shells had created. McIntyre took me out with him on a patrol. We went what seemed an endless distance, being out three hours and never seeing a sign of a German outpost or patrol. There was talk of a raid on the Hun lines, and Arthur called me in and said I was to go out with an officer and six men. The officer was to learn the strength of the German wire; we had all the night for it.

I had only seen the officer a few times, as he was a newcomer from Fifteen Platoon. But I did not like his appearance. We went out at 9:30 and the officer suggested I lead the way, saying he understood I had experience in scouting. He sounded sarcastic but I made no reply. When we reached any new sector I always took time enough to see what landmarks could be used as a guide when in no man's land. On this front there were four old stubs two-thirds of the way over, ranged so that they were parallel to the space between the lines.

We went out slowly. It was a close dark night and not a flare was going up, which meant the Hun had patrols out or listening posts or both. There was a feeling of rain. A machine-gun far over on the right chattered nervously at times but there was scarcely any shelling. I headed for the four stubs. Because some of the men were lagging and I did not want to walk into any ambush, we were a long time getting to the stubs, which were in a slight hollow. We took about an hour getting there.

The officer was nervous. He stood by the stubs and asked a dozen questions. How far were we from the enemy lines? Why were there no flares? Was there likely to be an enemy patrol operating? He received indifferent answers. I told him every front was different, every German unit had different habits. You could not be sure of anything. It could be quite probable that as we talked a German patrol was between us and our lines. Everyone must be quiet as possible and ready for any unexpected occurrence.

He stood silent a moment and then issued sharp orders. It was too risky, he said, to try and get near the German wire with so many men. So I could pick the best man of the six and go with him to the wire. He and the other five would wait right where they were. He did not want me to be too long.

You don't argue with an officer in such a situation. Especially when you consider it safer not to be with him if anything unusual happens. So without hesitation I chose Baillie, and off we went. Baillie and I were supposed to be the scouts of the group. We went carefully. I kept looking back at the stubs, and when I judged we were near the German line we got down and crawled, stopping to listen at every five or six feet. The air seemed closer than ever and the night was uncanny, as if it were peopled with unseen groups and all of them listening.

Time and again I was sure we must be near the Hun, but we would go still further. Then, at long last, I heard voices ahead of us. Sentries were speaking as if they were sure no one could hear them. I whispered to Baillie to stay right where he was and if he saw anything near us to give a low whistle. Then I resumed crawling. One of the most foolish arguments I hear is that there is no such thing as luck. How any reasoning person can make such a statement is beyond me. Fifty percent of the triumphs in this world are the result of lucky breaks. And throughout World War I, pure luck was with me time and again. As I reached the wire I discovered a gap, and the worn grass told me it was used by patrols and listening-post groups going and returning. Off to my right two Huns talked with the casual tone of those simply passing the time. I felt for the posts at the exit and found they were about four feet apart.

All I had to do was creep in the gap and feel for the wire. The Hun drove wooden stakes and strung wire along them, then tossed in loose wire to make tangles. I counted one, two, three fences, rested and crawled further, found four, five and six. Six fences meant an unusually strong wire. As I reached for the last fence a long barb entered my tunic sleeve at an awkward angle. I found it difficult to release, so I had to put my revolver down, lie on my back and work with my free hand.

At that moment, scattered heavy drops of rain hit my face and I knew we were in for one of those sudden drenching French showers. The whole evening had forecast one. At the same time a faint drumming reached my ears and my heart almost turned over. I knew instantly what the sound was. A German listening post was hurrying in to escape the shower. My ear close to earth had caught their tread. I dared not yank hard to clear my sleeve, as the wire might make a twanging sound; and when I was free I knew I dared not risk getting out of the gap. I had no choice. In a split second I had slid into the German trench and turned left. The voices had been on the right.

Now the drops were coming faster. As I rounded a bay a bright flash of summer lightning revealed a dugout entrance with a sentry in front of it, engaged in throwing a rubber ground sheet over his shoulders. His eyes widened as he saw my Canadian steel helmet but before he could cry out I struck him in the face with my revolver. His heels caught on the timber nailed across the dugout entrance to keep out water, and he went down backwards without a word, leaving his rain cape entangled on my revolver. I heard his body thud on the stairway and bump down like a sack of potatoes. And in that instant of time I had thrown the rain cape over my steel helmet. I was just pulling it down over my shoulders as three Germans hurried around the bay. They squeezed past me, breathing heavily, and went down the dugout. It was now simply pouring.

The last fellow was scarcely on the dugout steps before I was going all out. I jumped up into the gap and raced out. Baillie was standing up near the opening. He ran with me and we did our utmost. It is likely we were a hundred yards from the trench when flares shot up and machine-guns opened. We dropped at the first shots and lay with our heels toward the German lines, the rain pelting down on us. Bullets tore into the ground beyond us, to the right of us, but none came near. They fired a dozen "darts" and they went far over us.

When all had quieted we got up and ran again. The air had chilled and the shower was over. There was light enough to see the tops of the stubs and at last we were there. The officer's voice shook with anger. He wanted to know why we had taken an eternity to go a hundred yards or so. What had we done? What was the shooting about?

As he stopped sputtering I told him I had been in the German trench, that there were six wire fences.

"Don't tell me your lies." He was almost shouting. "I'm going to report you. Now lead the way in and no more nonsense."

All of us were soaked to the skin and not another word was said until we reached our trench. "Come with me, Bird," the officer snapped. "The rest of you can go back to your platoons."

He led the way to company headquarters and soon we were facing Captain Arthur. "I am sorry to report no luck," said the officer. "There were too many of us to try and get near the German wire so I sent Bird and a man with him to explore. They were gone an incredibly long time and only stirred up some of the German posts. They opened with machine-gun fire which came near us and we had to flatten on the ground in a downpour of rain. There were also some trench mortars."

There was no exclamation from Arthur. He sat as if waiting, and the officer largely repeated all he had said, sputtering nervously. Then came that quiet voice "D" Company learned to love.

"But I told you to examine the wire."

"As I said," stammered the officer. "There were too many to go near the German trench and I daren't leave the men out in the open as they might run back to our trench."

There was much more in this vein, a man talking against himself, getting more and more disturbed by the eyes watching him.

"So you did not find the strength of the wire?" Arthur finally cut in.

"It is six fences," I interrupted.

"He's lying," said the officer. "All he did was stir up a hornet's nest of machine-gun fire."

"Now we will listen to Bird," said Arthur. "Just what happened?"

I described the way in which Baillie had spotted the German listening post as they stirred around, but dared not try to warn me lest they see him. Then I offered the climax. "I have the rain cape, sir."

Captain Arthur jerked forward in his chair, then stiffened. "You can go," he said crisply to the officer. "And I want a report in writing by tomorrow noon."

We examined the rain cape and found on it the name of the owner and his unit.

"I doubt there will be any raid attempted," said Arthur. "Do you wish to keep this cape as a souvenir?"

I said I did and he let me take it. It made a neat little parcel in my pack and had no weight to bother me. A party from "A" Company went out and captured two German patrols. Lieutenant Crood was in charge, and two of the men with him were Walter Jackson and Art Leslie from our old unit of the Nova Scotia Highlanders Brigade. They each received the Military Medal.

We made a second trip into that same front, but over on the left, where the lines were closer than where we had held before. McIntyre had me go out again with him and in two hours we did not see or hear any enemy patrol. Twice I was out with other patrols from our company but we never saw a Hun. Word came we were to be relieved by the 22nd Battalion, and I was sent out with two men, Hickey and Egglestone, who had come from the 73rd, to act as guides and lead the Van Doos in. We had a long wait for them at the top of the Ridge. As we watched the ten-mile arc of Verey lights glimmer and sink, we saw a German attack on a battalion on our far left. Shells burst along the lines in a winking chaos, and we saw our S.O.S. soar aloft. In another minute red flashes marked the German front, a fury of explosions that lasted twenty minutes. We could hear the rattle of our machine-guns and Mills bombs. Later we learned the attempted German raid never reached our trench.

The Van Doos would not be hurried. Slowly, and with long halts every half mile, we wended our way down the Ridge and out onto the plain. The men smoked in spite of all orders posted along the way and I was thankful when at long last we reached our trenches. Our men moved away with unusual alacrity-recalling the relief at the crater posts-and soon the trench was handed over. They posted no more sentries than we used in daytime. When I mentioned it to one of their sergeants, he shrugged and said: "If he wants to come over-let heem come!"

Chapter 4: Passchendaele

It was now October. We moved away to Magnicourt, where there was to be an inspection of our brigade by General Sir Henry Horne[10]. There was the usual attempt at spit and polish and much fussing over the "sizing" of platoons, making sure no short fellow stood alongside a six-footer. Then we were out almost an hour before the big brass arrived. The next night I was placed on guard. We had quarters in a decent building and the officer of Sixteen Platoon was orderly officer for the period. He warned us that too many high-ranking Imperials were in the area for us to relax in the least. We were to act as sentries and fire patrol combined, making prescribed rounds every hour.

The arrangement was such that it was the hour before daylight when I did my last round. Everything was in darkness and not a vehicle was passing. But as I went along a shot rang out in the house I was passing. It was so unexpected that I stood a moment, wondering what a guard was supposed to do. Then I went to the door and tried it. It was not locked and light shone from an inner room. I stood undecided, expecting a voice or voices. None came so I looked in the room. An officer was lying on the floor in his pyjamas, a revolver beside him[11]. No one else was there.

One look was enough to see the man was dead. Then I saw a written note lying on the table beside the lighted lamp. The pen was there as if it had just been used. I scanned the note, went out and down the street to where I knew a senior officer was billetted. He was rather gruff at being aroused, until I told him my errand. Then he dressed very hurriedly and went back with me. He read the note and told me not to tell any person what I had seen. He would look after everything. I was to carry on with my round.

There were rumours afloat the next day, but I never mentioned a thing to anyone. Our platoon was feeling like laughing every time a person spoke. One section was in a barn. Giger, the near-moron, made his bed in a corner away from the door. There were cattle in the rest of the building and during the night a calf managed to get its head through a small opening and licked Giger's face. He woke everyone with his yells of sheer terror.

Our section was in what had been a coal shed. A brick ledge ran around the wall and on it ran three or four generations of mice, so that we moved to the barn loft and slept on straw. But it was a useless effort. The mice were there as well, and after battling them a time I went down and outside. It was quite mild but dark and uncanny. Men were on the move. You heard nothing but the steady tramp, tramp, tramp on the road as the shadowy files marched past in a cloud of dust like river mist, silent and half-asleep. They were, like us, headed Ypres-way. Bulky ghosts loomed alongside the column, the non-coms, watching for stragglers, but there were no shouted orders. The only sounds besides the tramping feet were the dull creak of equipment and an occasional muttered curse as someone trod on another's heels. All at once the line halted. Men slumped down on the roadside without waiting for any "fall out" order. Mostly they reclined on their packs, but here and there a match flared as a cigarette

[10] General Sir Henry Horne (1861-1929). Commander of the First British Army, which included the Canadians, 1916-1918.

[11] Lieutenant Walter Wrixon DeRossiter, of Dublin, Ireland. Age 49.

was lighted and there were glimpses of tired, sharp-lined faces. After the battalion had gone I wandered along the road. The night was still and warm but a shower threatened. A dozing sentry was leaning on his rifle. Back from him, under two big trees, several men were sleeping on the ground. Then to my surprise I met McIntyre. He had probably been visiting some other unit and was feeling talkative. He asked me what I was doing and said I should be sleeping. I mentioned Ypres, and he cursed the place. Then he talked about the platoon and praised his "boys." And his voice seemed to go husky, making me think that he had to censor the company letters that afternoon, perhaps finding them more poignantly inarticulate than usual. It began to rain as I left him and went back in the mysterious silence only broken by the steady beating on the cobbles. The bent still figure of the sentry had not moved, but under the trees the sleepers were stirring and muttering as drops from branches overhead fell on their unprotected faces.

We moved again the next day, seeming to leave the main route, for we stopped at a little village prettier than any I had seen. Trees shaded most of the homes and a brook gurgled its way among them, flowing under a stone bridge that looked a century old. The men had become restless. The *estaminet* had a penny-in-the-slot piano and they made merry, singing too boisterously for harmony. Giger got drunk and semaphored to a mademoiselle until incapable of motion. The men were noisy during our evening meal, and afterward smoked the Army gaspers, Red Hussars and Beeswings, as if in a contest. Rumours of what waited ahead of us had disturbed everyone.

That night was the wildest I had seen in billets. Two-thirds of the men had too much liquor. We had two new men who were different. One was Corporal Jimmy Hughes, who came from the 73rd. The other everyone called "The Professor." He spoke with a precise manner and never used slang. The platoon thought him a granny who considered even a knowledge of French immoral. Our men shouted at each other about the three kinds of "cases" we might expect, "walking," "sandbag" and "stretcher," asked each other grisly questions concerning "next-of-kin," made vows to get either a Victoria Cross or a "wooden one." Then the ones who'd had too much went up the street to get more, but the *estaminet* had closed. Probably our military police had something to do with it, but, as in almost any country, there were ways and means of getting drink. About eleven Tommy and Childs and I went out and began helping lads back to the billet. Some cases were so helpless we got a stretcher and carried them in.

Tommy and Old Bill helped them undress but I went out to the old bridge and sat there. I hated the smell of a place where a man had been rum-sick. The moonlight fell flat on things and gilded them, and there was the night's faint moist smell of trees and grass and brookside. A man came along, walking slowly, and sat beside me on the old stone wall. It was Stewart, our stretcher bearer, a fine man in every way, and he began talking, telling me of his boyhood in Scotland, of his going to Canada, what he intended to do after the war. As he left I looked at my watch and it was one o'clock, but The Professor came along and told me he had found friendly folk at the far end of the village who talked English, and had spent hours with them. As we went back to billet we found Mickey lying on the brook bank. One turn would have dropped him in a deep pool. We carried him in and put him to bed.

The train took us to Hazebrouck, packed in "40 *Hommes*" coaches. Some were nursing hangovers, but the stronger ones were singing in harmony while Old Bill made a type of music with tissue paper on a comb. In our coach were Bill Brown, Baillie, Ira Black, Glenn Lunn, Corporal Hughes, Bunty, Kennedy, Lugar, Hickey, Egglestone, Flynn, Cuvilier, Mickey, Tommy, Dykes, a broad shouldered newcomer, and a lance-jack named Alway. The boys persisted in calling him Always.

Hazebrouck was quite a town. Baillie, Ira Black and I went to have a feed of eggs and chips but discovered we didn't have quite enough money. As we considered our problem we looked in a place and saw Howard Gordon sitting alone at a table. He was a good-natured lad and everyone liked him. He could not speak a word of French, so we decided to go in, order our food and tell Madame that Howard would pay the shot. Howard greeted us warmly as we went in and asked us to sit with him, so there was no difficulty.

We dallied a time after finishing and looked at each other. Howard noticed our glances. "I bet you haven't got a franc," he grinned. "You planned to stick me for the eggs and chips?"

"It's the sad truth," admitted Baillie. "Can we borrow from you?"

"No, you can't," came his retort. "I'm flush and I'm going to pay the works myself. You can treat me on our way back."

It began to rain that night and continued all the next day. We went to Ypres and waited four hours in the desolated town. Tommy and I went exploring an old ruin that had once been an elegant home. There were actually lace curtains at the one unbroken window in the building, although the roof was gone. There was a sort of path through the debris to the remains of a large marble fireplace, but our noses told us the place had been used as a latrine. As we emerged, a man with Pioneer badges came and begged for a smoke. Tommy obliged him and he began pointing out places in the fan of the great wheel before us, Railway Wood, Hooge, Sanctuary Wood, Mount Sorrel, Hellfire Corner, the Crab Crawl, the Bluff and Zillebeke Lake. Then a whistle blew for us to fall in.

We went to California Trench, relieving the C.M.R.'s, and found it a dreadful, smelly ditch with make-shift shelters. The rain was a constant drizzle so we dragged out into the mud until we found some corrugated iron and contrived a sort of shelter for three of us, Tommy and Baillie and myself. There was considerable shelling but it had no pattern whatever. Shells dropped here and there, as if the gunners did not care where they went. Water had formed two or three inches deep in the big ditch they called a trench and there was no way to make a bed under our four-by-five roof. So we huddled together with ground sheets spread on a bit of plank for a seat. We sat there the night, soaked by constant dripping and chilled to the bone.

Dawn came slowly, with a clinging penetrating mist that made even our rifles clammy to the touch. We ate our rations but had not been issued tommy cookers and could not make tea. At eight we climbed from the ditch and were formed in small sections of seven or eight men, then stood in oozing mud while an officer came to "inspect" the swamp hole in which we had cowered, to see if any cigarette butt or can were in sight. *Wheeee-wump!* We heard it coming but had not energy enough to try and run for cover. The big shell arrived with heart-stopping threat and exploded in the spot where we had sat all night-leaving the inspecting officer a lifeless bloody pulp[12].

There was a long wait as a party was detailed to take the body to Ypres, and then we moved to tents in St. Jean, where we were told to take off our equipment and leave

12 Lieutenant Charles Kenneth MacPherson of Clinton, Ontario.

it where we would bed down at night, along with our rifles. The tents were leaking and the floor boards either broken or tilted with long usage, but we did as ordered, then lined up outside. An artillery sergeant joined our officer to act as a guide. We followed duckboards for a distance and began to see dead mules and horses along the way. Some had been there a long time, but the whole Salient had an odour beyond description, and one never felt the dead mules added much to it.

When we left the duckboards it was to go through mud knee deep. Progress was slow, as each man tried to avoid sinking deeper than necessary. We stopped and the sergeant waded over to an "island" of broken timbers and got a heavy coil of large rope. It was soggy and muddy, all he could carry. We kept on and arrived at a battery of five guns. The battery horses had drowned in mire as they tried to move the guns to the left where a slight rise afforded more solid ground, so now thirty men of the 42nd took hold of the rope and tried to pull a gun. It was soon evident we could not move the guns in the usual fashion, as the mud gripped the wheels like glue, so we turned them over and over until they were at the new emplacement.

It was tremendous labour. Each man had to keep getting a new footing, and often we sank in mud and water of gruel thickness until the slime rose above our hips. The only thing solid underneath was a huddled dead man, and we stumbled over five or six during the morning. The job had to be completed before we went back to the tents, but there were just two thirty-man teams, so it was almost three o'clock when the last gun was in the new position. At that moment over came two big black-winged German Gothas and dropped bombs. Their aim was bad. They missed us by one hundred yards, but some ammunition mules were packed in line on a shaky "board road" made of planks and one bomb made a direct hit on a broad mule rump.

The Gothas flew off, and we saw men pull three dead mules into the mire, an addition to the many carcasses beside the way with legs stiffened toward the sky and bodies distended so that they afforded footholds for rats. Shambles of heads and entrails were shovelled into the mire and then the ammunition train went on. We had stood knee-deep in the slime and watched proceedings, and now we turned and made our way toward the duckboards. We had just reached sound footing and were trying to stamp off clinging mud when we heard shells coming. The Hun was still after the battery. He seemed to have uncanny knowledge of the slope. Most of the shells went into the mud to raise small harmless geysers, but one gun was wrecked by a direct hit and two gunners were killed. We watched dispassionately from two hundred yards away, as if we had no part in such actions, then went back to our tents, sodden, shaking with exhaustion, plastered with mud, and were cheered with messtins of hot mulligan and hot tea. The rations were up and better than usual. After eating we had energy enough to scrape mud from our kilts and bare knees, but only to a degree. No man tried to get clean. It began to rain again, to get colder. Some hardy spirit ventured forth and found where we could get water, as we had been issued plenty of tommy cookers. So we made tea by the messtin around six o'clock and ate again.

It was impossible to escape the leaks in the rain-soaked tent. The sagging floor pooled with icy water. We put our ground sheets over our shoulders, kept our helmets on and sat on our equipment, doubled to keep us from the wet floor, jammed together in a huddle about the tent pole. Through the night we sat there in the dark, unmoving, sleeping in fitful snatches, wakened by someone starting to fall over, not speaking, our brains numbed by the awfulness of everything, each trying to attain the comatose state that answered for sleep.

At daylight we made and drank messtins of hot tea. More rations arrived and we ate. Around nine o'clock orders came for us to put our equipment on, ready to move. There was still a slight drizzle as we waded over to the duckwalk. We proceeded slowly as we were continually meeting men, some walking wounded cases, going back. One dared not yield too much right of way, because to step from the wooden bath mats might mean immersion to the waist. On and on we went, with the occasional halt as we waited for guides or runners. At noon we reached an area dotted with rusting derelict tanks and stood there, sideways on, as the remnants of a relieved battalion edged by us, men who looked like grisly discards of the battlefield, long unburied, who had risen and were in search of graves. Not one of them spoke, nor did we.

Three sausage balloons had gone up above Ypres as the rain had stopped. A German airman came over, flying deliberately, swooped down and sprayed bullets into the nearest blimp. There were forked flames, billowing smoke, a meteor of fiery fabric, charred fragments, and two swaying figures attached to parachutes. They dangled a moment and sank from sight as two of our planes appeared. The German had spotted them and was away. The other two balloons remained aloft.

After standing around an hour amid much going back and forth of runners, we were told we had to stay in the place and make any shelter possible. There would be no chore for us until after dark. Some of the men managed to get into the derelict tanks and slept there. Tommy and Baillie and I went to one and could tip it with our weight. But there was water in it, and water around it. As we rocked the monster, a head squeezed out of the muck, a face without eyes, the skin peeled as though from lard, a corpse long dead and frightful.

We left the tanks and wandered about, being lucky enough to find a mound of solid mud, enough to make our bed, and there we stayed between sandbagged walls, with a roof of salvaged corrugated iron. Nearby was an old trench revetted with German stick work, blocked at one part with broken wire and the black dead of forgotten fights. About dark we wriggled outside to make room enough to set up our tommy cookers, and hot tea put life into us.

An hour later our platoon was called to form up on the duckwalk. We were led back to a "dump" where each man was told to take up and carry a section of new-made bath mats. All around the giant horseshoe of the Salient there were red flashes and winking glows, and the misty light of flares. The man in charge of the dump told us not to linger on the way but to make good time, as the German shelled the duckwalks with considerable accuracy. We were not to worry, he said, as only a direct hit would maim or kill. A shell could go in the mud just twenty feet from where you stood and do no damage, save splattering you with mud. He said mud had saved at least ten thousand lives in the Salient and was saving more every day.

We moved up toward the front line, past water-logged trenches, a nightmare of scummy holes, an indescribable desolation, and our burdens, plus occasional gaps in the duckwalk made by shelling, made our going slow. The sky became illumined by a thousand strange flickering lights, the reflection of a thousand gun flashes, and quivered with the passage of shells. As we neared the end of our duckwalk flares soared up ahead of us, alarmingly near. Their fitful gleams made strange moving shadows over the swamp. A machine-gun fired nervously, and its bullets buried themselves with vicious thuds in jagged tree stubs close by. We hurried, then met the leading carriers returning. Each man, as he came to the end of the bath mats we trod, threw down the one he was carrying, butting it to the one on which he stood. Thus the path grew with amazing speed. But the boards were new and their light colour was detected. Suddenly a hurricane of shell fire was all about us. Fortunately it happened just as I got clear of my load. I ran back where men were hustling, jostling and cursing. In a moment all was confusion. High explosive rained all around us-stunning, terrifying, but not a shell actually hit the duckboards. The shell eruptions sent mud and slime in all directions and roused new smells of old gas and mud and blood.

Some of the men had simply got clear of their bath mats where they were as the shells came, but no officer was with us and the sergeant did not shout any orders. We were about one hundred yards away from the scene when suddenly the Hun began sending salvos ahead of us. Some sharp mind in his artillery staff had calculated our actions. But we were not in a panic. Without an order being shouted, every man stood where he was and there we waited, until after a few minutes the salvos ceased. At midnight we were back in our shelters and everyone made tea. We were away from all water tanks but there was plenty of rain water in shell holes, and if the water were boiled a time, we were told, it was all right to use. No one debated the point. We simply boiled and drank.

Orders came in the morning that we were to move again. We went to Abraham Heights and relieved the R.C.R.s. Our platoon was lucky enough to reach a spot where the mud was hard enough to make a shelter. Baillie and I made a small shelter, and Brown and Tommy had one close by. Hickey and Alway came over and said they had trouble with water where they dug. So they began making a short bed-length shelter about thirty yards away.

We had just finished our new abode when we heard the distant report of a high-velocity gun. One got to know the differences between reports in a comparatively short time. "I don't like the sound of that one," said Baillie. It came with a rush that made us duck and hit about fifty yards beyond, sending up cartloads of muck. Another one came and it was much nearer. Hickey yelled a warning, but we were already crouched like rabbits in a hail storm. The third shell plowed deep beside Hickey. He vanished in the cloud of filth. We rushed over, half-blinded by the falling slime and choked with fumes. Neither man was to be seen. We dug frantically and found Hickey. He had been killed by concussion. Alway was dead too, doubled beneath him.

Shaken by the explosions and our efforts, we awaited a fourth shell, but it did not come. Half an hour later slim rations arrived, some mail and dry socks. I read my two letters and then carefully peeled off my mud-hardened puttees, removed my boots and put on the clean dry socks. Baillie had received a parcel from his sister. He could not read or write and I read to him the short note enclosed. She was sending him four plugs of his favourite chewing tobacco, "Napoleon," and hoped it would do him until Christmas when she would send more. She was well and they were having very mild weather.

He took the tobacco and went over to visit Bill Brown, who also chewed. I could hear their talk and saw him give Brown a plug. Next he made his way down to another section and when he returned he had only one plug left. "You're too big-hearted," I said.

Map 3: Passchendaele, the Attack on Graf House

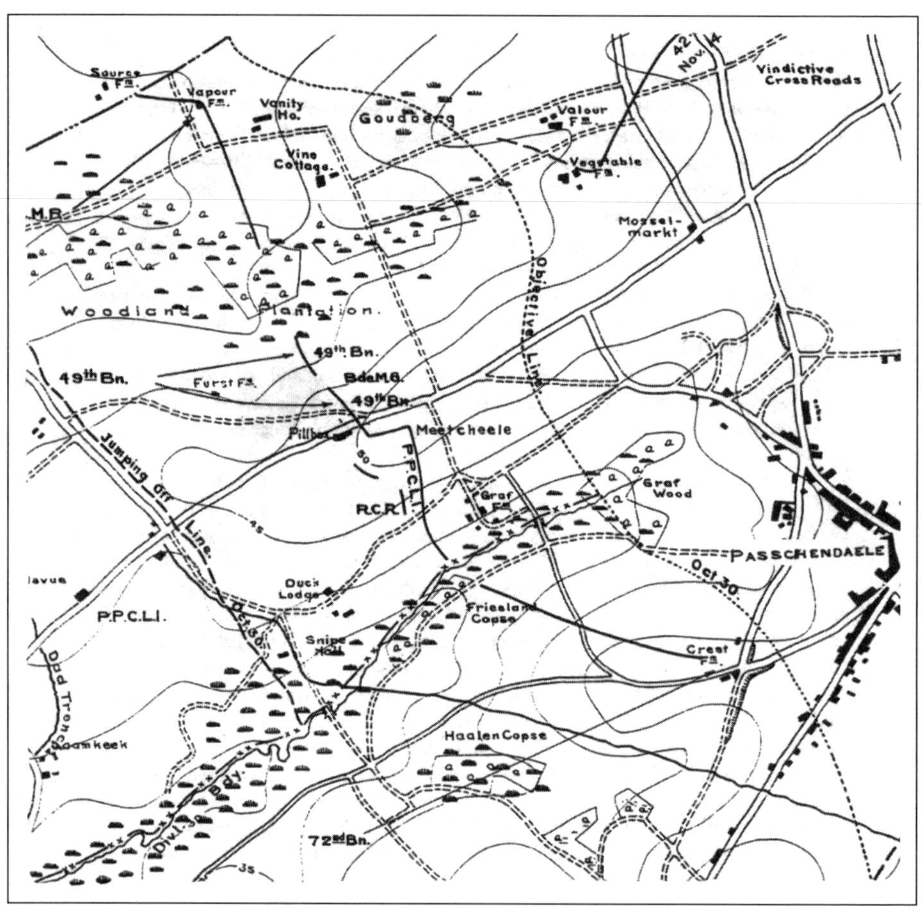

"No, I'm not," he said. Then he handed me the socks he had been issued. "Put these in your pack," he went on. "I won't need them."

"What do you mean?" His manner startled me.

"Don't argue with me, Bill," he returned. "I'm not coming back from this one."

For a moment I was too stunned to think of words. We had been through all sorts of action together, and he was one of the best to have with you in a tight corner. Nothing could faze him.

My acquaintance with Baillie had begun back in Aldershot, Nova Scotia. We were not given many passes for late evenings, and as there was entertainment in plenty in the town a mile away, many men tried to slip back to their tents without being seen by the guard. Camped above us on the slope were the Cape Breton Highlanders. Their battalion sergeant-major was one of those men whose greatest joy in life is to make someone else miserable. He had nothing to do with us, but we would come down the transport road through their lines and slip into our tents from their camp corner. He got a flashlight and would station himself there, grab some of our lads if they did not spot him first, make them give him identification and send in their names to our officers. Such action naturally gave rise to many threats, but after he caught Baillie there was more than threats. Baillie was a big fellow and powerful. He went to town and bought a bottle of whiskey, came in late by the same route; when the B.S.M. grabbed him, Baillie threw that individual on his back, knelt over him and by holding his nose forced him to swallow all the whiskey.

Someone found the B.S.M. some hours later, making queer noises. He was rushed to hospital and recovered. He had glimpsed Baillie before being overpowered and sent in a report that might have committed a man to life imprisonment. But our officers did not like the manner in which the B.S.M. carried on, and Baillie was only given three days C.B. (Confined to Barracks). The conscientious military police thought he should be required to do something during the period and hunted jobs of whitewashing which were well performed until, just at noon time, he was taken to the company commander's tent. There was a neat flower bed ringed by stones, and the stones would look better whitewashed. The policeman got a call and was leaving, so Baillie asked what he was to do. "Whitewash," came the answer.

"Whitewash what?" asked Baillie. There were posts marking off the tent site, and they had not received attention. "Everything," yelled the police officer, by then almost out of hearing. "Everything." He felt Baillie ought to know what he had in mind.

An hour later an irate company commander found his tent and cot and all covered with a heavy coat of whitewash, and the police officer found that five men, good and true comrades of Baillie, had heard the specific shouted directions. Baillie was acquitted.

The P.B.I. (Poor Blinkin' Infantry) were really supposed to earn their $ 1.10 a day with free board. So when not in combat with the enemy, they did the work that was supposed to be the lot of the Pioneers. One chore was the digging of cable trenches. The cables had to be put six feet down to escape shell damage, and always the areas selected for such trenches were in the hardest chalk zones. We were out one night on such an errand. We were digging six feet in depth and six feet in length, and an engineer officer was in charge. His manner indicated he thought the P.B.I. the lowest form of humans in uniform. He had a pole with the six-foot level marked on it in luminous paint, and when a man said he had the required depth and distance, long past midnight after five hours' hard labour, he was not believed. He was not to leave until the officer had tested the trench with his pole. And the officer was far too smart to be outwitted by any P.B.I. dullard. He always put the pole down at least three feet away from where the slave pointed.

On this particular night half the crowd had dug their required stint and were gone. Baillie had struck unusually hard going, and the officer had been most sarcastic, hinting he knew a slacker when he saw one, etc. So when a spot of soft earth was unexpectedly encountered in the centre of Baillie's bit, he sunk a well there the depth of the shovel handle. Around came the officer and wondered aloud if he had to stay all night for the lazy ones. Baillie simply stood and pointed where to put the pole down. The officer snorted contempt, made a lunge at the centre part and went down with a great crash. The pole snapped off and there were deep groans. Baillie told us about it when he returned. We did not know how long the officer lay in the hole before being found. He was sent away for repairs, and efforts to locate the cause of the disaster were not successful.

But now this rough and ready lumberjack had assumed a quiet seriousness. It was easy to sense he did not want to discuss the matter. "Let's just not talk about it," he said. "You and me have got on grand and I don't want to spoil it."

So there was nothing to do but carry on as if nothing had been said. Our spot was the driest in that area and seemed a bit higher. I stood to look around for landmarks and noticed something about one hundred yards on our left. Baillie came and gazed, and then we set off across the mud without saying a word to the others. Nearly all of them were lying in whatever temporary shelter they had devised.

We reached a level of planks, covered with mud. It was evident they were the same type as used for the "board road." And in the middle were lying two sacks partly covering three jugs of rum. We peered into the first sack and it was filled with bread, most of it turning green at the end of the loaf. The other sack had meat, cooked meat in slices, such as we had never been issued. We felt it must have been intended for an officers' mess, and ate what we could. Then we carefully carried about a pound or so with us to put in our haversacks. We sorted out a loaf each of the bread, finding two loaves with no green tinge. The rum seemed a waste but we agreed not to mention it, and remembered that many of the R.C.R.s we had relieved had seemed half-drunk.

It was soon dark and orders came to move. So we filed in the darkness up Gravenstafel Road and halted by shell holes occupied by the 49th. It was higher ground and much drier than any place we had seen. As they left we dug and connected many of the holes, then cut places in the trench sides, hung ground sheets over them and boiled messtins of tea. One boiling and our water was gone. There had been no sniping, so I took off my equipment and crawled out a distance to find a hole filled with rainwater. After two trips we had all the water we needed. The tea was wonderful as the night turned chilly.

All at once we heard a low moaning sound from somewhere in the sea of mud fronting us. It was faint but sounded like a man in deep suffering. Once at Vimy a sentry had heard a man moaning in no man's land and went out to help him. Then he was shot and badly wounded by a German sniper who had simulated suffering in order to lure a victim over the parapet. So I said this might be another such decoy and Baillie agreed with me. But Sergeant Ormandy heard the sound and told Sergeant Clark. Out they went, moving with extreme care, and found a German in the swamp. He was badly wounded, having lain in the muck so long that gangrene had set in. He hated us and snarled like an animal. A stretcher party was organized and carried him back to the nearest dressing station, leaving him there alongside a wounded R.C.R. officer. The pillbox was filled with other cases and evacuation was slow. The stretcher party was no more than fifty yards on their return trip when a shell dropped between the German and the officer. Its explosion sent mud, bodies and stretchers into the air. The party hurried away as a dozen more shells ringed the place. The Germans shelled dressing stations frequently.

Ormandy came and told me I was wanted at the end of our newly made trench. In the dark I made out the officer commanding Sixteen Platoon. He told me I was to go on a patrol with him, as some of his men asserted they had seen several Germans beyond a hedge on their front. He said the area was marked Furst Farm on his map. He had not been long with the company and was very nervous but seemed the right type. I asked if I might shed my equipment and he agreed at once. Some extra clips of ammunition and two Mills bombs in my pockets seemed enough.

We moved out very slowly. The mud carried us in places but after a time we reached a farmyard and there was slime on the mud. The place was nauseating, with a putrid stench that had both of us close to gagging. Shelling had started at the right of us but nothing came our way and flares were at a distance. We had just worked our way through the farmyard when up went flares about two hundred yards in front. I froze there on my hands and knees. Directly in front of me, revealed by the flares, was an outline of pot helmets!

The officer, behind me, had not seen them. I turned and whispered, and he became agitated. Perhaps, he said, we should go back. More flares arose and I stared, saw the line of German heads. A patrol seemed bunched there, waiting for us. But before the last light faded I had noticed something. Not one head had moved!

A whisper informed the officer. He said to wait for more flares and for me to be absolutely sure. So we lay in the mud and presently up went five or six more flares. The German was not taking chances on a surprise attack. This time I made sure that not one helmet tilted a fraction. Everyone seemed immovable, so we crept forward. Halfway there we stopped and waited for another lot of flares. This time there was no doubt. Every German was dead!

They were in rifle pits. They had been killed by overhead shrapnel and were so wedged in the mud that only four had fallen over. We crept completely around them and not one was alive. I realized they had been dead for quite some time, and the foul stench was drifting from their decomposing bodies. So back we went, sickened with smells, my legs raw in places rubbed by my mud-hardened kilt. Baillie made me a messtin of hot tea and I curled up on a ground sheet he had found and slept.

When I woke it was growing light. Rumour had it that we were to be relieved that night. There had been no shelling of our area, and many of the men were chatting happily. Bunty and Brown were near us in the trench and they wanted more tea. They asked if I would go out to my shell hole and get water. So out I went and as I dipped in their messtins there was light enough to see a dead rat at the bottom. The hole was fairly large so I went back and said nothing, but insisted the water be boiled an extra time, saying every water hole must be polluted. Baillie and I had good meals. The cooked meat was delicious.

All day we sat in those connected shell holes, dozing as much as we could, waiting for word of relief. Then a runner arrived. McIntyre was with him, and they talked with Ormandy and Clark. The runner left and McIntyre came into our trench and asked us to gather around. His manner, and breath, told me the worst. The 42nd was to make a big attack on the enemy. There would be five parties in all, and ours would be called Number Two. There would be twenty-five of us, with Clark as our second-in-command. We were to capture a pillbox.

Every man sitting or squatting in that trench knew two things. First, that McIntyre had no sure idea of where the pillbox was. Second, that he had had much rum. He told us it was not far to the pillbox, that the main attack was to be on a strong point called Graf House, that one party was to be on the bank of the Gravenstafel-Mosselmarkt Road to protect our advance. There would not be any barrage. We were to work up a road as quietly as possible and to reach our objective at two a.m. The Stokes guns were moving into position and would send over salvos if they received a signal.

When he had finished talking, McIntyre climbed out of the trench and had another session with Clark. Then he called to me. "You are to follow close to me all the way," he said. "When we have our objective I want you to take the message back to company headquarters. I can't trust it to a runner."

"How far is it up the road to the pillbox?" I asked.

McIntyre said it was about one hundred and fifty yards. Clark said it was twice that far, and to the right of the road. McIntyre said he was wrong. He had seen the map. It was left of the road. Never through the war was I more sickened and discouraged than at that moment. The whole affair was cock-eyed. We were new in the sector. None knew the terrain. None knew what defences the German had or his strength. The place after dark was a swampy wilderness without anything to use as a guide. Half the men had never been in an attack, and that included the officers. Furthermore, in those few minutes I discovered that Clark had also had too much rum.

Word came to get ready. Every man was to have two Mills bombs to throw if need be. Baillie came and shook hands with me, a long hard clasp without a word spoken. Then I was amazed when Ira Black came and whispered he was glad we were on our way. The waiting was deadly and now we would have action and get from the hateful swamp when it was over. Then a sergeant came with a jug of rum and every man who would take it had a stiff jolt.

At least we found the road. It wasn't much. Shell fire had almost erased it in spots. We started in four little parties, McIntyre leading on the left. I was crawling directly behind him and told him if I saw anything of the enemy I would pull his foot. Lugar was back of me, then Charlie Hale, Stewart, Mickey, Tommy, Brown and Johnson. On the other side of the so-called road was Clark, and back of him were Baillie, Ira Black, Jennings, a big man who disliked the French but who was religious and often got the boys to sing hymns, Neath and Flynn. The rest of the twenty-five followed in two groups.

There was quite a drop of bank on our left. McIntyre did not look left or right but kept scrambling along as fast as possible. I peered over the bank from time to time and suddenly saw three or four Germans raise their heads no more than twenty yards from us. I seized McIntyre's foot to signal him. He yanked it away and spoke angrily. The Germans fired instantly. A bullet creased the top of Lugar's head, slicing his scalp and causing him to be temporarily insane. Hale and I had to hold him down by main force, as had he raised he would have been shot. In our struggle Hale raised up higher than he thought and was likewise creased with a bullet. Now it was Stewart, the stretcher bearer, and I holding Lugar, but he began to quiet and the moment I could let go of him I threw my grenades over the bank. Both exploded as they went down, and the Hun shooting stopped at once.

The next thing was to get Lugar's bombs to replace mine, which I did. McIntyre had never stopped and was quite a distance ahead. Clark's party kept up with him. Brown had crawled forward and now he and I left the group and ran to catch up with McIntyre. Machine-guns opened up on all sides. The night was an uproar. We dove into the mud and saw the signal go up for the Stokes support. The German Maxim stopped firing and we jumped and started running again. There was a flaming white-hot instant-and oblivion!

When I recovered consciousness my head was splitting with pain and a terrible nausea had seized my stomach. The Stokes shell had dropped beside us, throwing me bodily across the road and knocking Brown down. He was rolled over on his back, feeling for wounds, as I saw him. All around us was a clamour of machine-guns, bombs and rifles. I heard McIntyre shouting "Five rounds rapid!" Then his voice shut off abruptly. I discovered my nose had been bleeding, and when I tried to get up I collapsed again with dizziness.

The burst of shooting stilled. There were no more bomb explosions. But far on our left another eruption of shooting began to dominate the night. Brown had tried to stand and had just slumped down again when we heard plunging noises in the mud and two dim figures came toward us, puffing and blowing, carrying something and grunting in conversation. They were Germans, big men, and had a machine-gun on a tripod. They went past us, apparently thinking us dead, and set up their weapon about thirty feet from us. One man yanked at a long cartridge belt, while the other grunted something. I pulled the pin from one of my grenades, held it for a count of two, then hurled it at the Germans and flattened myself in the mud.

The bomb burst between the two gunners. Not a bit of metal touched Brown or myself. One German never moved but lay on his back, dead. The other pawed at his side feebly for a time, then was still. Brown and I struggled up, went over and made sure both Germans were dead, then heard a voice calling. We found a 42nd man in a shell crater, holding his left arm and groaning. He told us he was from "A" Company, that his group was lost and most of them had been killed or wounded. His left hand dangled, held only by a strip of skin. I cut the skin with my trench knife and bound up the stump with his field dressing, poured a bottle of iodine over it, slit a hole in his tunic and had him thrust his arm through it for support. Then I took off one of his puttees and made a tourniquet of it as best I could to stop the bleeding. We helped him from the crater and away he went, past the dead German gunners.

At that moment Clark came from somewhere behind us, trying to run and reeling all over the place. "Come on!" he shouted "Let's give them hell!"

His shout ended and he pitched into the mud ahead of us. He was dead when we tried to raise him. Another figure emerged from the murk. It was Neath. He said

McIntyre was lying to our left, shot through the stomach and dying, unconscious. Neath wanted to get a stretcher and carry him out. We asked him where the others were.

"The party behind Clark's never came along after the shooting started," he said, "and I don't think the ones behind us did. The others are just ahead a few yards in a big shallow crater."

We went on and soon found the place, the limit of our advance, not one hundred yards from where I had yanked McIntyre's foot. Mickey and Old Bill Childs and Johnson were there, crouched low and taking quick shots at a German gun that streaked sparks a very short distance away. Its bullets tore at the crater lip. Brown gave me one of his bombs and we threw at the same time. The bursts must have been right on the gun, since there was not another shot from it.

A look around showed us three still figures on the bank beyond Mickey. They were all dead: Baillie, his premonition proved correct, and Ira and Jennings, lying together, rifle in hand, all shot through the head by one sweep of the German gun. Back of them was another dead man, Sam Burnett. He had been with one of the rear parties. Neath came with a stretcher and Childs helped him get McIntyre on it. They carried him away, and Johnson went with them as relief in the carrying.

Suddenly I was sick again and vomited severely. Brown and Mickey stayed with me. There was comparative quiet now in our sector, but heavy firing to both our right and left. Machine-gun bullets whined about so that we had to crawl, and when we were back a distance we found The Professor lying on the road bank, riddled with bullets. He was plastered with mud and had lost his glasses and steel helmet. Evidently he had got lost in the darkness and there he lay, after years of study and culture, a smashed cog of the war machine, with not a hope of burial save by a chance shell.

Ten yards on we came into a light vapour rising with the chill of the night. Over on the high bank of the road, we saw Stewart stooped over someone. We called to him softly and told him to get down in the ditch. He did not answer and went on bandaging someone who was lying perfectly still. There was the report of a German rifle. Stewart pitched head-first across the man he was bandaging, so that his kilt fell over his back, and lay there, dead, while the sniper shot again and again, as if venting a crazy hate. The wounded man was still. I had lost a bomb and we had none, but we wormed back to a spot on the roadbank and from there all three of us fired at the rifle flashes. They stopped instantly. We started back. Mickey was at the limit of his endurance. He was not rugged and we had to rest him now and then, so it was an hour before we were back in the trenches. And there I suddenly lost consciousness again.

When I came awake it was late in the morning. I was lying in a corner of the trench, plastered with mud, and Mickey was beside me. Brown was curled like a dog in another corner. Mickey told me I had been violently sick twice and then had lain as if in a coma. He said there had been a heavy shelling of the area. I became aware of the acrid reek of explosives. None of the other survivors were near us. Not a runner had appeared. We huddled there until noon, then I roused up and peered over the side of our refuge. A few yards away were three green-scummed pools. White chalky hands reached out of one, and from the farther one a knee stuck up above the filthy water. In another bit of old trench, where the parados had disappeared, a soldier stood rigidly, feet braced apart. He had been killed by concussion, and his body was split as if sliced by a great knife. Some German bodies were lying on a bank and one, bare-headed, looked as if he were reclining on one elbow.

A shell came as I looked and erupted almost beneath the body, and the dead man stood straight up a heartbeat, as if saluting, then tumbled down on the other side. I lay down again and saw that neither Brown nor Mickey were moving. They were huddled side by side, mud-splattered, sleeping.

Night found us still in our cover, and I got up and explored until I found Old Bill and Johnson. A runner had told them a relief was due but there had been no orders. The attack had been a flop. Lieutenant Crood's party had got into Graf House, but he had been killed and they had to withdraw. All the 42nd losses had been for naught. Sergeant Ormandy had been wounded. Corporal Jimmy Hughes had gone on leave from St. Jean. We did not know who would have charge of what was left of Fourteen Platoon. Then a corporal from Thirteen Platoon came and told us we were to go back to Ypres, the 16th Battalion was relieving us. We went with him and met our relief coming in by our old trench, and heard that Glenn Lunn had been killed.

All that drag back was a hideous nightmare. The track was worse than when we came in, and the shelling was incessant. We moved with infinite slowness, every step a struggle, a physical effort, a vast noise over us and all about us, a rolling clamour that dulled thinking and helped us forget some of the frightfulness of the night before. We went back to the Watou area and there were given trousers to replace our soaked and muddied kilts. A big draft came and refilled our ranks, and then came the dread word that we must make a second trip into Passchendaele. One unit of every brigade had to do so, and it was the 42nd in the 7th Brigade.

The November rains became more chilling. Our feet were always soggy, and some of the men were on the verge of becoming despondent. K. K. McLeod and Farmer had died in the mud. Poor old Flynn had been killed. Egglestone had been wounded and was on a stretcher going out when he and those who carried him were killed by a big shell. A chap named Upham, who had been out before, joined us and stayed in our section.

Once more we went to California Trench and hated it more than before. We went on the next night through heavy shelling to an abomination of desolation, finding tangles of wire in absurd places, men squatting in the muck, staring, stiff-moving men who muttered to themselves as they got up and moved away. It was daylight before we could learn where we were to dig in. Captain Arthur came among us then, the first officer we had seen up there save McIntyre and the officer of Sixteen Platoon. He told us to dig for shelter, and no more, as we might move at any time. Orr and Hayward were wounded on the way up and one man killed.

As we worked the Hun began to shell our position with "whizz-bangs," and some of the men grew panicky. Arthur climbed through the mud from group to group, speaking to the fellows reassuringly. Tommy and I were digging together and watched him come near us. Dykes was working just a few feet from us. He straightened to say something to us, and the next instant a shell cut the top of his head away, leaving but the jaw and neck. The body rocked a moment and then toppled backward. Arthur saluted as he passed.

Sure enough. No sooner had we got partial shelter from the shelling than word came to go on and make a new line. The Hun seemed to spot us there. He shelled us and machine-gun fire raked around us. Upham scrambled over a mud heap to join me and suggested we work together. We had good digging but the bullets and shells came closer and closer. I peered ahead and saw a body, that of a big man with equipment over his greatcoat. "Catch hold of this stiff," I said. "We'll pull it back here and use it as part of our parapet."

Upham jumped back, horrified. "Don't!" he yelled. "Don't touch him."

So I seized the corpse myself and dragged it into place. Upham sprang from the spot and began digging ten yards away. A salvo of shells came and exploded. Whizzing fragments sang all around me but I was not touched. Upham tumbled down and was dead when I reached him. As I left him I heard a weird sort of cry in the darkness on our left. It was C. S. M. Kennedy, the grand "original." They had tried to get him to go to the base on rest but he had insisted on one more trip. His jaw had been carried away by shrapnel and he died before morning. Two other men were down, Johnson and Barron, both wounded.

The shelling continued all night and the next day. We dug deep v-shaped pits, connecting some of them, and there we crouched, grey faces under muddy helmets, staring, our brains numbed by incessant explosions. At noon there was a small avalanche of mud, and a young lad slid down alongside of me. He wore an English uniform and I asked him where he had come from.

"Just yonder!" he pointed. "Sergeant were killed, then six more. I coom."

He was so plastered with mud I could not identify his unit, and he was shaking uncontrollably. Twice I asked him questions but he was too dazed to answer. The shelling was heavy and never let up. Soon the lad snuggled tight against me. I moved over and he followed. Each shell that lighted near made him cringe. He kept saying something in a high-pitched voice. I caught him by the shoulder and shook him. "What on earth are you saying?" I asked.

He shook more violently. "I'm a shepherd boy from Hawes," he gasped. "That's the way we count sheep. I can't stop."

It was no use to try aud do anything with him. He stayed tight against me, shouting in my ear the count of the shells landing near us. A new man in the next pit with Mickey had half-risen as if to go somewhere when a shell burst just over their parapet. One arm was sheared from his body and he pitched down dead. Mickey came slithering over the mud hump between us and squeezed tight against my side, his arms and legs twitching convulsively at every near burst.

A shell landed in the trench section on our left, scattering mud over us. A steel helmet struck our parados, then a haversack came hurtling through the air and fell apart at our feet. We gazed stupidly at the contents, a pair of socks, a towel, a toothbrush, a razor and a tin of bully. The shepherd boy never stopped his count. A new man came sprawling to our shelter. His helmet was gone and he had lost his rifle. He shook as with ague, making animal noises, then suddenly went where Mickey had come from, going on hands and knees in a grotesque manner.

C. S. M. Davies came from the other direction, tripping over the armless body in his path. I shouted questions at him but he never answered. He sat down beside Mickey and there we four huddled. Mud showered down on our legs and buried our Lee Enfields. Then came a tremendous shock. The way through which Davies had come was blocked by the upheaval, and the dead man slid toward us until his one arm was outstretched beside our boots. There was a watch on his hairy wrist and, strangely, it was going. I looked at the time. One o'clock. Each hour had grown to be a grim possession, something held precariously.

We heard a small noise through the din. It was the new man crawling back where Mickey had been. Fear had relaxed the muscles of his face and it had become like dough. His mouth dribbled. I could not look at him. All that afternoon we huddled there and, oddly, it seemed but a short time. Nothing was clear to me. Explosion succeeded explosion, a concentrated clamour, until the noise beat on the brain itself, and when the firing finally lulled to solitary shells it became the torture of dripping water. We stirred and freed our rifles of mud. Davies went to find Arthur and said we might be relieved. An hour later a runner came scrambling over the debris with a message. The Hun had been driven back on the left, and we were to move our line forward as soon as it was dark. I was to go with an officer and help stretch a tape where the company would dig in.

There was only casual shelling as the officer and I ventured into the no man's land beyond our battered line. He was from another company, but the men had a name for him. He was extremely nervous and plunged through the mud so blindly that he lost his direction. It took me some time to convince him of his mistake. Then we swung about and went forward and some "whizz-bangs" dropped quite near. The officer jumped at each explosion and yelled something at me. I paid no attention, as I had just located the old stub we were to use as a guide. As I tied my end of the white tape to it I looked up and saw the fellow running away like a wild thing, taking kangaroo leaps, falling, sprawling. Fear had mastered him. He had hurled his end of the tape away and was leaving me there alone in the dark, with the company due in five minutes. Nerves were bad after that afternoon, and before I realized what I was doing I snatched up my rifle and took aim.

Before I could press the trigger a quiet voice said: "I would not do that if I were you. It will be on your conscience."

It was Captain Arthur. He had come up alone, without a batman, probably because he was unsure of the officer. We stretched the tape as though it were our regular chore, and just had it in place when the first men arrived. I waited for a further reprimand but none came.

We dug in as fast as we could. One man was wounded and Christensen, the stretcher bearer, had a hard time, as the fellow was in a frenzy. Christensen was the only real fatalist I have ever met. He had been shipwrecked twice and almost drowned but he never ducked or hurried in exposed places in spite of orders or anything else. "When my time comes I'll get it wherever I am," he said. "And until that time I am quite safe."

A runner came and said our platoon was to go with Thirteen and help assault a pillbox ahead on our left. The battalion beside us was making the attack. I hunted up Corporal Jimmy Hughes, but he knew nothing of the order. Then we saw men from our left starting to advance so some of us, Tommy and Mickey, Howard Gordon, Brown and some others, scrambled over to join them. All at once the strongpoint loomed through the murk and a Lewis gun hammered its rat-tat-tat-tat. Others joined us. We found the going hard but managed, somehow, to get to the pillbox in remarkably quick time. Cries of "Kamerad" were loud and seemed to come from all directions.

We realized a German relief had been on. The first attackers had reached the spot just as the old garrison was all outside the concrete fort in full pack, and before the new garrison, also in full pack, could get in. In five minutes those who tried to fight had been killed and the rest made prisoner. The new garrison had thermos bottles filled with hot coffee. Never did anything taste so good; Tommy and I each got a bottle. We stood around until an officer came and said we could go back to our company.

Our trench was in fairly dry ground and easy digging. The men seemed to like to dig, and we soon had it a good depth and made fire steps. We were well spread out. Tommy and Mickey were far along. Then came Bunty, a tall man named Murray, myself, then Murray's chum, Babson. Farther to the right was a machine-gun post, and Jimmy Hughes and Howard Gordon were beyond it. In the next stretch of twenty yards there was no one, then came a short trench with three men from Thirteen Platoon. Brown was with them. On the left there was no one for fifty yards. There Barney Guiney had a Lewis gun. With him were McPhee, who was always grinning, and Russell, an eighteen-year-old from Newfoundland who could take a man's place anywhere. Beyond them was a gap, then the Camerons. Sergeant Geordie Taylor was in charge of the platoon but we did not know where he was.

At daylight a thick, clinging mist obscured everything. No officer came near us. We had neither orders nor rations, and we were ravenous. I peered around and made out a hillocky sea of mud in the rear, crawled out among mounds and hollows to find a number of dead South Wales Borderers in full pack. I looked in their messtins and found MacConachie rations, a tin of jam and, in a pack, a full loaf of bread. It was green with mould, but we cut away the outside and ate the centre. We had tommy cookers, so we boiled tea and heated the meat rations. Babson looked over in front and saw a dead officer who had on high boots of excellent workmanship. He went to get them and Bunty begged him not to, saying that robbing the dead would bring disaster. But Babson got the boots and put them on.

When our meal was ready a lone shell came over and exploded directly on the parados of the Lewis gun post to the right. One man was killed and three wounded. We rushed over but there was not much anyone could do. The wounded set off to find a way out, and some whim made us fetch their Lee Enfields back with us. No one touched the Lewis gun.

Once more we made ready to eat and had just finished the meat when I heard the unmistakable report of a German high-velocity gun. An instant later the world seemed to come to an end. There had not been a sound but the shell buried in front of our trench and heaved over us an avalanche of mud and debris. In that split second all sound of gunfire ceased. I could not move hand or foot. There were five feet of earth piled over me. But I had one grand bit of luck. My head had landed at the butts of the four rifles we had brought from the Lewis gun post, and the three belonging to Murray, Babson and myself. Air came down to me from the surface, as each rifle had a bayonet fixed on it.

Then I heard voices. Geordie Taylor was saying all hands had better clear out before another shell came. He said we three were undoubtedly dead and there was no sense in digging us out. Bunty's voice was high pitched with resentment. He told the sergeant to start running but announced that, if no one would help, he himself would dig us out. There was silence and then some faint sounds of digging. I did not know how far along the trench had been filled, and suddenly thought that if they found Murray and he was dead they might not dig further. It was mental torture not to be able to shout or move.

Fortunately Murray had only a couple of feet of earth over him. But he had been shell-shocked by concussion and would not listen to anyone. Tommy had to take him out in search of a dressing station. Bunty kept on digging, and the sounds became stronger. Howard Gordon had come over and was lending a hand. Then a spade touched my foot and I wiggled the toe. It was enough. They became careful and after a few minutes I was helped out of my bed. I shook all the earth from me I could, then sat down. A queer physical sensation spread over me. I perspired heavily. Finally it passed and by that time they had uncovered Babson. He was as deep under earth as I had been and had smothered. They lifted the body over the parados, and Bunty shook his head. "I told him to leave them boots alone," he said.

Twenty yards or so back of our trench was a small ruin with a roof over one end. Gordon said he was going to have a sleep in it, as water was seeping where he had dug. Over he went and was not there more than ten minutes when another velocity shell made a direct hit. We had a look. He would never know what happened. Hughes came along and talked with us. Taylor had vanished. Bunty and Mickey and I remained. There was a stench that seemed to penetrate one's inmost being, the awful stench of death. Mickey became ill and we persuaded him to start for out.

As the darkness came, early and foreboding, only Bunty and I remained in that bit of line that Fourteen Platoon had held. Then I saw something moving directly in front. I watched and made out a patrol of nine Germans. They seemed uncertain of direction and would remain a considerable time at one spot, pointing as if they were arguing. Every bomb had been buried. Our rifles were clogged with mud. We cleaned them in haste. The patrol moved over to our left and Barney's Lewis gun chattered at them. They ducked low and came back in our direction on hands and knees in the mud.

Suddenly a file of men came overland directly to our trench. It was an officer with a company of Black Watch, Imperials, and he said they had come to relieve the Camerons. I pointed to where the Camerons were, and he asked what we were watching. He had no trouble detecting the patrol, as they had started walking directly toward us. "You two give a hand," he said, "and we'll soon take care of those lads."

Bunty shook his head and stayed where he was, but some quirk of pride made me want to give him a good impression of the Canadian Black Watch, so I climbed from the trench and went along with him. It was a weird mix-up. The Huns seemed to think we were their own men and came toward us. We let them come until they recognized our steel helmets and then rushed at them. Four or five of them appeared eager to use their bayonets. The Black Watch officer shouted at the Germans, telling them to surrender, and shot their non-com with his revolver. Two bombs changed the situation though only one German fell, and then I made my first and only kill with cold steel.

It was like a bad dream. I hardly realized what I was doing. The officer had expected the Germans to surrender, and when one lunged at him with the bayonet he only escaped the thrust by falling to one side. Between his assailant and myself was the body of the Feldwebel killed by the pistol shot, and as I flourished my bayonet to bluff the German, he drove headlong at me.

He tripped over his dead comrade. But I was too surprised by his ferocity to try and jump away. Instead I tried to ward off his weapon. Then I felt, not tearing steel in my own flesh, but the jolt of my bayonet as it brought up on something. The German groaned once and sank down. I tugged the bayonet free and saw the fight was over. Two more Germans had been killed and the others had surrendered. The Black Watch officer got to his feet and began wringing my hand, scarcely able to form words. When he fell he had become entangled with wire just below the surface and could not tear himself free, at the mercy of the man with the bayonet. He got out a book and took down my name and number, assuring me I would receive a suitable award.

The others had gone while this happened, although no relief had come for us. No officer had come. No runner with a message. Corporal Jimmy Hughes was the only authority and he was dead beat. We started back and found Mickey seated by a crater. He was ghastly white, had no food all day. Hughes was not in much better condition. We reached the pillbox that served as a dressing station and Bunty was there, seated on two dead men covered with a ground sheet. He said he was too tired to go further.

We met incoming men and there was considerable shelling. I had Hughes by the arm and fairly dragged him through the mire. Then we came to a ruin where a man sat on a fragment of wall. I went to him and asked if he could spare a drink of water. He did not answer. He was not wounded, but absolutely everything in his mind was dead. I took his water bottle from his equipment, took it to Mickey and Hughes in turn, then took it back and replaced it. We went on down the road and there came a salvo of "whizz-bangs." As the last soul-tearing smash crashed in my ears I saw Mickey spin and fall. I let go of Hughes and jumped to him. He had been hit in several places and could not live ten minutes.

"Mickey-Mickey!" I called his name and raised him up and he nestled to me like a child.

"I'm through," he said. "I don't want to kill people anyway. Tell my mother. . . ."

His voice was so low I could not hear, but his lips still moved. Little white-faced Mickey. I held him in my arms until he stiffened, then laid him by the roadside and took his pay book from his pocket. Hughes stood where I had left him, as if unable to comprehend, and I suddenly knew he was in a worse condition than I had thought.

We reached the long duckwalk. All around us were flashes and glows. We were in the great Salient's maw, with shells whining overhead or exploding in the sea of mud. There were red and yellow flashes, flares that looped high and floated in ghostly fashion before falling. On the duckwalk we were just a pair on a straggling line of steel helmets and hunched shoulders, outgoing units of bone-weary, shell-dazed men who had reached the walk after an exhausting struggle with the Ypres mud, treading on old dead and new dead, slipping in the foulness of slimy ditches.

Somehow I kept going. Hughes had become querulous, mumbling all the time that he wanted to sit down. I was carrying his rifle and equipment, so had to take out my entrenching tool handle and threaten him with it, as one would an unruly child, making him go on and on and on, until in that blurry darkness just before dawn we reached tents that were to shelter us. The quartermaster met us. He took Hughes and led him away to give him a hot drink and put him to bed. I staggered toward the nearest tent-and pitched into a crater filled with stagnant water. Both rifles I carried were embedded in the mud and I left them, with Hughes' equipment, under the water. Shaking so I could scarcely speak, blinded with filth, I got to the tent. Tommy was there, had been for an hour. I stripped naked, then lay down on a pile of five blankets, and Tommy piled a dozen more over me. The quartermaster came to ask about me and when he heard what had happened, returned with a great mug of rum. I downed it and when they woke me it was afternoon.

We went in lorries to Bourecq, so crowded we had to stand. In the dark of one village we passed through, the driver swerved to avoid a great crater newly made at a crossroads and ran head-on into a brick wall. We were badly shaken and the lorry was damaged. But another came and we loaded into it and before morning were in our barn billet.

By now the entire company did not muster much more than the strength of a platoon. We sat around after being roused for a late breakfast, unshaved, not speaking, no one so much as asking about mail. At noon we had better food than we had for many weeks, then slept again or stared at the traffic on the streets. The second day we formed up for the first time, shaved and clean.

Captain Arthur was kind to us. He stood and gazed at our pitiful ranks, gazed without speaking, and I saw in his eyes things of which no man speaks-the things that words would kill. We had little drill, but rested and slept and had good food until finally we were more like human beings. But every man who had endured Passchendaele would never be the same again, was more or less a stranger to himself.

Chapter 5: Winter-Spring 1917-18

A draft arrived and Earl Black was in it. There were not many of our old unit in the company-Christensen, Brown, Tommy and Cuvilier. In the afternoon we heard a shrill yapping voice in the *estaminet.* "Red" Herron, from the 73rd, a very good man in the line, was being confronted by a short individual who, like the majority of the "originals," had been on a safe job far back of the lines for well over a year. But too much drinking had got him in wrong with the authorities and he had been shipped back to the battalion. Now he had been drinking again and was yelling that Passchendaele was nothing to what he had seen, that all the real battles had taken place before the "umpty-umps" came over. Red grinned at him, and the cocky little man took a swing at his chin. He woke up about ten minutes later, all by himself.

Most of the men in the draft were veterans wounded at Vimy or the Somme. Sykes was a stretcher bearer, a great reader when books could be found, who could make excellent rissoles of bully, onion and hardtack. Boland was a friendly, well-built lad. There was Thornton, with black hair and high cheek bones, dubbed "Pocahontas," and Lockerbie and Williams, finely built men. We also had an officer. He was new to France, and one glance told you how much politics had to do with his getting a commission. When he formed us up his first morning and said "Number," we numbered in French. Just to test him. He flushed and scolded, and so lost all our respect immediately.

Orders were posted saying the 42nd was now privileged to wear the Red Hackle[13]. "Red Hackles!" snorted Tommy. "What good are they? What about Mickey and Baillie and Ira and Gordon and all the boys? Red Hackles, bah!"

No one said anything to him. Nerves carried too fine an edge to permit any argument. The short "original" got drunk again and found his way into our billet after we had all turned in and lights were out. It seemed doubtful that he would escape hospital treatment, for his reception was very harsh. He never opened his mouth again when any of us were around. Before the month was out he had wangled another "cushy job" back at the lines, and brief enquiry discovered he had just three months service in the front line and had never been in a real battle.

A morning later I was told to report to company office. Wondering what had happened, I went over, and a laughing clerk told me my leave had come through. Leave! Officers got one every four months at least. I caught a lorry and arrived in Boulogne just as the leave boat was leaving the harbour. The group with me swore furiously, but I wandered into a book shop and purchased a funny little book containing statements made about France by people of other nations. One of the first was by Mark Twain. He said France had neither summer, winter nor morals, that Napoleon's monument outside of Boulogne had been erected to celebrate his triumphant invasion of England. I was walking slowly and reading when a squeaky voice said: "Drop that damn book and salute an officer!"

Automatically I thrust the book into a tunic pocket and looked around. On a cross walk leading ten feet behind me was a smirking pip-squeak in officer's uniform. He stood about five feet two inches had no chin and no shoulders, but hanging to his arm

[13] A red feather worn exclusively in the headdress of the Royal Highlanders, the Black Watch. It was an honour bestowed on the 42nd.

was a female in atrocious hat and gown, giggling like a fool. I had not met him as he was crossing the street, but I thought of my leave and had to turn and salute the miserable excuse for a man. His companion tittered and whispered something and he yapped, made me salute again. "Cut your hand away sharply, my man. Try again."

How I restrained myself I'll never know. My blood boiled every time I thought of the incident during my leave. But finally I was allowed to go, the blonde atrocity still giggling. Worst of all, the officer wore Canadian badges.

That night I slept with the leave crowd in a big barrack-like room and talked with men of the 2nd Division. But mostly I listened. There were long and bitter denunciations of the folly of Passchendaele. The "brass hats" were raked over the coals in lurid language, and the opinion of all was that there was not a single brain in the Army Staff. The man beside me from the 6th Brigade said he had never seen a good officer. I told him that he was unlucky, that we had several, and officers were exactly the same as the men, good, bad, and indifferent; but the advantages were theirs. The weak-kneed ones used S.R.D.[14] to fortify them. All of them had good food and comfortable billets, and servants. As a rule the average officer did not see more than a third as much of raw, undiluted war as did the men under him. The men stayed on post, six hours on and six hours off, and saw relays of officers doing two hours out of the dugout in twenty-four, and that a hurried tour of the trench. The men who did the fighting, not the Pioneer battalions, carried barbed wire and ammunition from dump to front line, in all weathers, under all conditions, and the officer leading them had the job once during the trip in the line. The men went every night. The men had to stay on post and endure the strafing, dig out dead and wounded comrades, stick it and carry on. Meanwhile the officers were in the dugouts. During the worst two days at Passchendaele I never saw an officer except Arthur.

Victoria! Leave men thronging everywhere, hungry for a change of food, for girls who spoke their own tongue, for shows and a clean bed. I checked my equipment and Lee Enfield, went out and bought clean underwear, soft boots, breeches, and a British warm, found a place to stay on Vauxhall Bridge Road and there had a hot bath. After putting on my clean clothes, I hunted up a barber shop. Then I went to a restaurant, ordered a meal I had long pictured, and ate it leisurely.

The Strand was inviting, but my thoughts were on a long night's rest in clean sheets on a soft bed. So back I went to my room. For a year I had slept in barns, on hard floors, on chicken-wire bunks, in the mud, and now I was going to enjoy something different. To my amazement I did some tossing and turning. Had I been in the usual billet and eaten such a dinner, I would have been asleep in jig time. But it was not too long before I was into some happy dreams. Then there came a terrific thundering at my door. I sat up dazed, realized where I was and asked what was wrong.

"Zepps-the Zepps are over!" the fellow shouted. "Come quickly. I'll show you where to go."

Zeppelins! After Passchendaele! "Go away and leave me alone," I yelled back. "What's a Zeppelin!" There were sirens going and I saw long fingers of light in the sky, seeking the raiders. I listened a moment to the rattling crashes of anti-aircraft guns-then went to sleep again.

In the morning I had a delicious breakfast and heard that two of the sky ships had been brought down. Five or six civilians had been killed. It seemed a minor affair to me. I had a wonderful rest. There had been no dreams of a Boche on my bayonet. That

14 Service Rum, Diluted.

killing had bothered me more than the sniping or anything else. Strangely, it seemed perfectly my duty to shoot all Huns, but to put cold steel in one was another thing. It made one remember the "Thou shalt not kill."

Away I went to Nottinghamshire. The girl I had left in Canada had been born in that district, and I was going to visit her people. They made me welcome and I had wonderful times in the small villages, had a visit to Lincoln, then was back in London. I took a taxi out to Bramshott to see my brother, Hubert, who was still there, and the brother of my fiancee. He had been wounded at Vimy and was at the depot of the 85th Highlanders. Both he and my brother asked what it had been like at Passchendaele. "Not too bad," I said, and changed the subject. What I had noticed in others had come to me. No soldier who had been in that fighting wanted to talk about it.

When I got back to the battalion it was still in Bourecq. I traded my finery to Wakling, the quartermaster, for a new regular issue. A few days later we moved to Lieven and relieved the 16th Battalion there. One experienced an inexplicable thrill in being back again in dark, smelly confines and frost-bound trenches, where only Death was sure of his billet..

We did carrying parties up Cow Trench, that long and crooked trail known to so many Canadians. Soon we were as lousy as ever and having a hard time to keep warm. We made several trips each night, laden with barbed wire, "A" frames, corrugated iron, anything the engineers could load us with, while they walked along and gave the orders. Tommy got a particularly evil burden one night, some wooden frame work to be used in an O-pip, and he expressed himself in no uncertain terms when three engineers, privates like ourselves, simply walked along behind us to where we took our loads.

"The front-line soldier," he orated, "does more work than anyone in a labour battalion, gets less food than anyone else in uniform, does three-quarters of the engineer's work, is used like a mule, bedded and freighted like horses, and officered by asses." Jimmy Hughes had a hard time quieting him, and our new officer stood in the shadows, silent.

The houses left in Lieven were booby-trapped, so we stayed away from them and used cellars. On Christmas Eve a few of us were in one such haven that was little better than a corner of the yard. The bunks were a mass of broken wire and foul sandbags. Rations were very slim. We had no fire, and it became so cold we could not sleep. Tommy produced a candle and set it on a long board. Each man produced the biggest, most active louse he could locate on his person and we raced them, three heats, the length of the board, the prize being three dirty paper francs. After that sporting affair, won by Tommy, we shivered until in desperation we tore down the bunks and made room enough for one common bed on the stone floor, piling all the sandbags on it. There the six of us lay, packed tightly with our greatcoats over us, and slept, warmed by the heat of each other's body.

A while after daylight there were steps on the narrow stairs, then flashlight beams. We sat up, expectant. Parcels, rum, or rations? It was the officer, wrapped in muffler and holding the flashlight in heavy gloves. "Merry Christmas, boys," he chirped.

It was unbelievable. "Go to Germany!" said Tommy roughly. The rest of us lay down again and never spoke.

We stayed in the line, relieving the 49th. The officer of Thirteen Platoon came to me as we finished a particularly wearying task of trench repair and said I was to go with him on a patrol. We crawled under barbed wire furred with heavy frost and found no man's land scattered with loose tiles and bits of timbers, flung there when our shelling took the roofs from the miners' cottages. It meant very slow progress, as each tile and stick had to be removed from our path with care, lest there be noise. We went no more than a hundred yards before the officer had his fill. We turned and went back. "I'll turn in a report," he said. "There is no need for you to say anything."

The next night we were in a brick cellar used by the cooks, waiting for a mug of hot tea, when there was a shout of "Gas!"

We rushed out and found that gas shells were dropping everywhere, long slim containers that simply broke on contact. The officer from Thirteen Platoon was suddenly beside me. "Put on your mask, man," he shouted, "and follow me."

I put on my respirator and followed him as well as I could, but he made many turns and you could not see well through the goggles. We visited three company posts and when we headed for the fourth he was soon away from me. I found him waiting. "Can't you keep up with me?" he demanded.

I yanked off my gas mask. "I certainly can, sir," I said. "You had no mask on, and expected me to keep up with you. That is silly. You have yours off so I'll keep mine off. See if I can follow you or not."

"You feel quite competent, don't you?" he sneered.

"Not especially," I returned. "But I'm as good a man as you are."

"You think so?" He was almost hoarse with anger.

"Absolutely," I shot back. "Mentally or physically, and only too happy to prove it in any way you like."

"If you say any more I'll have you arrested," he rasped, and turned away. He never talked to me again, and when he lingered at the post and I saw the shelling had stopped, I turned and went back. It was hard to understand the man. He seemed a good man in the line, but after my experience with him he was disagreeable.

On New Year's Eve I was on a listening post four hours straight, shivering with cold and hunger. I watched flares trace their patterns in the night, wondering what 1918 would bring, and whether or not I would see another New Year. Finally I heard the Germans. They had waited well into the night and now they were working to establish a machine-gun post. There were four dark figures. They were clearing debris and building a wall of brick from the ruins. Very carefully I got back to the trench and suddenly there was a perfect deluge of Stokes mortars on the workers. They did not try to erect another post in that area.

The battalion moved back to Souchez when relieved, and our company was placed in miserable huts, half the regular size, with vents to admit the cold wind and without stoves or any other means of heat. The second night was very cold. Tommy and I got up, as we could not sleep, and went along the old Vimy shelters, searching abandoned quarters. We were rewarded by finding a small stove and enough pipe to do. We carried it back two miles to our hut. The others turned out and demolished a small wooden shelter at the head of the camp, which supplied the needed fuel. Then, with everyone taking turns to keep the fire going, we were able to sleep comfortably.

There was a parade, and an officer grandly told us there was to be a fine Christmas dinner. There had to be, however, a working party to assist in the preparations. Tommy and I were two who were detailed. We had to carry tables and benches from the engineers' quarters over a mile away and set them up in a big marquee. By the time we had made the last trip the dinner was under way. Only a company could be fed at a time. We had to wait our turn, and "A", "B", and "C" Companies were ahead of us. We had started carrying tables and benches at seven in the morning and we did not get into the dining tent to eat until four in the afternoon. A lump of cold pudding, a mug of cold tea and a few biscuits were shoved at us. "Where's the turkey, the Christmas dinner?" demanded Tommy. "What's the bloody joke?"

"That's all that is left," growled the cook. "What the. . . ." Tommy hurled his lump of cold duff at the fellow, followed by his mug of cold, greasy tea. The platoon took their cue from him, and there was a barrage of cold soggy pudding that drove the cook to shelter. Then, as we stood in the road, starved for food, debating what was to be done, the fellow had the nerve to yell from cover: "You guys can't beat it. They told us you would stay and wash up the dishes."

Enamelled plates and mugs had been borrowed for the occasion and "D" Company was actually supposed to wash the dishes after doing all the work that was done that day. The boys wanted to go and report to Captain Arthur, but Tommy and I were able to discourage them. Arthur would not know what was happening, and nobody else cared. Two months later one of the boys from Montreal got home papers describing the "wonderful Christmas dinner" given the "happy boys of the 42nd." "No pains had been spared"; all the rank and file had been stuffed with turkey and all the fixings. He wrote a letter telling the truth and addressed it to the paper, but we were able to get him to destroy it, as we pointed out no officer would let it go through and he would be in trouble.

Tommy and Old Bill and I went up the valley to the Y.M.C.A. canteen and tried to get some lukewarm cocoa and dry biscuits. But we had no money and were refused. Old Bill told the man in charge he hoped the next German shell that came over "will blow that blinkin' Y loose from its triangle." Desperate, we walked another mile and found the "Sally Ann." We told the man our story and that Salvation Army fellow made us bowls of soup, gave us biscuits galore and a wonderful dessert of canned fruit. Every front-line soldier of World War I knew that his true friend was the man in the Salvation Army canteen.

The night we were to go back in the line, our Christmas parcels arrived. They had been mailed in mid-November but had been side-tracked somewhere. It did not help matters when one of the batmen told us the officers had received their parcels the week before Christmas. We were determined we were not going to be done out of a Christmas feed, so we scrounged cord and went into the line that night looking like anything but soldiers. Some had two parcels tied together and carried them atop their packs.

We marched into Cite St. Theodore, a place of underground passages and concrete chambers. Our part of Fourteen Platoon was in a room the Germans had made waterproof and almost shellproof. There was a good stove in it, and coal in the passage outside. The first night we were in, more letters and parcels came. The parcel contents were shared generously and we had a grand evening.

In the morning Tommy and I roamed the street and explored. Passages crossed the street from cellar to cellar, and other tunnels opened from strong points. The Hun had used concrete lavishly. We found a cellar that had German blankets, ground sheets and shrapnel helmets, as well as two German rifles. A low passage led from it and did not look as if it had been used. We went along it, then up steps until we were blocked by wreckage that had fallen over the stairway during heavy shelling. It was well we were stopped, exceedingly lucky we were not talking. We saw, at the same time, a vent about five inches square permitting us to look at four German soldiers. They were leaning against a wall in lazy fashion, smoking and talking.

Two of them turned and went away, and the two remaining called out to someone we could not see. They were answered by a voice that seemed directly above us. A footway ran alongside the wreckage and another German appeared, walking along it. Had we spoken, or been smoking, we would have been discovered. Softly as possible we stole back the way we had come, and in our own quarters tried to formulate some plan whereby we would capture one of the Heinies and surprise the troops.

At dark we were called to do a ration party. It was raining, and the sergeant tried a short cut coming back which took us through a mud hole knee-deep. We were sorry figures when we returned. The stove was stoked up, and we stripped off all our wet clothing and strung wire to hold it for drying. Soon everything was steaming. The door opened and in came our officer. "The orders are," he said, "that no man is to take off his boots, and you must have your rifle and equipment where you can get them at a moment's notice."

"Yes, sir!" we chorused. He looked at us through the steam from wet socks and trousers and went away.

The 87th Battalion relieved us and we went back to Fosse 10. Tommy and I did not tell anyone about our tunnel that led to the German line. Something nasty might be entailed, we thought. From Fosse 10 we went to Noeux-les-Mines and were billetted in the town. The Hun shelled it the next day and killed seven civilians, one a little girl from the house where Tommy and I were staying. She had been outside with other children and I helped the mother get her in. She was a frail little elf who had smiled at me and called me "Canada."

That evening I was ordered to go with Eddie Cuvilier to Ferfay and report to the 3rd Divisional School there. "You are to be a corporal," C.S.M. Davies told me, "and don't try to refuse it." The boys laughed as I took my pack and left them, but the last laugh was mine. There were other 42nd men at the school and we had a good time together. My partners in class were Siddall from "B" Company, and Turner from the 49th Battalion. Our course was just one week and we passed with honours. Then came my laugh, when I saw our "D" Company shined and cleaned, drilling long hours on the school parade ground.

There were 85th men about, and one told me the battalion was at Rimbert, nearby. I went there at once, as I had word my brother, Hubert, was in France with the 85th. It was easy to locate him. His first information was that he was starving, had no rations and no money. I had no money either but I told him we would make out. There was the usual popular *estaminet.* We went in and I ordered eggs, chips and coffee, also one of the cartwheel loaves of dark French bread for my brother to take to his billet. Madame was very busy, as there were other soldiers willing to spend money, so I left my brother at our table, went around to the rear of the *estaminet* and, inserting the blade of my issue knife under the window, was able to raise it. In the middle of the room was a pile of army blankets four feet high. I took off the top three, took the next two, replaced the others, went back out the window, lowered it carefully and rejoined my brother. When Madame came with our food, I asked her if the blankets were a good payment. She said they were, examined them casually and took them to the rear room.

"How long," asked my brother, "does a battalion do in the line?"

"About six days," I said. "Sometimes more, sometimes less, never in the front line more than seven or eight days."

Back at Ferfay, I was told the course was over and I was to report to the company. I went in the morning, rather proud of my stripes, and got a real surprise. I had been requested to return because I was needed to take over the guard. It was the usual thing to use a corporal as orderly sergeant in charge of the guard.

The weather was unusually mild for the time of year, and there was a closeness in the air that made one feel sleepy. It seemed to be worse at nightfall. The orderly officer made his last round at 9:30 and advised me to take the guard out and run them around the chateau yard a few times if I saw them getting sleepy.

After a time I found it most difficult to keep awake myself. Once I went out and walked about. The second time I roused with a jerk and knew I had been dozing. I looked at my watch. It was almost midnight. I went outside and blew my whistle. The guard fell in at the double. I ran them around the yard twice then headed out through the chateau gate to the roadside. There I halted them and gave the order "Present arms."

Just as each rifle came down smartly, a car with a pennant roared by. Then a second car. The third one slowed to a halt about thirty yards from us, and a very English voice called, "Sergeant! Come here!"

I went over and saluted. "What unit?" asked the voice.

"The 42nd Royal Highlanders of Canada, sir."

"Oh, jolly good! Who is your commanding o officer?"

I told him and he said: "Just wanted to tell you, sergeant, your guard is the first to salute us in sixty miles. Our compliments to you. That's the General's car ahead."

It would have been fantastic to tell him the true circumstances, so I merely thanked him. The guard shouldered arms and we went back to our quarters. The incident was a lucky one as far as I was concerned. The men argued for hours as to which General was in the car, and there was no further trouble about sleepiness.

On March 6 we relieved the 116th Battalion, taking over a part of the line on the left of Avion, near the embankment. Part of no man's land was under water, flooded by the Hun, and wire had been thrown out near the shore so that anyone trying to wade across would become entangled. On the left the line ran out to a listening post. Its garrison stayed in a cellar there, a squalid little hole with a make-shift roof, and you could not show yourself in daylight as the place was in plain view of a big slag heap on the German side. There, in that foul hole, I had my first little garrison of six men.

Opposite us, continuing our line, was an Imperial battalion. They had no post at the canal bank, but used a "flying patrol" that came once every two hours through the night. A heavy wire had been thrown to the other bank and was used for signalling. The Imperials tugged on it when they arrived. If all was quiet we tugged twice in reply. If we had heard or seen Germans near their part, we pulled the wire three times. Barron had come back to the unit and was with us. The others were Brown, Tommy, Thornton, Johnson and Millar. On the way up we had smelled buds and green things and had hated thoughts of the front line. It was hard to force to the background all fear of death at that most hopeful season of the year.

Suddenly we heard the flying patrol coming. They were making plenty of noise, and when they reached the bank they gave the signal wire a tug that almost jerked Barron from the post. "O-kye, Canada?" shrilled a Cockney voice. "I sye, o-kye?"

"Shut your trap and get out of that or I'll 'o-kye' you," flared Barron, so savagely that the patrol did not come again all night.

It was dreadful in the daytime. The weather continued balmy, and we were cooped up in a small space. The cellar was foul with slime from the canal and stank dreadfully as the days got warmer. Big blue flies buzzed about. Rats climbed around in the dark making small noises that startled one. We were lousy and the air made our heads ache. The water we carried got stale and unfit to drink, and we had no warm food, only bread and cheese and bully, and the tea we boiled at night. It took all sorts of cautioning to keep the men under cover during the day.

During the third night we heard a German patrol. They came to the other side of the canal, but we dared not shoot as it would give away our position. The Huns came to within feet of our signal wire and every moment we expected to hear the Imperials coming. But the Germans were gone some time before there came the familiar tugs on the wire. Six awful days we endured that cellar, and six nights we enjoyed the cool air, every man going outside as soon as it was dark. Then we moved back to support. The boys had a few lines they used to recite about that post.

When the war is o'er and I'm home once more
To the land I love the most,
When the sewers stink I'll always think
Of the Isolation Post.

I cursed my luck when that place I struck,
And I cursed the Kaiser's host,
As I waded through the bloody glue
Of the Isolation Post.

I sat by that cesspool of disease while the sun my back did roast,
With your cover the sky and a wall three feet high
The Isolation Post.

If evr I get the drop on Bill I'll make him drink a toast,
From a dead man's shoes filled with slimy ooze
From the Isolation Post.

To one who's been and smelt and seen this will seem no idle boast,
I've been to hell for a six-day spell
At the Isolation Post.

The La Coulotte Brewery was the support quarters, a large place covered with sod and reinforced by concrete. The Hun was supposed to be contemplating a big attack. Orders came for us to hold ourselves in readiness for anything, and everyone became tense. When an alarm came we were outside in jig time. We lined a fire trench and waited there, but nothing happened, so we suspected it was a practice exercise. The Germans shelled the brewery one morning and our batteries replied. The clamour beat down on our underground retreat, and every quaking told of a big one landing near. Next day we watched a shelling of the area in our rear. Every little while there would be a great rushing sound followed by the roar of explosion, and a cloud of black and yellow fumes would rise from the brick-strewn slopes.

Then, instead of going back to billets, we moved into the front line again, and the men groused wholeheartedly. An officer swam across the water to the German side one warm afternoon and located one of their posts. Its garrison of three were dozing in the sun. An expedition was formed to raid the post at night, and two crude rafts were made to carry bombs and ammunition, plus a jug of rum. The water was cold. The next day rumour said one of the raiders had been seized by cramps, had reached for the rum jug and upset it into the pond. Trying frantically to recover it, he had upset the raft and the bombs were lost. There were other versions but no one cared. We were spending time as if we were in jail.

Some of our company had a post in the support line, and I was sent to them with a message from our sergeant-major. There was no hurry after the message was delivered, so I returned by the long way around the brewery route, noticed a long-disused German gun-pit and went to look for souvenirs. I had already taken three lots to the French house at Divion and was always looking for more.

As I reached the old emplacement somebody rushed out from a corner. One glance told me it was the miserable half-pint officer who, had made me salute him at Boulogne Ah-ah my good fellow, he spluttered. Can you tell me where I am? I'm lost. What part of the line is this?"

It was easy to see he was not only lost, but completely craven, and suddenly I lost control of myself. How about some snappy saluting. I demanded. Always salute before you speak to your betters."

His badges showed he was attached to an artillery unit. He started back, mopping his face with a dainty handkerchief. "Come, come, my man," he said. "I'm an officer and I want you to tell me where I am."

"You're almost up where the men are," I said. "How did you get away from the doll you had at Boulogne?"

He started back as a shell exploded about two hundred yards from us, muttered something and snatched at his revolver. I had it from him on the instant and threw it far over the bank, just managing to stop myself from slapping his chinless face. He darted from the place and turned right-luckily for him the way out and the last I saw of him he was going for all his worth, a queer knock-kneed style of running that a circus clown might display. In a moment I was out of there and on my way back, sweating as I wondered whether or not he had noticed my badges. All that afternoon I expected a summons to company headquarters, but none came. I had to tell someone so gave Tommy the story. He told me I had been very foolish. I was compelled to agree with him.

When we were relieved, the men groused loud and long that we did not leave the trenches but stayed up in reserve. Each night we went out on working parties, cleaning trenches and strengthening defences. One morning was heavy with sounds of a terrific bombardment somewhere near the Somme. Rumours began to circulate, and every man forgot his grousing. They said he would attack us next. We went about in a tense way, awaiting orders, expecting a move. But nothing happened. We were told we were holding and responsible for a very large frontage.

On March 27 we were told all leave was cancelled, all training schools closed and the personnel returned to their units. Rumour said an attack on the Vimy zone was certain. We thought it had come the next day when the Germans opened up at three in the morning, bombarding a line extending from Acheville to Vimy. The shelling continued until eight in the morning before it gradually died away. Each platoon had a little meeting with its commander, and we were told the Germans had broken through on the Somme, that a great battle was raging, that we were to hold Vimy Ridge at all cost.

There were constant patrols. Headquarters wanted all possible information about the movements of the enemy, and the sergeant came and got me to go with him about ten o'clock at night. Someone in our trench unthinkingly sent up a flare just as we got away from our wire, and for a moment we feared we might be discovered. We could see the black wall of the parapet we had left, the wire like frayed ribbons, the sentries-two white faces under mushroom hats-and then the darkness was intense as the flare died. We were an hour going out one hundred yards. Much of the way was through what had been a vegetable garden. At last we could hear German voices and after waiting a time we went back in.

The next night I was told to report to Fifteen Platoon. The officer seemed a good man and he had a patrol of six. He said he had seen a German in some long grass but had watched an hour and the man had not moved. Possibly he was dead. I mentioned booby traps and we went out very carefully, with two men each side of us and two in the rear. We found the German. He was quite a distance from the German wire and had been dead for some time. His hands clutched his middle, and blood was dried there as if he had been caught by a full burst of machine-gun fire. He had a machine pistol strapped to his chest, an unusual weapon with a barrel about fifteen inches long. After it was examined in our line they found it would fire fifteen shots with one loading.

A draft came from the MacLean Highlanders[15]. Many of them were Americans and they were a fine lot. Two inseparables, Thompson and Tulloch, were assigned to our cellar, and calmly tried to take possession of the best corner until gently shown the error of their ways. The next night I was told to take a carrying party to a certain point and get some wire. Ten men were in the group. One of them was very tall and had a white bandage around his neck. When I asked him what was wrong, he said he had boils. It was not a very dark night and I was afraid the white would be seen, so went to his officer and asked if he might be excused. The officer agreed at once when I explained. So I told the man he would not be on any carrying parties until he could shed his bandage. He was unusually grateful and spoke like an educated person. I saw him twice in the daytime and had a long chat with him, finally asking him his name.

[15] The MacLean Kilties were the 236th Canadian Battalion, recruited in Nova Scotia. It reached England in 1917 and was broken up for reinforcements.

It was Robert E. Sherwood. Later it would be a name known all over America.

It was Sixteen Platoon's turn for a patrol. There were only four men with us and it was still and warm and very dark, an ideal night for travellers in no man's land. Our escape from harm was due solely to the sergeant's puttee coming loose. When he sat up to fix it, his hand touched some tin cans. He whispered the information to me and it made me suspicious. Why would a little pile of tins be out there? We moved the men back toward our line. Then the sergeant went in and got a short stick and a length of light wire. We crawled out to the tins again and, attaching the stick to the wire and carefully placing it on the other side of the tins, paid the wire out and came back to a crater large enough to hold both of us. When the sergeant pulled the wire, the tin cans rattled. Instantly there was a perfect spray of machine-gun bullets. The tins were tossed by it. Bullets thudded against our parapet. The sergeant, at the last minute, had sent his men in. We lay still for an hour and then heard someone crawling toward the tins from the German side. We pitched two-second Mills grenades at the spot, and an awful scream was part of the explosion. Two stick bombs were thrown in our general direction but came nowhere near us. As soon as we got back in the trench we sent up flares and saw two bodies lying where the trap had been. In the morning they were gone.

Over on one flank there was more line, covered by a flying patrol. It was "C" Company's area. The patrol one night was Lieutenant Baber and four men. They were in what we called August Trench when a group of fifteen Germans showered them with stick bombs and jumped them, firing revolvers. Three of the men got away in the dark, but the Jerries seized Baber and a private named Grant. They hoisted them out of the trench and started overland with them as one of our patrols headed that way to find out what was going on. Baber took advantage of the situation to trip his captor and plunge away in the darkness. Shots missed him, though he had four wounds from the grenades, and he got back to our trench. Grant was not so lucky. He was a prisoner of war until the end. There was much enquiry as to how the Germans had penetrated so far without being detected, but nothing came of it. It was the only time a German raid had any success against the 42nd.

"C" Company returned the compliment with a raid supported by the artillery. But the guns apparently served warning of what was to come, as all three enemy posts were found vacant.

The German was really nervous on the front where the sergeant and I had uncovered the tin can trick. Each night he sprayed the area with machine-gun fire, and put up flares continuously. We did not go out again on patrol and then went back to the brewery instead of going out of the line. They boys were grousing about it but all really knew the situation. Rumours were a dime a dozen. The Huns, according to some reports, were within reach of Paris. Passchendaele had been recaptured and we were being surrounded.

We went on a working party. A sudden shower at dawn soaked everyone, so rum was issued. The sergeant in charge of the jug bypassed Old Bill, who had not been out, and Bill resented the omission with such heat that he was taken before Arthur for discipline.

Everyone was becoming highly strung, and there should have been more excuse for the veteran. He had his troubles. Giger had been fired from four positions as batman, and after a session with red and white wines had told a kindly member of the military police he should be inflicted with an inferiority complex, or words to that effect. The net result had been seven days in the clink, and on Giger's return to the company he had been placed in Old Bill's charge and was occupied in looking after the latrines. Giger liked telling new men he came from a part of New Brunswick so tough that the canaries there sang bass. He heard someone talking about Junkers, and when questioned about them said they were the Germans who demolished French houses.

From the brewery we went to the left front, the Lens area, and relieved a battalion of the Staffords. They seemed in no hurry during the changeover and chatted freely. They possessed a cheery compound of optimism and tenacity that made them grand frontline holders. We had heard they were invaded by a raiding party and had lost three men as prisoners. It was right enough, they admitted, but old Jerry had not been on the level. He had made his raid when they were thoroughly exhausted after a hard night's work. "It's the wye he is," remarked the corporal I was talking with. "They ain't got no sense of humour or honour. They give you the camel's 'ump."

Each night a German machine-gun had been firing from a position that could not be detected during the daytime. I was told to take a man with me as far as possible along the top of the railway embankment, and there to watch for any unusual movement or German patrols. Tommy went with me. There was a place to the left where it was comparatively easy to get up without being seen. Once on the embankment we stayed between the rails, worked well over toward the enemy and lay still. The spot was ideal. There was a comfortable hollow between the rails, where two sleepers had been taken out by a shell explosion. We lay so we could watch two ways at once. The air was mild. The usual shelling went on, and machine-guns fired at intervals. It was our luck that the gun the Staffords had reported did not fire a shot that night. And there was not a sound of a German patrol. Once in a while there would be ten or fifteen minutes of quiet save for the faraway rumble of guns down on the Somme, and not once did we hear a voice or any movement. After about three hours Tommy had to crawl back carefully the way we had come to attend to a call of nature, and when he returned we could hear faintly, on the German side, the sound of someone playing a mouth organ. We listened carefully and stared at each other. The Hun was playing "Annie Laurie"!

"Let's take turns sleeping here," whispered Tommy. "The air is wonderful, and I could go to sleep in a minute."

"The trouble is that both of us could drop off," I returned. "Another hour and we'll go in."

The sound of the mouth organ ceased. There was some firing away on our left, and once in a while machine-guns on both sides would chatter challenges, but on the whole it was more quiet than usual. We were both becoming drowsy when we heard the mouth organ again. It was farther away but playing some catchy tune.

"That chap is really good," whispered Tommy. "Let's go along a piece so we can hear him better."

"All right," I said. "I'll watch while you crawl, and you watch while I go. I'll go first."

I went about fifty yards between the rails on my hands and knees, moving with care. When I found a good spot I crouched there. Tommy came along without any trouble and hardly was settled when once more we were treated to "Annie Laurie."

Then one of our batteries began shooting, one gun at a time, as it had done the hour before. The second shell had not enough elevation. It struck the steel rail where we had been lying and detonated in a sharp explosion.

Tommy gasped. "Boy! Are we ever lucky! If I knew that Jerry's address I'd send him a post card of thanks. From this day forward my favourite bit of music is going to be 'Annie Laurie'."

After the shell explosion the mouth organ was silent a long time, and we were getting sleepy again when it began a beautiful rendition of "Old Black Joe," played with quavering sentimentality. It was fantastic. After four verses the player switched to "My Old Kentucky Home." Tommy declared the Heinie was surely some German who had spent years in America, either in Canada or the United States. We stayed until he stopped playing, then went in.

The weather turned warmer than ever and in the morning we could hear skylarks overhead. Dandelions dotted every patch of sod that remained in our area. The enemy tried to raid trenches near Hill 70 and we saw our S.O.S. go up. The response of our artillery was heartening. It did not seem an instant before a barrage was falling on the German lines. Brown had a narrow escape when a single shell dropped near the daylight post he was on and created a baby volcano that covered him with debris. No shrapnel touched him, but he had quite a shock and the medical officer sent him out. Many reported sick in the hope of getting away from the trenches, but good old number nine[16], Queen of the Movies, was the prescribed treatment for would-be evacuees.

By now a bath had become imperative for everyone, so small parties were sent by light railway to a mines bath. French girls were the attendants. They handed out towels sparingly and were not embarrassed in the least by our presence. We received clean shirts and socks and felt much better. With me, the unbelievable had happened. I no longer belonged to the membership of candle searers of kilt seams. There was not a louse on any of my garments. At long last I was free, and all through accident. Some impulse had caused the girl I was to marry to send a tin of Zambuk in a parcel. I had a scratch from barbed wire and at once applied the ointment. Being itchy where the crawlers were most active, I rubbed dabs here and there. Peace, perfect peace. Toward morning I woke marvelling, explored my person, and not one crawler could I find. The first time I reached another canteen I looked at the shelves. They had two tins of Zambuk. I bought both, and thereafter kept my stock strong.

We moved to supports. A party was sent up to do wiring in a corner too difficult to approach on ordinary nights, but this night it was dark and raining, so seemed a good opportunity. Our party carried stakes and wire, and by the time we had navigated Cow Trench and reached our objective we were literally soaked. The officer from Sixteen Platoon whispered hoarse instructions to me. Somehow he found it necessary to stay close to the trench exit. I took two men to use as a covering party and we went thirty yards beyond the workers. Tommy was one of the men I had with me, but we never whispered or looked at each other. The pouring, slashing rain made us indifferent. The three of us stood together, rain running off our tin hats, down our necks, down our legs. We did not want to move. The workers did a grand job, since the deluge drowned any small sounds.

Tommy nudged me with an elbow as we stood shoulder to shoulder. I glanced

[16] The Number 9 pill was a purgative pill prescribed by most Medical Officers for a variety of ills and complaints.

where he indicated, but it was too late to do anything. Two German soldiers had appeared from somewhere on our right, heads down, their feet squelching in the mud. They passed within ten feet of us, panting with haste, and never noticed us. We did not move, but every moment became an eternity until the workers said the wire was in place. The officer didn't speak when we arrived at the exit. He was as drenched as we were, and not interested in any report. The third man of our trio was called "Sparky." He had come with the MacLean draft and was a good soldier. I suggested that neither he nor Tommy mention how near we had come to contact with the enemy.

A day of hot sunshine dried us. The sergeant-major came to our cellar and asked for volunteers for a raid. There were many questions, and when I heard who would be in charge I kept quiet. Williams, Lockerbie and a Russian named Waldvogel, whom everyone called "Waterbottle"-an extremely good man-volunteered at once. The raid was to be at the embankment. The officer in charge had a fiery nature and appeared anxious to get at the Hun. But he had no experience. Another old-timer, an "original," had returned to the company after two years on a cushy job, and was looked upon as a wonder. Someone circulated great stories about his worth as a raider. The needed men were chosen and sent back to the rear to rehearse their raid.

Tommy and I went back to Lieven. The rain had pooled water in many cellars and we wanted to have a bath. The street was blocked with debris, so that we had to detour in many places. Every living thing was absent, with the exception of two cats, which stole about the wreckage as wild-eyed as evil spirits. In a small garden we found rambler roses in bloom and Tommy made a garland for his steel hat.

We entered a shaky ruin. A shell had made a great gap in the floor, revealing a cellar lined with bunks. We lighted candles carried in our gas masks and found it had been a German billet. Equipment in good condition as well as tunics and greatcoats were lying around. Two things were evident: the occupants had left in a great hurry; and the place had been visited by someone afterward. Pockets had been turned inside out. Letters had been taken from envelopes and were mouldering on the floor. The peculiar German odour lurked about the place. Tommy turned over a corner bunk when he detected hinges, and the bunk was the top of a great box in which were five German caps with badges, two spike helmets and belts. We divided the souvenirs and went back to the upstairs to find it was nearly dusk. The floor boards creaked under our tread, and from a shell opening in the rear wall came a glow of red as the sky behind it was lit by gun flashes. The glows played on the walls of the next ruin with a fascinatingly bizarre effect. The batteries were not a great distance behind us, and for fifteen minutes we stayed and watched the light flicker, dance, vanish and reappear. Then the shelling stopped and a waiting silence ensued.

As we reached our cellar again the Hun began shelling the front line. Then a message came for me to go to company headquarters, taking a man with me. It sounded as if there might be another patrol in the offing. The shelling became heavier as we reached our Company H.Q., and a sergeant told us to wait in a cellar where some runners and signallers were congregated. A game of banker was in progress and Tommy, after watching a few moments, borrowed ten francs. He lost it quickly and borrowed the last five francs I had. The play turned his way and did not change. We could hear shells tearing along Cow Trench, down by the cook's quarters, and all along our sector, a general strafe. Our ears were attuned to every explosion, and we looked at each other whenever a heavy one seemed near, but the play went on.

After about twenty minutes of heavy shelling, things quieted. Our lads sent up flares immediately but there was no attack. I was told to report to the captain. By that time Tommy had about one hundred francs in his pocket. We made a tour of the company front and found trench sides smashed down in several places, but no serious harm done. Two old buildings had been knocked down but no one had occupied them. Not a man had been wounded, although Sparky, on sentry duty, had a near one when a shell fragment knocked the helmet from his head. After an hour's wait in which the Hun remained quiet, orders came to restore the broken parts of the trench. Out went the men and everyone turned to with a will. Action was better than sitting and waiting the night away.

Next night Thirteen Platoon made a routine patrol: four men, myself and the officer. It was dark and quite still. We got within twenty yards of the German advance post and did not see or hear anything.

Each day grew more monotonous than the previous one. It seemed years since we had been away from trenches. Food became more tasteless and appetites lessened. We had turned night into day for so long that it had become difficult to get to sleep when there was an opportunity.

The raid had been postponed twice, but at last it took place and, though more successful than some attempts, was more or less a fizzle. Under a screen of smoke bombs the party pushed over, but tumbled into wire that had been put up the previous night, after the scouts had reported the way clear. The Germans spotted their visitors and gave them a harsh welcome. But the raiders used rifle grenades, and got into the German trench and chased the small garrison, the fiery officer leading and the "original" with him. One German did not run too fast but threw a bomb, and the officer was badly wounded. While the men were trying to carry him back the Germans got in from the other side, and but for some courageous work by the "original," things might have gone worse than they did. As it was, they did get their leader back to our lines. We met them in the trench, their faces blackened, winded and much excited. Next day there were hot arguments about the unsuspected wire.

Hopes rose each time we neared the end of a tour, but again we went to hold the front line, this time the sector about the "Minnie House." It was a ruin that had, beneath its cellar, a concrete shelter that would turn any large shell. It was dry and roomy enough for a platoon to live in comfort. I was warned for patrol and went out with a sergeant known, behind his back, as "Flighty." He was with one of the other platoons. After we were about forty yards from our wire, he halted his crawling in a huddle of ruins, whispering that it was a very dangerous place and we should not go too far. "You're in charge," I said, and made no other suggestion. We did not go ten yards further toward the German lines, but worked to the right where a shallow emplacement gave some protection. There we stayed for almost two hours. Then we carefully worked our way in. Next day I heard the sergeant-major saying Flighty had been very near the German posts and had brought in a fine report.

There were no orders for me the next night, but at dawn Sparky came hurrying to find me. An officer wanted me to come to a post on the right. He was a new man and I had not talked with him. It was just breaking light as I reached him. Two of the MacLean men were on post, staring over the parapet. The officer was pacing back and forth and was very nervous. He told me there had been some wiring to do, some work at a spot well out in front, and he had been in charge of it. He had, of course, had a covering party out, and to ensure his safety while he superintended the work, had put them well out, near some trees of an old garden. There had been some machine-gun firing just as the work was finished and the party had hurried in. The officer had completely forgotten his covering party. Now he said he did not remember exactly where they were, and it was nearly day. He was in a state bordering on hysteria. He was new to the front, he said, new to everything. Would I go and get the men?

All this was said in the hearing of Sparky and the two sentries. I asked who were out there and was told that Tom Mills was one, Millar another, and Bob Jones, an "original" and one of the best chaps in the battalion. He had been on a job for sixteen months and said so, praised all the men and did his bit. All the officer could tell me was that the men were behind some stunted trees.

There was no time for crawling, as the sun was nearly due. I left my steel hat and rifle and ran in a stooped position to where there were a few stunted trees. No one was there. A German machine-gun just to the left let loose a few rounds that sang into our wire, helping to speed me to a second bush clump. No one was there either. Each second I expected a fusillade from the German trench, for it was getting lighter every heartbeat. There were some bushes further out. In desperation I ran there, and stumbled over Jones. They had their rifles ready, wondering who was coming, and followed me without a word needed. But when we reached our trench there were some very harsh and bitter speeches. They had lain there five hours after the job was done, awaiting orders to go in, and Mills spoke his mind freely. The officer flushed and stammered, and I got away quickly.

The next afternoon the sergeant-major told me I was to go out on patrol with the "original." At first I was sure he was kidding and passed it off as a joke. But he was serious. I asked him who had given the order and he would not tell me. In my own mind I was certain the "original" despised any "umpty-ump" and would not want me with him anywhere. However, I reported at dark and found him waiting with the sergeant-major. He did not speak to me as the sergeant-major said a new enemy machine-gun post had been bothersome on Fifteen Platoon's front and was to be eliminated by Stokes mortars if it could be located. We were to do the locating. Still the "original" did not speak. He crawled out without looking to see if I were following and he did not ask a question or give an order. We went out until we were among ruins that I thought housed the machine-gun, and there we wormed around brick heaps and up ditches until I was sure we were in German territory. But not a Hun did we see or hear, and we returned slowly, listening for long intervals. He made his report without saying a word to me, and I went back to my dugout, where I was amazed to learn we had been out over three hours.

On the third night it was the turn of our platoon to do a patrol. Davies very kindly offered to send another in my place, as I had been out two nights. I refused and only asked that Tommy go with me instead of the three men he had detailed. He agreed, and when the time came we shed our equipment and steel helmets, and took revolvers and Mills bombs instead of rifles. My intention was to stay out until we had located the German machine-gun post. Tommy was willing. There was enough cover to protect us from any sudden machine-gun fire, and enough moon to let us see where we were going. We found a ditch that was dry and crawled up it, one ahead of the other. Not a German was to be seen or heard. I was dumbfounded. Something seemed wrong, for we were in territory that fronted Fifteen Platoon's holding. We lay there and thought we heard voices far in the rear, and were just going to move when three Germans appeared as if by magic. There was only a pile of rubble between where we were lying and the path they followed. The three walked along as unconcerned as if they were in a back area, veered over to the path beside the ditch we had crawled along and entered a post formed by an angle of walls. The ruin there was about five feet or more high, and its corner was part of the post. A wall made of salvaged stone and brick added to the protection. The place was roomy enough to contain the three men, and their machine-gun was on a tripod and fired through an opening the size of a shoe box. During the day it was evidently lowered into a corner. They fired a few rounds and then were still. The moon grew brighter while we lay in the ditch and watched.

We dared not move. A jumble of rubbish blocked our going to our left, and to go the way we had come would be to cross their path in plain view. Now and again they moved the gun somewhat and fired twenty or thirty rounds. For an hour this went on. We were cramped and stiff when suddenly the moon went under a cloud, so we rose at once and, keeping crouched, walked back the way the Huns had come, circumventing the rubbish heap and crawling into rough ground beyond. It was the longest way back, but we had to use cover that would protect us from the machine gun.

At last we crawled through our wire gap and into our trench. Our officer was on duty. We got him to go with us and after much pointing made him understand where the gun was hidden. He said he would go to headquarters and report in full, and told us to go and have a drink of hot tea.

We went and had plenty of tea, but when we tried to sleep it was useless. We were too excited. Finally Tommy suggested we find the officer and inquire what the captain had said. The officer had a batman so furtive-looking and small that everyone called him "The Rat." This night we could not locate the officer in the trench so we went to his dugout. The Rat had a brazier at the foot of the stairway to allow fumes to exit and was cooking something on it. Just inside the gas blanket at the top of the steps someone had left an empty rum jug. As we hesitated by the entrance a runner came up, a happy-go-lucky boy known as "Doggy," who was not frightened of anything. He struck the rum jug and it went bouncing down the steps. "Look out!" Doggy shouted. "Rum jar!"

Bang! The rum jar struck the brazier fairly and over it went, frying pan and all, in a flurry of sizzling flame, smoke and fumes.

We looked at each other. What would the officer say? So we backed away and waited in the trench until Doggy appeared. He was convulsed with laughter and said that when he got down the steps, both The Rat and the officer were trying to get back off the iron cot. "Rum jar," of course, was our name for a large German shell.

As we talked, Earl Black came along the trench with water cans and asked if I would go with him in search of "do-loo." The men were parched. Water rations were exceedingly slim, and rumour had it that The Rat had pinched the supply in order to provide a bath for the officer.

We walked and walked and walked. The moon vanished a last time and it became pitch dark. We had to feel our way around corners, so that it took us an hour to reach a water line the engineers had laid. There we filled our tins. First light of dawn showed us a Y.M.C.A. sign in the trench. It pointed to a cellar some distance away, but a passing soldier told us the place was closed, and was never used in daytime as it was under enemy observation. I had some money with me and had not seen a canteen for some time. We sat our tins down and ran out over the footpath. The door was fastened, but I used a short plank and broke the staple, walked in, selected tinned fruit and chocolate, laid the money on the counter and left. The Y man slept in a cellar close by and would be in the canteen as soon as anyone.

Then we did a quick trip back to the Minnie House and breakfasted in style.

Tommy had cramps in the morning but would not go sick. At Vimy he had a severe case of cramps after three days of wading in slush and water, and had joined the sick parade. It was the time when rations were very short. All the new men circled the cook wagon like gulls, and even the sick men were hungry. The padre was generally in the medical officer's quarters at sick parade. He was a fluent speaker, a nice singer, and led a smooth church service, but his place was with the officers and every man knew it. This particular morning the padre made some joke about food, and Tommy cut loose in his usual fashion and was hoisted out by Captain Hale without ever being asked his ailment. From then on he never reported sick and would have died in a dugout before reporting.

Nevertheless I went to Davies and got Tommy excused from duty. The long strain was telling on our nerves. Twice outposts in the ruins had shot at each other, thinking they saw the enemy. A rumour came that we were to be relieved, but we hooted at it. We were past believing any rumour. But it was true. After fifty-five days we were withdrawn from the trenches and taken back beyond the reach of machine-guns.

It gave us curious feelings to be back in civilization, even to see French people. We were billetted in a little village, and there some of the boys went wild. They got hilariously drunk and marched around the houses and their billets. Others walked into the fields, along the hedges, and sat down and stared about them. After the one riotous night the boys sobered and became more like their old selves. We marched again, our legs unused to such exercise, on cobbles we had not trod in a long time. Flowers were everywhere and all the world was flooded with glorious sunshine. We inhaled the sweet breath of the fields and trees and gardens, and there were spasms of singing. We passed places where the "outside" soldiers lived, and saw hut frontages adorned with flower pots, white-washed doodads and crests that did not seem to us connected with war at all.

Then we came to St. Hilaire, a village of friendly people, with shops and places where we could buy eggs and chips. We were billetted in barns on clean straw, and after a vigorous bathing in a nearby stream and clean shirts, we felt more like living again. It was wonderful weather. Poppies were like blood drops on banks of green, and the white-walled cottages seemed to enhance the verdure of the fields. Rations improved and parades were sensible. It was good to have survived the spring. The second day there I told Davies about our locating the German machine-gun. He made enquiries. The officer had never reported our finding. It had been his turn to lead a raid.

We slept in a ring around the floor of the barn. Old Bill was near the door. Walton and Morris were with him. They had come back to the battalion after being wounded at Vimy. Then came Harvey, a strongly-built MacLean Highlander, Rees, a young Welshman with a sweet tenor voice, Thornton and myself. Along the end were

McMahon, another singer, Ted, a Liverpool lad, Tommy and Sparky. Rats were very plentiful and McMahon hated them, feared them. The mud-and-straw walls of the barn were honeycombed with rat tunnels. Some of the boys slept with ground sheets over their heads. McMahon had his bed directly under a tunnel, and one of the boys cut up some cheese finely when we came back after supper, scattering it in the straw where McMahon would lay his head.

Everyone retired early the first night, tired by the march. No sooner was the last candle out than there was a wild yell from McMahon. He sat up and declared a rat had jumped on his chest. Voices said he was crazy, to lie down and go to sleep. He went to his equipment, got his entrenching tool handle and returned to his pillow. In no time he was striking furiously with his club, sputtering and saying two rats had jumped on him. Each time he lay back another rat came from the tunnel. Everyone got to rolling in mirth. McMahon thrashed about like a madman with his tool handle, but the rats merely waited for a lull. It ended with McMahon taking his blankets and rubber sheet into the orchard where he slept beneath an apple tree, quite unmolested.

In the morning when we fell in, we learned our officer was gone. Three months in the line was really a long time for one of his kind.

Thornton, or, as we called him, "Pocahontas," always slept on his back with his mouth open and snored. One night I was awakened by stiff whiskers on my face. I opened my eyes to see a large rat scanning me gravely. He backed off a trifle as I looked at him and pushed himself into the palm of my hand. The feel of his feet was revolting and I pitched the thing from me. My revulsion lent strength to the movement. The rat rose in an arc and descended, head down, straight into Thornton's open mouth. Its weight drove it in and Thornton's jaw closed convulsively. For a heartbeat there was a picture of the rat's hind legs kicking wildly, then Thornton put a hand each side of the rat and threw it across the barn. He sat up and spat furiously, giving me a tug. I was almost strangling myself with mirth but pretended to be stupid. "What's up?" I asked.

"A rat-sfut-jumped-sfut-into my-sfut-mouth!"

"You're crazy," I said. "They wouldn't."

"But I'm-sfut-telling you they-sfut-did."

Soon he had everyone awake and was describing, with much spitting, how the horrible thing had jumped into his mouth. All hands asked questions and shook with laughter.

Often the majority of the men slept outside. The nights were deliciously cool and fragrant, without heavy dews. Our cooks were down the street a distance, and when reveille blew we never roused. At the breakfast call we simply reached for our messtins. Shortly there would be a straggling parade that never failed to bring mirthful cackles from peasant women driving into the village. We went without our kilts, in shirts and boots, digging the sleep from our eyes, and paraded back with steaming tea and porridge on which reposed strips of bacon.

One loss all of us regretted was R.S.M. Percy MacFarlane. He was wounded and did not return. In his place was a good soldier but a man never intended to be an R.S.M. He walked as if he were following the plow, and his only name among the men was "Farmer." He had no sense of humour, handing out drastic discipline at every opportunity.

While we were in billets, Sykes got books from some source and spent much time reading. Cuvilier was made a sergeant and was a good one. Two tall men, Haldane and Peeples, from the MacLean Highlanders, became popular with the platoon. We had some grand singsongs at night in the barn. McMahon, who hated rats so much, would sing "O Love That Will Not Let Me Go" with a little encouragement, and I have never heard anyone do better. With McMahon and Rees as tenors, and three very good bass voices, the entertainment was excellent. McMahon was a character. Many of the men declared he was French, for he spoke French fluently. But he maintained he was Scottish. He never drank or smoked or played poker, was thirty-two and could outrun any man in the platoon. But he became confidential with us and owned he was married to a girl in the next village. He went there at every opportunity and lived well. When his leave came through, I was surprised that he went to Scotland-until he confided he was married to another girl in Edinburgh, who operated a small pastry shop. He frequently received parcels of food from her. I asked if he were not married before the war, and he said he had a wife and three children in Quebec.

One day I saw the driver who had taken me to the old chateaus. I arranged to get a day's leave, as his "boss" was on leave in England. We drove around the back areas and at one place stopped and watched Chinese labour battalions digging ditches. They used round shovels with very long handles and always had earth in the air, keeping the shovel going as if it were a machine, and only taking a third as much earth and chalk as an ordinary shoveller would do. Yet they worked with no rest at all and dug a great length of trench in a single day. They carried their dixies of rice and tea level-full, having them suspended from bamboo poles that sagged and allowed the dixies to swing, but they never spilled a drop as they walked in spring-kneed fashion. Some of them were enormous in size, and worked naked from the waist. They had their own foremen, although British sergeants were in attendance. That night as we returned through the district a Chinese band was playing. Each instrument had one string. It was weird, doleful music.

Wherever there was a chance, the Chinese slept under bridges, fearing German bombing planes. One night a plane did come and dropped its load about two miles away. The Chinese ran all over the fields, we were told, and some were found six miles away in the morning. Later some of the 42nd found the Chinese would buy tins of bully, and the cooks had a hard time keeping a stock on hand.

On Sunday Earl and I walked to Lozinghem, as the 85th Highlanders were there. I saw my brother, Hubert, who laughed about the "six days" in the line he had spent. Many lads from the home town were in the unit, and we had dinner with them. On the way we saw many more of the Chinese, and Senegalese, strange, soft-eyed fellows with their hair done up in black buns.

We heard rumours of field manoeuvres. Lorries came to take us over the country, where we marched into imaginary positions and had day-long picnics. Some of the officers took all the proceedings seriously and bawled us out in harsh language, but the war-wise ones were calm. It did not break their hearts to see us lying on the grass and drowsily regarding skylarks overhead. Messages would be sent and mixed into mystery. We would go where we were not supposed to go. Smoke bombs would be used at the wrong time.

Some of the manoeuvres were huge affairs. One nice morning we were disturbed by furious voices and saw the Corps Commander[17] arriving with some of his staff.

[17] General Sir Arthur Currie (1875-1933) was the Commander of the Canadian Corps, 1917-1918.

They did not seem pleased with our lack of enthusiasm, and our officers covertly implored us to show signs of action. At one point a village was designated as our battle ground. We were told to be prepared to make a wholesale attack and charged heartily-right into a Y.M.C.A. tent that was in our path. An enraged major ousted us from the place. He sent a platoon in one direction and when it vanished over the wrong hill, sent another after it. He left for a minute and returned to find his other two platoons had vanished. At night we lay around the billets and laughed over the incidents of the day. It was a wonderful vacation.

One afternoon one of the red-tabbed beauties from the safety zones came on the scene and declared my section had become "casualties," as we were in a wrong location. We had to lie on the ground and await further orders, so when left alone we visited a French home nearby. Madame could speak good English. She made coffee for us and said she wanted to help us, as she had a "Tommy." We laughed at our Tommy, who reddened, but our grins faded when she went to the door of an inner room and led an apparently old man into view. His hair was white and he walked feebly. His eyes were distended, staring. "He is twenty-three," Madame said, "and my only living son. There were two more but they are dead. This boy, Henri, was at Verdun. His mind is what you call at the halt-it cannot get past Verdun. He was wounded badly and a man fell across him and died. He could not move, was like that a day and a night. In his mind, he is still there."

We thanked Madame for her coffee and all of us shook hands with her as we left her. Two hours later we found the rest of the platoon-asleep in a grove.

There was a little *estaminet* a mile from our village on the Bourecq road, managed by a gaunt woman with skull-like eye sockets. A varied company used to gather there each night, as she made the best coffee in the district and served the best eggs and chips. It was there we met old "Peter" from the R.C.R.'s. We never knew him by any other name. He had been nineteen months in the line without receiving the slightest recognition of his worth and it grieved him.

"Some bleedin' pup comes over wot has money and goes in the line five minutes and has a Military Cross on his chest. Wot for, I awsks yer. Nobody knows. Maybe he won the trinket, but wot would he be like if he had a year first in the muck?"

He had been crimed once for striking a sergeant. Up in the crater line at Vimy one night when it was raining in French style, a message came saying the sergeant wanted to see him. Peter asked if the morning would not do, as he would be obliged to go overland to get to the sergeant's dugout, and the sap had been blown in by a bomb. No, the message was urgent, so after Peter finished his turn on post he wallowed through the mire, got caught by machine-gun fire and had to lie in a crater half an hour. Then at last, mud from hoofs to horns, dead beat, wet to the skin, he reached the sergeant's abode where that three-striped authority had remained in dry comfort-and the non-com wished to know the number of his rifle!

"I soaked him a good one, I did," said Peter. "Number of me blinkin' rifle! On a night like that! There ain't, I'm tellin' yer strite, an ounce of common horse sense in the runnin' of this war."

Tommy's leave came through and away he went in high glee. Giger's leave also came through, relieving Old Bill. He had discovered Giger roaming around a melancholy female, the attendant of two bony porkers and a cow, who wore her hair in a frowzy knot and was dressed mostly in soldiers' discards. Giger had been trying to talk to her in sign language.

The battalion moved to Bellacourt. All of us realized we had not been taken back and fed well, and trained in a sort of way, if there were not some big attack in the offing. We had learned, however, to live each day as it came and not to worry about the future. From Bellacourt we moved to support trenches at Neuville-Vitasse, relieving the 27th Battalion. It was a quiet sector and the weather continued warm. We lay in bivvies and slept during the day, and at night went on working parties. The MacLean men thought we had a "jake" war. A draft came to us, and among the dozen or so was a man named Morris, a tall chap with queer eyes. He pushed himself into Tommy's bivvy, which was fairly large. The last morning there Tommy roused me and I went out to see Morris lying in the trench, rather badly battered, and to hear a strange story.

Tommy had been sleeping until he was awakened by a terrible grip on his throat. Morris had him pinned and had a revolver to his head, saying he would shoot if Tommy did not agree to come with him. Tommy agreed, convinced the man was crazy, and hoping to see a sentry who would help. But none was near. Morris pressed the revolver to Tommy's back and told him to get over the parapet and walk to the German lines. At that moment a shell landed not far away and Morris ducked down. As he rose Tommy whipped over a beautiful right-hander, sending Morris down for the count. He grabbed up the revolver. It was empty! It enraged him to think a new man had so scared him, so he waited till Morris revived and got up, then knocked him down again. Morris caved completely then and begged for mercy. He said he would not make further trouble. Tommy made him move to another bivvy and that was that.

After another brief spell at Bellacourt we returned and relieved the C.M.R.s at Mercatel Switch. It was a very dark night when we took over, and the relieved unit got away without leaving any information about our company front. We did not know how far it was to the German lines or what the front was like, so a call came for me to go to company headquarters. I was to go with the sergeant of Fifteen Platoon and explore.

We went slowly and carefully. The sergeant, Ross Young, was an old hand and a good one. Not a flare was going up, nor was there much shooting. The 2nd Division had been on that front and had raided the Hun regularly, so we figured there were some surprises in store for us. We crept on and on. The area was mostly grass and weeds with occasional craters. We lay and listened a long time but did not hear any movement about us. Young began to get nervous. The lack of any sound made us think we might be in a no man's land of greater width than usual. Just then flares went up on our right, and they seemed no great distance from our lines. There must be listening patrols out, Young whispered, so we better lie and listen for some time.

It seemed the sensible thing to do, so we lay with our heads on the ground to catch any footsteps near us, and stayed and stayed. Nothing happened. We could not hear or see a thing. The only thing left to do, we decided finally, was to go in and have someone put up flares from our side. "But let's go on a bit further before we do," I whispered. "Let's stand and walk. The ground is fairly level here. Put your hand between my shoulders and dig me if you hear or see anything."

He agreed and we stood up, listening again. Then we started off. About the fifth step I took I descended through space-I had stepped off solid ground into a deep trench!

As I pitched downward, my steel helmet struck a strand of barbed wire that spanned the trench. The helmet saved my face on the right side, but not on the left. There the long barbs of German wire tore the skin above my eye, ripping to the bone. I landed with a crash but was not otherwise hurt. I found my helmet, put it on and stood up. On my right at a distance a voice asked, "Ist du Otto?" On my left at a distance another voice asked, "Ist du Fritz?"

I put out an arm, waved it and struck into the grip of Ross Young. I just had time to put a foot against the trench side when he yanked powerfully and I was out, and we were running as fast as we could go.

We ran side by side and really sprinted. Suddenly the earth left us and we crashed into a crater about four feet deep, knocking the wind out of us and jarring us badly. For a moment I could not move. Then the night opened wide with flares and machine-gun fire. There seemed about a dozen German machine-guns going. Twice bullets knocked earth over us as we lay. Stick bombs began to shower all along the front, but none reached as far as our crater. The explosions were constant. When they had ceased, out came the "darts." They were really dangerous but only three came near us. The majority fell on our right, but the three near ones scattered earth and debris over us.

Finally the flares stopped. Then the "darts." For a moment all was quiet as before, and then someone put up three or four flares on our side.

When they subsided we climbed out of the crater. My eye seemed badly damaged. It was full of blood. We reached our trench, and I left Young to do the explaining and hunted up Sykes. He got a candle and made an examination, told me my eye was badly torn and there was nothing he could do about it. He put a loose bandage over it and advised me to lose no time in getting to the medical officer.

Our shelters were along a sunken road and just at that moment the Hun began a heavy shelling. No doubt word of our visit to his trench had just reached headquarters. Sykes said it would be foolhardy to venture outside, but I could not wait. I just had to know how badly my eye was damaged. Earl was at our shelter and offered to go with me to the first aid post, by an overland route that was very much shorter. It would save time but was very exposed. It was a most unselfish thing for him to offer, as he had finished his work for the night and had no need to take more chances. But he insisted on going.

We were not ten yards from my dugout when a salvo of shells landed in the road ahead of us. There were cries for a stretcher bearer on the double, and as we ventured out again they were picking up a poor fellow who was making his first tour in a front line. He was dead before they could bandage him. We hurried on and climbed out to go overland, were part way across when more shells came in a hurricane burst. We dropped to earth and they fell ahead of us, to our left, to our right and behind us. Shrapnel whined over, but not a thing touched us. We got up as soon as there was a lull and ran again, reaching the second trench before another outburst came. It was just a step from there to the doctor's dugout and Earl said he would go back the safer way around.

Captain Hale was finishing a cup of coffee. He grunted out questions, gave me an inoculation and had me lie on a cot while he probed my eye. It was a painful procedure, but I did not mind when he gruffly told me my sight had not been injured in the least. "But the barbs cut to the bone," he said. "So you'll have to go out."

"What for?" I asked.

"Because we haven't any anaesthetic," he said, "and you will have to have quite a row of stitches."

"I don't want to go out," I said. "Will you please sew it up and right now."

He shrugged. "As you like," he said.

I reached up and gripped the handles of the stretcher while he sewed, with two candles on his table and another on a stool by my head. It was certainly a painful process but nothing to what I had imagined. "Now don't touch the dressing," ordered Hale. "You better go out to the transport lines and let a doctor look after you out there."

"No, sir," I said. "I'm going to stay in the dugout and I'll come to you."

He shrugged again and that was that. The sergeant-major was kind. He said I could stay off duty and let Captain Hale look after my eye. Ross Young came to see me, bringing me binoculars the second afternoon. Between our first and second lines there was an old ruin of brick, and from it I could look over our front. After a time I made out the German lines, then followed their wire and finally made out a gap about four feet wide. Pure luck had steered us to that point.

My injury saved me from a Fourteen Platoon patrol. Earl, Barron, Williams, "Waterbottle" and Lockerbie went out and explored the area to the right of our company front. They discovered the Germans had a post at a place we had dubbed "Long Alley." At once headquarters said it must be attacked. The next night a party with the sergeant in charge went out and worked in close until they got into the sap leading to the post. "Waterbottle" and Williams led the attack, throwing Mills bombs and shooting. It was so sudden and the Germans were taken so completely by surprise that not a prisoner was taken. Two jumped out in the confusion and escaped overland. The other six were killed, and not one of our men received a scratch. Williams and Waldvogel received Military Medals for their part in the action.

This success whetted appetites and immediately a second raid was planned. There were to be two parties, one to act as a covering crew. The orders were to "cut off enemy posts from the southwest under cover of a barrage with a demonstration to attract the enemy's attention to the northwest." The covering party was to go out thirty minutes before zero hour and take a position north of the attack, remaining there until the raiders returned or zero plus ten minutes. The signal was to be the opening of the barrage. Smoke bombs were to be released, red flares shot on the northern side of the enemy line and rifle grenades discharged at Hun trench posts. This was supposed to fool Fritz as to where the real assault was taking place.

When I learned the names of those in command I did not regret my damaged eye. As with so many elaborately planned affairs that look so good on paper, all did not go as expected. The covering party had the opportunities but the raiders did not. The covering party was barely in position before a German patrol came wandering along and dallied a few yards from them. It was a golden opportunity, as the patrol would not have a chance, but the officer in charge decided an attack might create a mixup, so the covering party lay quietly and after a time the Huns casually made their way along, almost contacting the man on the far left.

Over went the barrage, the red flares and the rifle grenades. Over went the raiding party, but there were no Germans in the post, only a small black dog and a loaf of German bread. The Germans sent up flares and golden sprays and retaliation fell on our lines. One of the raiders was killed by a rifle shot.

At any conference regarding raids I had but one point to make, and I adhered to it: never plan a raid on paper. There was continual change in enemy posts and in enemy tactics. Never take too many men on a raid. Have everything fluid so that any opportunity offered could be grasped. But I was always talked down. The sticklers for paper work were in command. So I would never go on a raid unless ordered to do so. The morning after the raid our doughty friends, the engineers, had a beautiful O-pip constructed. I sat in it two days with a telescope and watched two Germans working in their back area. I thought they were burying dead, as they seemed to be excavating a considerable depth. They were both elderly men and worked slowly.

Word came we were to be relieved by a battalion just arrived from Egypt, the King's Liverpool Regiment, and that we were to go to Wailly. My eye was improving rapidly. I had done a turn on listening post when the Liverpools arrived. In addition, I had a most interesting time with a new officer. He was on duty for four hours and was supposed to visit the various posts. He was well-educated and a good-looking man. When I offered to take him out to a listening post, he refused. He did not make any excuses but talked plainly.

"I'm scared stiff," he said. "It's all I can do to stay in this trench."

When a few shells came over, a considerable distance away, he dropped to the trench floor and huddled there. I talked with the officer, fearing the captain would come along and see him, and persuaded him to get up and sit on the fire step with me. There he told me the circumstances of his enlisting. Everything he said rang true. We talked for half an hour, and the longer I was with him the better I liked him. I could write pages about him but will not. He conquered himself until he could go over the parapet and was one of the finest men I have ever met anywhere.

The "Egyptians," as we called the Liverpools, were even worse than we had feared. They knew nothing about trench fighting or the Germans. An order came that a platoon from each company was to stay with the newcomers until just before daylight, showing them the rounds and the proper methods of trench holding. We had our first big surprise when a runner came, leading the commander of the company relieving us, and he wanted to know where he was to keep his horse while the battalion was in the trenches. He actually thought he could ride back and forth from headquarters under cover of darkness and so save himself considerable walking. Then he asked about rifle fire. His men, he said, had not used their rifles very much. Our platoon commander excused himself and was soon among the missing. We were not long in learning that all our officers had vanished.

The next startling thing was when we came from our dugouts with full equipment so they could go in and take over-and saw men out tying bits of rags to our wire. A sergeant explained they were going to do the "five rounds rapid" stuff in the morning and must have a target for the men to use. We advised him to do his shooting some other time, explaining how proficient all German snipers were. Then we asked him who would man our listening posts. He selected two heroes and out we went. I explained their duties carefully and in detail, and showed them how they were to use the signal wire. It took at least twenty minutes to get them to understand the situation. As I went in, a bomb came hurtling at me from the trench post I had left. The sentry there had the signal wire attached to his wrist, had felt the two tugs signifying a man was coming in, yet had hurled the grenade, and only the fact that he did not know enough to pull the pin saved me.

Tommy arrived just in time to witness the incident. "Where's our officers?" he demanded. "Why didn't they stay and give instructions? We'll all be killed if we stay here. I'm going."

He went and I looked for Sparky, who had a trench post. An "Egyptian" was there, seated, having a smoke. I turned and left. On the way I did not see another 42nd man. They had all left the scene.

At Wailly there was a flood of rumours about an inspection. There was to be a general cleaning of brass, and some military mogul would arrive after we had been standing an hour in the sun, walk up and down the ranks and depart. A tooth had bothered me just enough to make it a legitimate excuse, and I got permission to go to dental headquarters in the next village. Tommy also tried hard to think of some excuse to go somewhere. Everyone wanted to avoid the inspection.

It was only two miles to the dental place. I had to wait my turn and then was in a chair. *Crash! Slam! Crash!* Three heavy explosions. The building rocked. Bricks fell in the streets. Windows were shattered and dust rose in clouds. I moved fast, but the dental lads were out ahead of me. A trio of German planes, flying very high, had dropped their loads into the village. Two soldiers on their way to the dental office had been killed on the street. Eleven civilians were badly hurt and three had died. I ran until I was well clear of the area.

When I got back to Wailly it was to discover that all orders about a parade had been cancelled shortly after I left. There had been no inspection and no visitor. The laugh was on me. My brother, Hubert, came to see me and we went to an *estaminet.* As we finished a fine meal of eggs and chips, a drunken A.S.C. (Army Service Corps) corporal rode his horse through the open door and around the tables, wrecking some furniture. It was a real pleasure to see the military police arrive just as he was making an exit.

We were never at another place as filled with rumours and spy stories. They were a feature of Wailly. We were told about the military police making a man in engineer's uniform come down a telephone pole, where he was pretending to work. The story said the man was a German spy and his job was to tap wires and listen to military conversations. Another account said that carrier pigeons were seen flying from the village on several occasions, that police experts sent to watch the place discovered they were coming from an upper window of the most popular *estaminet* in Wailly. The police went in and up the stairs to find a stout old woman making a bed. She expressed amazement when they asked about pigeons coming from the window, which was still open, and said there was some grotesque mistake. Her family had never had pigeons. Very few persons in the place had pigeons. She sounded very sincere, but one of the police opened the closet door, and a large cage that had not been cleaned since it had been occupied by pigeons was found underneath a load of clothing hastily pulled from closet hooks. By this time one of the police had noticed that the woman walked very stiffly. He threw her back on the bed, and a pigeon emerged from her petticoats and was gone out the window before they could catch it. The rumour said the woman had confessed being a German spy, in an effort to save the rest of her family from suspicion, but she had been shot and the others were in jail.

But the natives were close-mouthed when we questioned them, and all we could find out was that a new family was in the *estaminet* from which the pigeons were said to have flown.

A man from the 8th Winnipeg Black Devils was in the *estaminet* one evening and said his platoon had a wild spree at Arras after doing a turn in the line. They had a patrol out the night they were to be relieved, and captured a young German on a listening post. When they got him to their dugout they saw that he was extremely handsome, with quite feminine features. No one wanted to bother taking him to headquarters and answering endless questions, so they simply took him along when they went out of the line. It was very late when they arrived in Arras, so they kept the German with them in billets till the morning. The place they occupied had been a fine residence. In a closet was an abundance of French feminine finery, and they stripped off the young German's uniform and arrayed him wondrously in a flowing skirt and waist, putting an attractive bonnet on his head and taking him down into the street. He was very afraid of what might happen to him when they let him loose and indicated he was to walk up the street ahead of them. Their hope was that some army buck would try to make the "lady's" acquaintance, but around the corner came a very fat and pompous major of the A.S.C. The German saw a chance for salvation, so he gathered up his skirts and did a wild sprint up the street, throwing himself on the major's expansive bosom. The Black Devils also took to flight-in the opposite direction. A last glance back revealed the lady still in the arms of the major.

We were paraded to baths, and an order was pasted in every pay book. It read: "Keep Your Mouth Shut," and finished with a warning not to talk to the French people or anyone else about our movements. There was plenty of talk among ourselves, however. Everyone knew something big was on the horizon. Soldiers were on the move everywhere. The very air was tense. We began moving without knowing where we were going, and the second day went through areas where no troops had been in a long time. In one little village the people were wildly excited when they saw our kilts and heard the pipe band. They all ran from their cottages or gardens and came alongside, chattering shrilly. When we stopped to rest by one farm, a girl came out with a bowl of strawberries and a big spoon. We opened our mouths like expectant nestlings and each received a tasty treat.

The route lay beside waving cornfields, little cottages with red roofs, old peasants driving big white Percherons with a single rein, poplar and willow trees along canal banks, and village ponds in which ducks swam. We marched endless kilometres in the hot sun, on long straight roads lined with tall trees, and a crucifix at every crossway. At night we stopped wherever we happened to be, too weary to do any exploring, our thoughts concentrated on the cook wagons. By the time they arrived and everyone had been fed it was dark and we were sleepy. One night at the place we were staying, we noticed a long pool formed in a field where someone had built a dam across a brook. So off went Tommy and Brown and I to have a bath, as we were very sweaty and uncomfortable. The water was a trifle cooler than we had expected but pleasantly refreshing. As we splashed around we were startled to hear the voices of some women very near. But it was too late to escape, and anyway our uniforms were lying on the bank in plain view.

Three women appeared, looking to be youngish farm wives worn with a hot day in the fields. They shrugged at the sight of our kilts on the grass, sat down and with a few motions divested themselves of all garments. Then they kicked off their shoes and simply waded in. We had moved to the far end of the pool and there we stayed, while they enjoyed themselves about twenty yards from us. Naturally we were not in any hurry, and neither were they. They surveyed us with candour and we returned the compliment. It was dark as we dried ourselves. Not a word was spoken until we were leaving, when all three of the mermaids shouted their version of "good evening."

A day later we reached Amiens. It was a big city, but looked and sounded empty as we marched through the outskirts. There were long halts while those in command made an effort to learn where we were to proceed. Finally we were allowed to enter a barnlike building out of the sun while messengers were sent somewhere to get information. As soon as the officers were gone there was singing, joking and frolicking that gradually died down to conversation. The scene made me think of our going up to Passchendaele. Tulloch kept talking about the type of "blighty" he wanted. Thompson said he didn't want one. Barlow, only eighteen, and Ted and Rees and Harvey kept singing softly. There was Old Bill, Barron, Waldvogel, Williams, Sparky, McMahon, Hayward, Cuvilier, Haldane and Norton. Our sergeant for the time was Jim Williamson. He was about six foot three, an "original," and had been two years, rumour said, on a cushy job. Sellars was back with us, and Ab Fordham, another old-timer and a good fellow, with Geordie Thompson, back for the third time after being twice wounded.

We left the city and marched out to a little village in the suburbs, a street of houses on a slope across the river. There was a small factory near the stream and the employees were all girls, a fact which did not deter the boys from having luxurious swimming in the sun-warmed water. At our billet a notice was posted forbidding soldiers to take anything from French gardens. Rations had not kept up with us the last three days of our trek, and we were unable to buy food in the little village. We waited until after dark but no bread and bully arrived. We were famished. Not far from us was a garden apparently abandoned. It was choked with weeds and the cottage was closed. In the cottage we occupied was a good stove, a large cooking pot and a supply of rough crockery. Tommy and I went out and filled the kettle with vegetables from the garden. After cleaning them we put them on to boil. There was plenty of coal in the shed back of the cottage and we soon had a good fire going, then we put out the lights and fastened the door. No one came near us. The dinner was cooked and though we were starved, we simply could not consume everything. So we called in Bob Jones and Sparky-who we knew were close-mouthed-and they finished the feast.

In the morning two Yanks came among us. They had cameras and were taking pictures everywhere. They got us to pose for them outside the houses, singly, in groups, with our equipment and without it. We gave them our addresses and they made solemn promises to send us snaps, but we never received one.

Then came a message that stunned every one of us. Our colonel had been killed!

Lieutenant-Colonel Bartlett McLennan, D.S.O., had been first and always a gentleman. He was admired and respected by every man in the battalion, and we tried our best whenever he gave an order. He had been out on a quiet afternoon to visit the line to which we were going, and a shell had come suddenly and struck him down.

There were colonels and colonels in the Corps. Some the men swore at and some they swore by. In my roamings back of the line I had visited practically every unit in our division, had talked with many members of various units as we relieved them or they relieved us, and had never found another battalion in which love for the commanding officer was as spontaneous and unanimous as in ours. We had bad eggs among us at all times, all kinds of soldiers, but I never heard one of them say a word against "the old man." His death more than shocked us. We feared we would not get another of his kind.

Chapter 6: The Battle of Amiens

We left our little village, St. Fuscien, on August 6, marching off at dusk. Our route lay through Boves. It seemed as if every other battalion and battery, every branch of the service, had also decided to move that night, and in the same direction. We did not make much more than one mile an hour. Limbers and men were close packed. Mules with transport, horses with field guns, tractors with heavy artillery, great lumbering, clanking tanks, followed each other in close succession. We were forced into ditches many times and in some places had to take to fields. In among the traffic we saw messengers on motorcycles, even cars with loads of "brass hats." Never had we seen such a jumble of traffic. If the German bombers had come overhead that night they would have made a ghastly killing.

It was early morning before we arrived at Gentelles Wood. Thousands of other soldiers were there, but all the wood was laid off in areas and each man stayed in his own battalion square. Some of the men made shelters of branches and ground sheets and some tried to dig in. Tommy and I spread our ground sheets on fairly dry moss that formed a sort of mattress, lay down together and slept. Overhead we could see stars twinkling above the tree tops. All around us was a humming, a murmur of voices and mild confusion. In the distance the tanks were still clanking and tractors were grinding. Farther away the guns were shelling in a spasmodic manner. Rumours of all kinds had run through the platoons all day. The most prevalent said we were to join in an attack that would extend over a front of twenty miles, and the fighting would go on until we had broken the Hun line. Each man had his own thoughts on the matter, keeping them largely to himself. Tommy and I slept warmly. When we woke the sun was playing on our faces.

Someone said it was Sunday, and we heard Giger asking if there would be a church parade. Orders came for us to lie low. No man was to leave his platoon zone. There was to be as little movement as possible. Tommy reminded me we had missed three church parades, so had something to be thankful for. Like the majority, he strongly resented being made to fall in a parade and go and listen to the padre and officers sing "Fight the Good Fight," and a sermon he scorned. But he would go to a voluntary service in a Y.M.C.A. or elsewhere and join heartily in the singing.

Tommy should have been a sergeant, but was too prone to express his opinion of the continual and irritating stupidity of the army. There was nothing to equal it. An ounce of common sense would have engendered good feelings, but common sense was seldom admitted to any army headquarters. When we were by the river each man bathed in the evening. We washed our shirts and socks and were cleaner than at any previous time. Yet headquarters did its stuff as usual. We were forced to fall in and march six miles over hot and dusty roads to baths. The baths were in an old building, and the pumps had been so mistreated by relays of men that only two were in working order. This meant an hour added to the usual time. The water was very scarce. The conditions were horrible. Torn and buttonless shirts were thrown at us in place of our clean ones, along with socks that did not match.

After all this humbug we had to march six miles back over the hot dusty road, which put us in such condition that every man headed for the river to wash away the sweat and dust. Then the shirts had to be mended and buttons sewn on, while we expressed our emotions in terms that would have reduced an adjutant to tears. Tommy had some bad luck at the baths. He was tossed a shirt made up of two materials. The front was flimsy cotton, the back was horse blanket. But as we ate our breakfast in the wood, I noticed he was wearing a good garment, and asked its source.

"I salvaged it from a batman," shrugged Tommy. "Probably he borrowed it from an officer. But I wouldn't hurt his feelings. I left my shirt, to make it an even trade."

Sergeant Williamson came around and asked if we had Mills bombs. Each man was given two. Fordham was a sergeant in our platoon and he was checking on field dressings. All through the morning there were great comings and goings of various non-coms checking on extra ammunition, ground flares and sandbags. Then we had dinner. The day was clear and sunny. Every time we heard a plane we listened anxiously, but always it was one of our own. They made sure no German aircraft came over us.

Poker games were in progress in many glades. Some men were writing letters home. The majority sat together, chatting now and then but mostly busy with their thoughts. "C" Company men were beside us and Leon Casey, a boy from our Amherst home town area, was there. It was the first time I had seen him in months, and though he was playing poker we had quite a conversation. At dark everyone was told to get his water bottle filled.

Major Arthur sent for me and told me I must go to the assembly point with a party, learn the route, and return and guide the company in. I left everything but my gas mask and went with the other scouts and guides. It was a mile to where we were moving, a deep trench south of the Amiens-Roye road, and it took us some time to find the men who were to show us the position. After ascertaining where "D" Company was to go, I hurried back to where I had left my equipment. There I had quite a shock. For the first time in my experience, some miserable character had stolen my rations. There was nothing I could do about it but go hungry, so I put on my harness and reported to the major.

It had turned cold and the men were impatient to get moving, but as we were leaving the wood a great rustle of movement stilled them. It was something we had not heard before. All at once no one was speaking or whispering. Thousands of men were moving by us as quietly as possible, and the only thing audible was the soft sound of men jostling in the dark, the swish of feet in grass. There was something in the night that seemed pregnant with sudden violence, as if at any time some crashing chaos might envelop the entire landscape. No one complained as we threaded in and out in snaky fashion to avoid other companies and other units, and all were too amazed to say anything when we saw field guns being wheeled into positions. There were no pits or camouflage for them, and it showed what the expectations were.

Companies seemed to be coming from all directions. One had to be careful to hold to the route. It was nearly three in the morning when we were finally in our position, and I had been walking since eight in the evening. It gave me a certain satisfaction to notice we were in place first in that area. Others were arriving for an hour afterward. Zero hour had been set for 4:20 a.m., and some units were still moving in at four. Platoon commanders came and told us we were not going into the attack until three hours later, but were to leave our position, go down the slope in front and cross the River Luce. After that we would be in the fighting. Five pontoon bridges had been made ready for the river crossing, we were told. They had been made of bath mats and were rather flimsy structures, so we would have to travel in single file and be careful. We would start moving at six a.m. to give us plenty of time in crossing.

It was so quiet we could hear men talking in Thirteen Platoon, even make out what they were saying. The next second the earth shook violently and a sheet of flame lit up the sky. The roar of the guns was overwhelming, making one almost tremble. Orders had to be shouted when we actually started to move at ten minutes to six. There was a thick mist that made it difficult to see fifty yards ahead, but someone had foreseen such a difficulty and there was a strand of wire strung along on stakes from the trenches to the bridges.

Suddenly we were conscious of enemy shells. The valley of the Luce was low marshy ground, and the shells went deep into the mud as they had at Passchendaele, throwing up geysers of muck but causing no damage. We could not hurry in the least, as the pontoon bridge was swaying under the tread of those crossing. Some shells landed with great splashes in the river itself. One bridge had a near hit, and those on it had to go through mud and water to cross the gap. It was about thirty more feet from the stream itself over the swamp approach. Our platoon made it without a hitch, but many made remarks about a stone bridge to the left we might have used. It had been preserved for the use of heavy traffic, and the sergeant quickly reminded the grouser that the Germans would know about the bridge and do their best to destroy it with gun fire.

It was not a good morning for me. Going without any sleep and having nothing to eat, plus all the walking, had made me very tired. And there had been nothing cheerful at the last moments. Eddie Cuvilier had come to me from his Thirteen Platoon and extended a hand. He was smiling but very pale. I gave him a hearty grip and said "Good luck, Eddie."

He shook his head. "This is my last trip," he said.

My words tumbled out vaguely, and he smiled again. "I know all you want to tell me," he said. "But this is my last morning, and I wanted to say goodbye to someone from home."

He turned abruptly and left. What could I say? And he was no more than gone when Bob Christensen, the stretcher bearer and one of the best, came over. He was a reader and he and I had argued a lot. He smiled and shook hands. He said he hoped he would get to my heaven, but was going that day anyway. We shook hands warmly and he went. What could one say to him?

Crossing the bridge took all else from my mind. The whole affair was swaying and dipping under our weight and the muddy river was swirling just inches below. I was almost dizzy. I could not hurry in the least, and when at last we were over we could not see more than a hundred yards in the mist. Word trickled through that our objective was a hill. Some said it was Hill 104. There was nothing official. When the last man of our company was over, we started off slowly and reached a wooded area. Presently someone found a trench. We moved into it as word came that our jump-off time would be 8:20.

That spring a reinforcement had come to us from a Montreal unit and he was very nervous. He said he had been a boxer, but no one believed him. He had been so nervous as we waited for our turn on the bridge that the sergeant-major had spoken to him roughly. And now as we rested in that wood trench a lone shell, almost spent, hit a tree and detonated. Our boxer boy received a nice "blighty" and it was evident everyone was glad. His presence did not help the morale.

As the sun grew stronger and the mist cleared, we saw more woods ahead. Soon we were filing from our trench. The woods turned out to be no more than a fringe of trees, with a brick wall to the left. At that moment a salvo of "whizz-bangs" came over and every man ducked for cover. Tommy and I jumped behind tree boles. One shell exploded ahead of us where some of Thirteen Platoon had scattered, and we saw their stretcher bearer running to the spot while we hurried along to where rising ground would give some cover. I looked around as we went and saw the stretcher bearer get up and shake his head. He was standing beside the body of Sergeant Eddie Cuvilier. In some way Eddie's premonition had been genuine.

There were trees ahead at the foot of the slope, but no one bothered to rush to them as the bank afforded protection. Just ahead was young Ted. He stopped, dropped his rifle butt on the ground with his arm resting over the muzzle and started to say something to the man next him. In some manner his rifle discharged and he screamed in agony. We rushed over to find he had a fearful wound. There had been a muzzle cap on his Lee Enfield, which had been blown through flesh and muscles. We tied a tourniquet around his arm and twisted it with a stick. The stretcher bearer bandaged the arm as best he could, but we had to leave him there as the signal came for us to right turn and advance.

We went up the slope. It extended much farther than we had thought. Some distance ahead three Germans rose from a covert back of a log and shot at us before turning to run. They missed by a wide margin, but Sparky, who was a crack shot, dropped to one knee and sniped one neatly. The fellow seemed to fling his rifle over his head as he went down. Sparky shouted with elation as if it was his first battle, and raced up the hill to look at his victim. Others were firing and another of the trio went down before he could reach the crest of the slope. The third German got away.

When we reached the top of the grade we looked down on a field of grain. A deep ravine lay beyond and we could see camouflage that told of gun emplacements. We were now in extended order, the men in good spirits. We swept down through the grain, and all at once a German popped up directly in my path. He rose so suddenly that I shot without taking aim. Experience had taught me to carry my rifle under my right arm, steadied by my left, a finger on the trigger. Only a pressure was required to beat the other man.

As the German dropped he gave a fearful groan, and to my dismay I saw he was a wizened old chap with steel-rimmed spectacles and a scraggly beard. Probably he used to do mean chores around the battery position, maybe as a sanitary man, and in all probability he was trying to surrender. He had no weapon of any kind. I wanted to stop and see if anything could be done for the poor fellow, but Tommy shouted to look out for Germans ahead.

They had appeared from dugouts and were sprinting like mad toward a cutting in the high bank. Our "C" Company men were on our left and a bit ahead of us. They bagged the lot neatly. The leader of the Germans, who tried to escape, was a fat officer with an Iron Cross dangling over his paunch. He had been remarkably agile for his size but was grabbed, and two men tried to get his decoration. All this I saw without stopping as we ran down the hill. We saw three guns with canvas covers still over them. There was a dugout entrance to the left, with some whitewashed stones in a neat pattern, and smoke was coming from a pipe at the side of the stairway.

We had fourteen successive officers in command of Fourteen Platoon. The most recent one, who was with us now, we loved with all our hearts. He was too elderly to be of much use, but he was kind. He was connected with one of the largest stores in Montreal, and after he got our names every man in the platoon received a very fine parcel from his establishment. He bought cigarettes for those who preferred Players to the army issue, and if he knew any man was without funds he handed out ten francs without a question. What to do with him during the attack had been discussed often, and finally it was decided that when we came to any tough fighting, "Granny," as we called him with affection, was to be taken to the safest place available and one man was to stay with him and try to protect him from harm. We did not want any other officer.

Three men had stayed behind with him to make sure he was all right in the hollow, and now they came down the slope with a gait suited to Granny's going. He was quite out of puff but vastly excited at sight of the guns. Why not turn them around and strafe the enemy? He shouted for everyone to take hold of the nearest, and while the men were trying to tell him that none of us were by any stretch of the imagination qualified gunners, I stole over toward the German dugout. I felt I would collapse if I did not get anything to eat.

Russell saw me and came running. Was it all right to go down into the dugout? Why not, I told him. The Germans had run away, he had seen them. There might be someone with a ready Luger but the chance was one in a thousand. The most likely occupant would be a cook making breakfast for the gun crews. Down we went into the dugout side by side, with our rifles at the ready. The place was brilliantly lighted. There were tables and chairs, and the beds were excellent with real mattresses and the finest linen. A clock was ticking on a shelf, beside newspapers, several letters and an unopened parcel. A frying pan with eggs rather well done was on the stove.

We sat down and ate in style. Hunger made the sausage quite acceptable, the eggs passable, and even the dark German bread was tasty. The coffee pot was still on the stove so we had clean cups and drank plenty. Then Russell opened the parcel. It contained a few candles, some candies, two silk handkerchiefs, contraceptives (most prevalent in France), and a huge cake covered with pink frosting. A card had some message for Lieutenant Fritz somebody or other. Russell cut a healthy slice of cake and gobbled it. I had another cup of coffee, glanced at the clock and watched him. We had been in the dugout twenty-one minutes. Presently I said: "How do you feel?" y

"Jake," he snorted. "Why?"

"Oh, nothing," I said. "It's time we got back to the war." I cut myself a good slice of cake and up we went, carrying the cake with us. The food and coffee had changed everything. I felt a new man.

Up above Granny was still examining the guns. The boys had taken the covers from them so he could make a good inspection. Russell blurted an account of what we had been doing in the dugout, and how I had him test the cake. The lads had a good laugh and soon all the cake had vanished. Then the sergeant decided it was time we carry on and do our part for the Canadian Corps.

No sooner were we on high ground than we met a party of German prisoners coming back. Some of them were almost trotting in their haste. There were twenty in all, and at the rear were three medical officers who spoke to us in good English and asked how far they had to go before finding someone who would take charge of them.

They were more than willing to assist in looking after any of our wounded, they said, and told us we were not likely to meet with any organized resistance for some time. As we talked to them I saw Tommy and two others making a quick search of the prisoners waiting on the officers. They had two Iron Crosses, several watches and quite a few German marks.

Thirteen Platoon was seen over on our right and not far away, and Fifteen Platoon was on the left. The sergeant said we were now well beyond our objective. He had a map with him. We were approaching Claude Wood, he said. The other platoons veered toward us and soon we were practically together. A shell had dropped near them and Cockburn, who had been wounded in the Quarry Line when Laurie was hit, had been killed. Christensen had been wounded and had gone out. The information made me tell Tommy about the Dane shaking hands with me and what he had said. We both grinned.

The company was extended as we went on toward the wood, and then came orders to lie down. The grass was soft and the sun warm. We were on high ground, with excellent observation of the battle, and could see Germans running everywhere on the horizon. Some had reached the edge of the wood and were hurriedly getting machine-guns in position, but the majority were fleeing on the other side, racing at top speed without weapons or helmets. There was a village not far off. The sergeant said it was Beaucourt, and we could make out the Amiens-Roye Road. An aeroplane crashed near us, startling everyone, as we had not heard its engine. The pilot was a boy of twenty and both his legs had been hit by machine-gun fire. We helped him to the ground and our stretcher bearers did all they could for him. He was quite calm, asking only for cigarettes.

Somebody shouted to us, and we left the airman to watch one of the finest spectacles of the whole war. We were privileged to have ringside seats, out of the danger zone. Over the slope came our cavalry, the Royal Canadian Dragoons, the Fort Garry Horse and the Strathconas, riding like mad, sabres flashing and lances glitter ing, in perfect formation. They swept by us with a thundering of hoofs and drove at the wood. Some passed to right and some to left of it. Following them came the "whippets", small tanks with remarkable speed and with guns mounted on the top.

The mounted men dashed into the wood, at the waiting gunners. Killing began as if it were a grand movie scene. The Maxims opened fire and men and horses rolled among the shrubbery or fell in the open. I saw an officer rise in his stirrups and strike a Hun across the neck with his sword so that the German's head lolled oddly on his left shoulder as he fell. I saw a lancer pierce a German gunner so that the weapon emerged at the back. Several Huns were trodden to earth under the hoofs of the horses, which swept in on them like a stampede. It was whirlwind fighting, so fast and furious that the machine-guns did not take half the toll we expected. One crew alone survived the cavalry charge. A tank headed straight for them. The Germans fired frantically, and we saw one of the men on the tank slide to the ground, but the tank went on and over gun and crew, so quickly that not a German escaped. After it had passed we saw a body rolled on the sod gleaming white, completely stripped of clothing.

We had more thrills. More horses came into view, pulling a battery of heavy guns. They thundered by us and over the wide plateau, swinging about and into action with astounding speed. We saw the shells striking in the village, sending up great clouds of smoke and dust, and soon the cavalry pressed on.

After noon a long column of men came into sight, battalions of the 4th Division going through to carry on the attack. I saw the 85th Battalion, but could not pick out my brother in the distance. No shells were falling near us. The only Germans in sight were the dead ones spread over the fields and in the wood, and a line of prisoners guarded by three Canadians with slung rifles. The medium tanks had gone and now the big ones lumbered up, one carrying water and ammunition. We went on to Claude Wood and some searched the dead Huns for souvenirs. I picked up a sabre from the grass, a long-bladed weapon with an elaborate hilt. Tommy found a Luger among the leaves.

We slept in the wood, happy that we had been in reserve all that day. Our cooks came up and served a hot meal, and the 49th moved into the same area for the night. The sergeant-major came over and spoke about Cuvilier and Ted. "Too bad about Christensen," he added.

"What about him?" I asked.

"He had a nice blighty and was well on his way out when he was killed by a shell. Tough luck."

There was no comment to make, and I was too dead for sleep to talk to anyone. Tommy and I had a snug place by the roots of a big tree. The last thing I heard was someone asking where we had left Granny.

They had to wake me in the morning. It was another fine day and we had our breakfast where we lay. Afterwards we were formed up and moved toward Folies village, but did not attack it. It was captured during the day by the Winnipeg Black Devils and we moved in after dark. All kinds of German equipment and clothing lay about.

A dressing station looked as if it had been abandoned in a desperate hurry. Doors were wide open, windows were up. We looked in and saw two dead Germans lying beneath blankets, awaiting burial. Clothing from cots lay on the floor, and packs and rifles. Helmets and gas masks were piled in a passageway, indicating heavy casualties. There was a kitchen in the rear, and a great vat of soup was not quite cold. We got bowls and spoons and had some of the soup, which was quite good. Poking into cupboards, we found five or six puddings, but they were cold and we did not like their flavour. A sergeant came in and told us not to do any looting, then when asked to explain said he was just carrying out orders. He said we would be staying in the village overnight and had better get a sleeping place.

We hated the smell of the place, so Tommy and I each got a clean blanket and we went outside just as the sun set in a riot of radiant colour. Years later at a reunion, someone spoke about the beauty of that evening, the streamers of rose and onyx, flecks of pearl, of crimson and gold. But at the rear of the building were grisly reminders of the character of the place-rough wooden coffins standing on end, leaned there so they would not collect rain water. We tipped down a couple and got into them. The wind could not get at us, and with a blanket folded double over us, and pillows from the beds, we slept warm and comfortable. Fifteen Platoon had been lucky. They had found a large underground fitted with good bunks, and a kitchen stocked with food. Each man had tins of this and that in his haversack.

To our surprise, there were no orders to move. No one seemed to know what was going on, and Williams announced we had become official observers for the 3rd Division. Word was that we must stay pretty well put, as we might have to move at any time, but after an hour we were exploring. There was no doubt that Folies had been a supply depot for the Germans. We found an enormous lumber yard with three loaded trucks by the gate. One had a German tunic in the seat, as if the driver had left in a great hurry, We discovered three dugouts and in one was a canteen that had been left intact. There was beer in bottles and kegs, drinking mugs on the counter. Seats and tables had been filched from French homes. Someone opened a till and found it well stocked with German paper marks. No one took any, even for souvenirs, but there was much sampling of the beer and three different varieties were noted. No one liked any of it, except Giger. He was overlooked as we left the place and was found in the afternoon by another platoon, so drunk they carried him back to us.

The whole 42nd Battalion was in the area and there were transport men in a big farm nearby. We had noticed a big pump in the yard. That night when we wanted fresh water, Tommy and I went over to fill our water bottles. The water was excellent and we drank thirstily. We got what we wanted and began to make our way back, and were just to the road when we heard the zoom-zoom above us of German planes. We started to run, then slowed. Where was there a safe place? We were too far from the dugouts. A great gash of flame spurted near the farmyard gate. Other bombs dropped farther over to the farm buildings. They were of the "spring" variety and seemed to explode a few feet above the ground. We huddled in the shelter of a doorway until the bombers were gone, and the first man we met told us a bomb had dropped beside a hut in which a platoon was staying and killed three men. Many horses had been killed in the farmyard, and several men there were wounded.

We stayed in Folies the next day as well, and by noon I am sure that every cellar and yard had been explored. Thompson had found a tub of pickles, which he had carried to our quarters. They were very good and so was some tinned meat Sparky located in a cupboard that no one had noticed, as it was behind a door. We had just had something to eat when orders came to move off at dusk. It seemed like the end of a holiday. There was much joking until we reached an old trench, and were told to make ourselves comfortable but to be ready to move at a moment's notice.

There was a grassy nook in a part of the trench we were in. There Tommy and I curled up and slept three hours. We were roused to hear orders to go to a front line and relieve a Border Regiment. We left the old trenches, moving along a main road where the walking was good, and soon we were near the village of Rouvroy. A group of men were waiting at a corner. We were told they were guides from the Border Regiment come to take us in. We were soon on an overland track with fair going and saw German flares rising and falling in front of us. They seemed quite near, and suddenly we halted. There was a long wait, then we were turned about and marched back to a junction of the main road to Rouvroy.

"The old army game," voices began to murmur. "Everybody's lost."

Another long wait was endured, then off we straggled, glad to do so since the Hun had begun to strafe Rouvroy. Soon we were strung out a long distance, muttering and stumbling. There was a call for scouts and I was told to take a man with me. Up we went. I had chosen Williams, as he seemed most restless in the platoon. We found three men from the Border Regiment and a group of our officers. Each man seemed to have a different theory, but at last we gained some knowledge of the situation. The Borders had had a rough time and heavy casualties. Slowly we made our way forward, and it was four in the morning before we had "D" Company in place in the front line.

When it came daylight we saw we were in old grassed trenches, with many concrete emplacements about, and wide tangles of rusting barbed wire at every corner. We stood where we were a time and then had something to eat. There was no shelling. The front seemed comparatively quiet.

It had become quite warm. We had lost Granny, and no one knew where he was. Then Major Arthur told us he was going to visit another part of the front, and to wait until he returned. The attack was not going to be made until two or three o'clock. The sergeant-major came and said nothing was definite. He had talked with some of the Border non-coms and they had told him the place was a warren of old trenches, a maze that would bewilder anyone.

It grew warmer and warmer, and soon most of us had emptied our water bottles. We became conscious of new odours, for there were many dead lying in full view from Thirteen Platoon's sector. A runner came and said I was to go to Sixteen Platoon. Major Arthur had not returned. I found the platoon in an old trench branching off to the right from the one we were in. The sergeant said he was not sure of anything; he had looked around the sector and found there were trenches in every direction and nothing to denote which had been the front line. He said that from what he gathered, each platoon of the company was to go in a different direction. Nothing made sense. Two dead of the Border Regiment were lying in a gap of the parados and they were covered with flies. There was not a breath of air. We sat, perspiring in the burning sun, and an hour dragged by.

A runner came and said he carried word there would be no barrage. It seemed an odd thing to attack enemy trenches without the support of a barrage, but we began to feel that nothing was real in this new area. The sergeant of Fifteen Platoon made us a visit and said he heard there were Germans in the trench further along, that we held about a third of it, the one in which we stood, and the Huns had the rest. We were to try and push them out of the trench. Then Geordie Thompson, acting as company-sergeant-major, came and told me I was to remain at the rear of Sixteen Platoon. Major Arthur would be along shortly and then we would move to the attack.

Major Arthur arrived, mopping his face. A whistle tooted somewhere and the platoon moved along the trench. Suddenly there was a wild clatter of machine-gun fire. It spread until it seemed to come from all directions. We ducked instinctively as soil was knocked into our trench and bullets sprayed the parapet. When we halted a moment I could swear that guns were shooting from the rear, from in front, from our left and from our right. The trench was narrow and had many bays. Thompson and Arthur and I were trailing, so we could see only three or four of Sixteen Platoon. There was a louder burst of firing directly in front of us and we heard the crashing of Mills bombs. All at once we surged forward about thirty yards in a rush. We passed a body in the trench, Haldane, the MacLean Kiltie, still grasping his rifle with fixed bayonet. He had been leading the attack with the bombers. We halted again. There was a wait and Major Arthur went forward. He returned with a worried look. The trench forked directly ahead, and there seemed to be Germans in both forks. Something was wrong. I was to go and locate Fifteen Platoon, as they were supposed to be behind us, then bring word of what they were doing.

How would I get there? I said I had no map of the place, had not been there before, and could not see any landmarks to use as a guide. The major agreed it was a problem but drew a plan on a piece of paper. I was to go back to where a small sap led left, follow it and, then, as I could see by his plan, I would be in the trench Fifteen Platoon was clearing, It was really fairly near us. Fifteen Platoon should have cleared the right fork of the trench we faced. As we talked the sergeant of Sixteen Platoon joined us. He said the Germans had suddenly withdrawn from the left fork of the trench. He had gone up it to a turn and no one was in it. He had also had a view, from there, of the trench that more or less ran parallel to the one we were in-where Fifteen Platoon might be-and no one was in it! This really complicated matters.

The major said I was to go just the same and take a man with me. We were to find Fifteen Platoon and bring back information as to what they had done. As luck would have it, the carefree "Doggy" was with Sixteen, and I at once asked that he go with me. He was headlong as a puppy but good-natured and sound.

We had no trouble finding the sap and soon were in the parallel trench. We looked at the earth carefully. There were fresh footprints going both ways! Furthermore, two trenches branched off at right angles and were not far apart, and there were footprints, quite fresh, on both. We could not see anyone along the trench. I thought Fifteen Platoon might have gone to the right on one of the trenches, but both petered out after a few yards. This was old ground, part of what had been an elaborate trench system in 1916. As there was nothing either way, we decided to go back, Doggy declaring that something was very wrong with the entire situation. It was often a joke in the platoons that runners knew more about what was going on than anyone else. Doggy had talked with Border runners, and they had told him they got lost all the time they were here, as the maps of the area were not correct. Trenches seemed to begin and stop without rhyme or reason.

There was a lot of shooting on our left, much nearer than before. In places the trench was not more than a glorified ditch, and we had to be careful we were not exposed. After going stooped over for some distance, we reached the fork-and no one was there!

It was true that Major Arthur had not said they would wait for us. But which way had they gone? Doggy said we had come much further than it looked on the map. He thought the platoon would have gone along the left trench, as it was more like the one we had followed to that point. I told him to go up the right one a distance, and come back if he did not see our men. I would keep to the left fork. Away we went, and shortly I had found three saps leading to the left from the trench, and was wondering where they led. Suddenly I heard German voices almost beside me. I could not see anyone, but jumped to a V-shaped place that looked like an exit, and pulled the pin from a Mills bomb. The next instant three German officers appeared as if by magic. They came from the bowels of the earth, out of a dugout entrance I had not seen because it was almost obscured by hanging grass and weeds. They were talking earnestly and didn't see me as they started along the way I had been going. I released the lever, counted two and tossed the grenade.

It exploded shoulder-high behind them and they went down like jackstraws. I was ready with my rifle, but no others appeared from the dugout and the three lay still where they had dropped. Two were dead, one with part of his head blown away, but the third man was breathing. He was wounded in the neck and spine and looked as if he would not live five minutes. Doggy had not come back. I returned to the fork in the trench but could not see him, then I came back and peered down the dugout and listened. There were no sounds, no voices. Suddenly the live German spoke, giving me a start. "You are Canadians," he said, in a good accent.

"Yes," I said curtly. "How many more are down in that dugout?

"None," he said. He was opening and shutting his eyes in the bright sun. "We came from the trench to the left. We used the dugout as it opens to both trenches." Then he began groaning and twisting in pain. I stooped over and took his Luger, also taking the pistols from the dead officers. It was impossible to carry them, so I hid them in the grass at a gap in the trench and marked the spot with a stick.

Still Doggy did not return, so I went again to the trench he had followed. There I met a fellow from Sixteen Platoon. He was wounded in an arm and said the platoon was travelling fast and had come to a road crossing. There was fighting. Major Arthur had gone back to see how the other platoons were doing. Where were Thirteen and Fourteen? I asked, and he waved vaguely with his good arm toward the left.

Back I went. It was terrifically hot. There was sudden machine gun fire on my right, and when I reached a trench leading in that direction, I glimpsed Canadian helmets and went that way. In a moment I came upon Major Arthur. It didn't take long to learn that here was another platoon not sure of its location. I told him about the three German officers and the passage through the old dugouts, said that Doggy had not come back and I had not found Fifteen Platoon.

He called the "original" with whom I had gone on patrol, telling him to go with me and others up the right fork where Doggy had gone, and report back as soon as we had located Fifteen. The others were Norton, Coleman, a happy-go-lucky lad, a Lewis gunner and his two crewmen. When we went back, I took the "original" to where the German officers were and told him where they had come from. He made no response and did not seem interested. The wounded officer asked me for a drink of water. I told him I did not have any, none of us had. He was getting weak and I had to bend down to hear him. "In the dugout is a good spring," he said. "Go down the steps and turn left about six paces. You will find it."

Coleman stared at him and shook his head. "A damn trap. Don't go"

Norton said that no dugout ever had a spring in it. But some impulse seized me. It would only take a moment and I wanted to prove them wrong. Besides, the officer was suffering intensely. The "original" started back to go up the left fork. He had not spoken to any of us. I took the other bomb from my pocket, held it ready, left my rifle with Coleman, and went down through the hanging grass and weeds on good steps. The dugout was of ordinary depth. I turned left, took six paces and knelt down, as the place was pitch dark. My fingers touched cold water. I had often seen seepage in dugouts, but this was the only time I had found a spring of excellent water. I filled my water bottle and hurried up, giving the German a drink. He had close-cropped brown hair and brown eyes. One of the gunners was bandaging his neck crudely. I gave him a hand and we moved the officer so he was in the shade of overhanging growth.

The "original" was waiting as if he were burdened with half-wits. It was fearfully warm. Even our rifles were hot. There was machine gun fire on all sides. You could not tell, by listening, where the real front was. There was wire along every trench, lots of it, and bullets ricocheted from it. We did not see anyone and suddenly were in a deeper, wider section of trench that crossed the one we were in, making a sharp T. There we halted. The "original" seemed more nervous than any of us and said he had never seen a worse mess. There were twice as many trenches as the maps showed. He was sure every platoon was lost. He did not like where we were at all. He told me to go with Norton to the left of the deep trench and explore about one hundred yards. He and the others would go to the right.

Norton and I went slowly. The trench sides were two feet higher than my head, covered with weeds and thistles. There were webs of black, long-barbed wire, and some wooden posts whose function we wondered about. Suddenly we heard German voices. I cautioned Norton to stand ready while I climbed up and had a look through the grass and weeds. There were five German pot helmets bobbing along about fifty yards away and they were going from our area. Just then I heard Norton give a sort of gasp and turned to witness a tableau that is vivid in my memory. Norton was about six feet three inches tall, and had not shaved for two or three days. He was holding his bayonet ready and his kilt was hitched high above his great, bony knees. In his hand, pressed against the rifle butt, was a Mills bomb. And facing him was a German, a young, white-faced fellow, a mere boy. He stood in a posture of recoil, cringing. And he was not armed!

Crack! Norton, after sixty long seconds of staring, pulled the trigger. He declared later that he had not meant to, that his finger simply tightened involuntarily on the trigger. The rifle muzzle was not six feet from the Hun and pointed at his stomach. The lad went down as if hit by a fist and groaned frightfully. I had never heard a worse sound.

The groaning upset Norton so much that he jumped about, dropping his bomb, and ran headlong down the trench. I dropped from my perch and dived at the bomb-but the pin had not been pulled. No other Germans were in sight, but I could hear a jabber of voices a few yards around the corner, so I pulled the bomb pin and hurled the grenade in that direction, then ran after Norton.

He was telling the "original" what he had done as I reached them and was so excited he hardly knew what he was saying. It was his first battle and his first kill. The "original" now suggested that Coleman and I go back to a traverse about one hundred yards away and watch for Germans. He and the others would explore in the other direction. We went back to the traverse, sweat running down our faces. We opened our tunics. And a party of Huns appeared twenty yards away, walking rapidly!

The Huns had their rifles ready, but I slashed at the trigger of mine and the bullet caught the coal-bucket helmet of the big leader, striking the earth-bank alongside them and scattering a cloud of dust. One of the Germans shot but his bullet struck the earth beside us, and then Coleman fired and brought the leader down. I shot a second time, catching a short, fat goose-stepper. Coleman shot at the third German as he turned and ran, and probably winged him, for the fellow dropped his rifle and clutched his arm as he vanished around the turn.

We hurried back and told the "original" what had happened. He decided we had better go back a distance up the trench, so the Huns could not come at us from both sides. It was a wise move. We had not gone fifty yards before Norton, using his height, saw pot helmets bobbing along the trench toward where we had been. At the same time he saw five Germans get up on the bank and start overland, so as to cut off the corner and rush us where we were. He was so excited he climbed out at a low place to meet them, and we, not knowing what was happening, followed him. The Lewis gunners jumped back in the trench when they saw five Germans with rifles ready, but for a second or so Coleman and I stayed with Norton. We fired at the Germans and they shot at us. The distance was about seventy-five yards and neither side scored a hit. The "original" yelled at us to get down, but there was a second exchange. Three of the Germans went down and both Coleman and Norton were hit. Coleman had a bullet through his arm and Norton had one eye shot out, a horrible wound. We tied him up and Coleman led him back the way we had come, as he had lost the sight of his other eye.

The Germans pressed us. They had jumped back into the deep trench, but they hurled "potato mashers" as if they had an abundant supply. We retreated to a corner, placing the Lewis gun in position. The "original" sent one of the gunners back to report to Major Arthur and to ask for help. We were not any great distance from him, and the major himself returned with a small party. To my great relief Doggy was with them. He had been forced to leave the trench, as a party of Germans had entered it from a sap, and he had stayed hidden for a long time before risking a return. Not finding me where I had been, he had kept going until he found Fourteen Platoon.

The Germans tried one rush and our Lewis gun played havoc with them. They left five dead before they retreated and vanished out some sap or down into some dugout. The major said we had better make sure there were no more of the enemy in the immediate area, as he did not want Fourteen Platoon attacked from the rear. The "original" said he would take the Lewis crew and explore in the direction the Germans had run. I was to take Doggy and four of the major's party and go the opposite way. A short distance along we found a 42nd man dead in the trench, his badges gone, his pockets ransacked.

We came to a dugout entrance. Doggy had bombs and a flashlight, so he and I left the others to guard the entrance and went down. It was a roomy place, with concrete walls and many benches about. In the centre was a table holding a big map and telephone. Doggy picked up the phone, and we could hear German voices speaking harshly, as if in great excitement. Doggy spoke into the mouthpiece: "Get off the line you blasted squareheads. You have the wrong number!"

The silence that followed was more eloquent than any retort could have been. We went up to the trench and moved on carefully, looking for another dugout, but found none. I did not want to go too far away from help. But then we saw a low spot where a road crossed, and we went forward to have a look and met three Germans head on. They were carrying telephones and wires, and were without rifles, but each man was armed with a Luger. The first man dropped his load and yanked out his pistol. He shot at Doggy from about fifteen feet away-and missed him! Doggy was carrying a revolver but in that split second handed it to me and took my rifle (Doggy hated pistols.). From the time the Hun shot first until Doggy lunged at him would not have been much more than three seconds. The bayonet of the rifle deflected the German's second shot, and then Doggy was at him with a queer, overhead drive. The bayonet caught the German in the cheek, tearing flesh to the bone and ripping up one nostril. The German staggered back and dropped his pistol, pawing at his face as blood gushed over it. Doggy did not lunge again. He simply pulled the trigger and shot the man. "You tried to plug me," he yelled. "There's yours."

The second Hun in the group had dropped his load and snatched at a stick bomb in his belt. He had it unhooked as the bayoneted man stumbled back, but threw it too high. It exploded on a bank behind us and showered us with dust. I fired twice with the automatic pistol as he grabbed for another bomb, missing at close range, but got him with a third shot. The third Hun had started to run, then stopped and threw a bomb that exploded very near, stunning Doggy. He sprinted on, but by good luck I got him and he went down like a baseball runner sliding into home plate.

After much digging at his ears with his fingers, Doggy said the ringing noises caused by the stick bomb had left him. We looked at the man I had shot and found I had hit him all three times. This was not much of an achievement, as he was within ten feet, but he had thrown the bombs after being shot through the chest. A moment's search showed us the dugout from which they had come. There was nothing in it except some dried black bread and a few bottles of soda water. We opened two but they tasted stale. We went up and invited the four who had been with us, but who had not dared risk a shot in the mixup, to come into the dugout. They drank some of the soda water but said it made them feel bloated.

After a time we finished exploring our sector and decided we had better go back and either find the "original" or go to the platoon. We talked for some time, and then one of the men looked over the high bank and beckoned to us. A dozen Germans some considerable distance away were going at a trot overland. As we looked a Lewis gun chattered and two of the Huns went down. The others took cover but farther on a German rose up carrying an enormous rifle, and a second man appeared and helped him with it. It was an anti-tank gun, the first I had seen. The four men with us fired at the carriers, and though it was a considerable distance they forced the Huns to drop their load and take cover. Suddenly a Maxim began firing and clipped the trench top beside us, and we simply fell back into the trench.

When we got back to where we had left the major, there was no sign of the "original" or his party. We went where the platoon had been and did not find anyone. It was beginning to get dusk. We were very tired but kept on, noticing much of the machine-gun firing had ceased. As we stood debating what to do, a man from Thirteen Platoon came along with nine German prisoners, and we went up the way he had come and found Fourteen Platoon. Tommy was seated on planks at a dugout entrance, binding up a man who had an arm damaged by a stick bomb. Ten feet away a dead Hun with both arms bandaged was lying in the sun, and flies were crawling over his face. Tommy said Earl Black and Lockerbie and Barron and Waldvogel made the greatest team he had seen in action. They had cleared many trenches, while an officer of the 44th had followed along, advising and cheering them.

"Old Waterbottle was worth four ordinary men," said Tommy. "He and Lockerbie rushed Heinie so fast he couldn't get set anywhere. Earl and Barron were right there to take their turn. Waterbottle twice caught stick bombs and threw them back. He and Lockerbie ran at half a dozen Germans who were slinging bombs and neither of them were hit. They were terrors with the bayonet and that's how Lockerbie got killed."

"Killed?"

Map 4: The Battle of Amiens, the Action at Parvillers

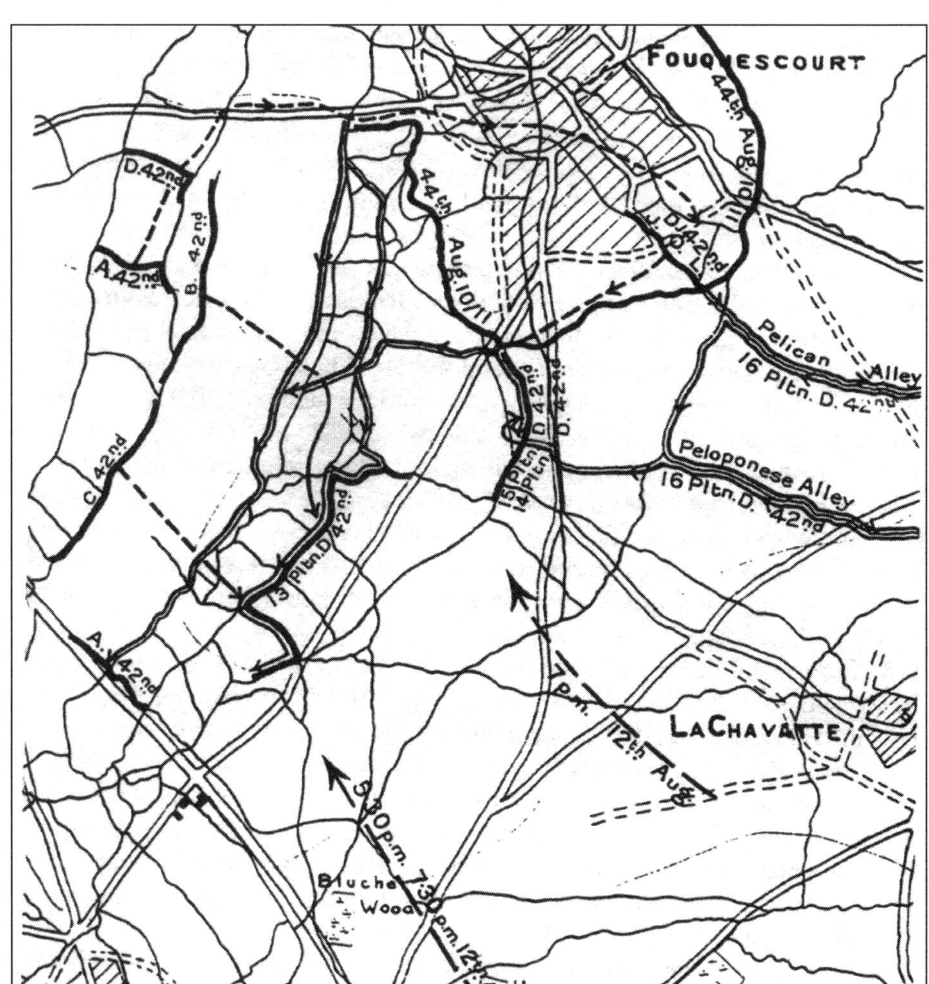

"Yes. He charged into four Heinies waiting around a bay and they shot him full of holes. A Hun threw an egg bomb at Barron so hard it broke his shoulder-but the bomb didn't explode. Thornton got killed when he stepped up the side of the trench to shoot at a machine-gun. Earl and Waterbottle got the gun a little later."

We went along the trench. There were dead Germans around every traverse, some killed by bombs, some by bullets. Old Bill and Hayward had been stationed at a sap when a trio of Huns had appeared with an anti-tank gun. They shot one of the three and the others ran. Tommy took me to see the "elephant gun," one of three in the sector. Morris, the new man, had been badly wounded. The boys had bandaged him as best they could and then had been driven back. It was an hour later before they were able to clear the trench again, but Morris was not where they had left him. They found him lying on a bath mat the Germans had used to carry him. They had taken his badges and the buttons from his tunic, and he told the boys there had been six dead Germans in the trench and all had been carried away as the Hun retreated. But poor Morris did not get out. The fighting lasted until dark, and when they finally went to take him out he had died.

Fourteen Platoon had made a name for itself that afternoon. Every man gave a good account of himself, and this in spite of the fact that they were handicapped with a new officer. This lad had spent most of the war in lecture halls and on parade grounds. He had weird ideas and no experience. At one point the platoon had reached a spot where a German machine-gun was placed so it could shoot directly down a deep trench. The officer ordered the men to charge up the trench and capture the gun. Waldvogel told him it would be suicide to try it. All day the big Russian had been foremost in the fighting, winning great approval from the 44th officer, while the platoon commander had been nowhere in evidence at the critical points. Earl said they were not going up the trench unless the officer chose to lead them. The officer whipped out his revolver. "I'm giving you an order. . . ."

He got no further. He was looking into the dark barrel of a Lee Enfield and hearing a voice tell him just one more move would be his last on earth. He sputtered and put his revolver back in its holster, tried to speak and in his consternation stepped ahead. He was barely in view of the Maxim crew, but there came a blast of bullets and one entered his neck. He bled like a stuck pig, yet after he was bandaged and helped away down the trench he insisted on sending a message to the major, reporting the outrage he had encountered. His effort was wasted. The major knew Fourteen Platoon. Being rid of the amateur, the platoon set about its job and in twenty minutes had driven the German gun from the place. Four German dead were found in the post when it was taken.

Earl and Waterbottle were the main cogs of the machine. Earl got out on the left and sent a rifle grenade over, then began sniping from a shell hole. The Huns at the machine-gun post gave him all their attention, tearing up the earth around with bullets and trying to throw stick bombs into the crater. All the while the Russian was crawling through foot-high grass and weeds on the right. When he was within a few yards of the cross-trench, he rose up and charged in like a great bull moose. The Germans were taken by surprise. Waldvogel speared the man at the machine-gun before he could swivel the weapon, and all at once the crew had their hands in the air and were crying "Kamerad!" One of the prisoners said the four dead men had been killed in a duel with one of our Lewis gunners.

Fourteen Platoon was established at the second road for the night. Tommy said he was sure the Waldvogel section alone had accounted for over fifty Germans, killed or captured. There were all sorts of rumours. Sixteen Platoon had been lost, going a mile into enemy territory before realizing where they were. Fifteen Platoon had been lost three times. By mid-afternoon each platoon had been on its own, not knowing where the others were and fighting desperate battles with Germans who appeared to be all around them. The Germans knew the underground and the 42nd didn't. It was said that over four miles of trenches had been captured. Another rumour said the Hun still held out in spots and the battle was to be resumed in the morning. Meanwhile all precautions against night attacks were taken.

Someone told me Boland had been killed by a sniper while his Lewis gun was driving Germans from the big trench. There was a rumour that I should report to the "original," but I gave it no heed. He was a corporal, and so was I. Then I remembered the three Lugers taken from the German officers and risked going back to the long trench to get them. Men were carrying out wounded on stretchers and I heard someone call my name. Going to where some wounded were lying, I saw Siddall, who had taken a course with me at the Divisional Training School. After our greetings, he looked up. "Tell me straight," he whispered. "Do you think I've got mine?"

He was frightfully wounded, and so were the cases beside him. It was easy to surmise why they had not been carried out. "I think you have," I said. "Is there anything I can do?"

"A drink of water, that's all, and thank you for telling me. I can get myself ready now."

But I hadn't a drop of water left in my bottle, so I hurried on in the dusk to where the three German officers were lying and went down into the dugout, where I filled his bottle and mine. A quick glance showed me someone had discovered the three pistols. They were gone. Siddall was grateful for the cool water and begged me to sit beside him till he "went to sleep." It was a strange experience to sit there without talking, for he was beyond a whisper, and wait till he was gone. The men on the other two stretchers were both dead, and shortly Siddall was too.

It seemed to me I might as well stay the night alongside Fourteen Platoon, so I found a good place to lie. There were several men there from other platoons of the company. Some had escorted prisoners to the rear and did not know where their platoon had settled. Others had acted as stretcher bearers. A wounded German lay in the next bay, moaning softly. Young Barlow was beside me. The night was not cold but I could not get to sleep, for I could not stop seeing all that had happened that day, passing in a kaleidoscopic procession. When I did doze about midnight Barlow nudged me. "Listen to that noise," he said. "I can't sleep." The wounded German was delirious and it sounded as if he were calling for someone.

A man the other side of us answered for me. "Go around and put him to sleep," he said jokingly.

Sometime later a rough foot wakened me. I looked up and it was Sykes. "Who stuck the Heinie?" he demanded.

"Don't ask me," I said. "I've been sleeping."

"The poor devil couldn't live," said Sykes. "That's why we didn't carry him out. But some character drove a bayonet into him."

Sykes was almost collapsing from fatigue, but he was angry. He hated such work and told everyone within hearing. I looked over and Barlow was sleeping like a child, his boyish face upturned.

Before dawn everybody was astir. There was work to be done. Two German posts on the road had to be cleared, and I was called to the trench block the "original" had established. Major Arthur was there and with him an officer from one of the other platoons. Someone told me the officer was going to lead an attack up the trench. It was the same narrow straight way we had retreated from the previous afternoon, where a Maxim gun was stationed in a position to sweep the trench. It would be sheer suicide to venture up there, and I took my courage in hand and went to Major Arthur, explaining the situation in detail. "Let us take a party and work around the place from the right," I said.

The previous day had been a really tough one for the major. The company had got lost. All had been confusion, even though the 44th officer had been a wonderful help. So Arthur, for the only time in all the months I served under him, gave me a sharp reminder that my advice was not asked for, that my job was to obey orders. Furthermore, I was to be one of the party to go down the trench.

It was like a death sentence to me, but I knew any argument would only make it worse. One look at the officer's face told me he had probably pleaded for another type of attack. He turned and shook the major's hand, said "Good-bye, sir." The major started slightly but made no remark. The "original" stepped in behind the officer. So I stepped up next, and one of the MacLean Highlanders of Fifteen Platoon stepped back of me. The other men hung back. Everyone there except the major knew the folly of what we were going to attempt. There was a sharp order, and a sergeant started to detail men to make up the party.

But the officer[18] did not wait for them. He pulled at his helmet and stepped around the bend, with us three close behind him. The German gun let go full blast at the "sitting-duck" target. We were swept down by the burst. The lieutenant took most of the bullets and was instantly killed. The "original" was shot through the neck. He reared back against me so suddenly as the Maxim blazed that I went down and bowled the MacLean man off his feet, while bullets whistled over us. The rest of the men had not had time to join us. I turned as I fell, and my haversack was partly shot away.

Major Arthur was white as paper and trembling as we scrambled back on hands and knees. The "original" was bleeding badly. A stretcher bearer began to bind up his wounds. I got up and began examining the remnants of my haversack. "Are you hit?" They were the first words the major spoke, and his voice was so strange I would not have known it was he speaking.

"No, sir," I said.

The MacLean man was shaking, licking dry lips with his tongue. He had just discovered blood running down his wrist. A bullet had clipped him in the shoulder, just a light wound, but he was terrified. The major turned and went back along the trench without speaking again or giving any order. Much as I deplored what he had done, I went along a distance behind him and when we came to a group with the sergeant-major in charge, I joined them. It was not possible to hear what the major said, but

[18] The officer killed was Lieutenant Sidney Peter Earnshaw.

about twenty men were selected from those available. Ten of us went down a trench on the right, making sure no Germans were about in any direction, climbed out of the trench and wormed our way toward the trench block.

The other group got out on the left with rifle grenades. We lay in wait about twenty minutes before we saw two grenades come over. The German gun began shooting like mad in the direction of the party, and we meanwhile got forward most of the distance between the trenches. The sergeant and I crawled ten feet or more as another pair of rifle grenades soared over and exploded beside the trench.

Both of us had Mills bombs with three instant fuses, and we threw at the same time. The bombs exploded in the trench block. Six of us were at the post in seconds, shooting as we came, and the party over the way rose and charged in also. There were ten Germans in the block. Four had been killed by the bombs and the shooting, and four more were wounded. There were wild yells of "Kamerad," and the job was over. y

It was sickening to think of the needless death of the officer and when we went back to report to Arthur I stayed at a distance and let the sergeant do the talking. Nothing else seemed important at the moment, and I was turning to go to speak with Tommy when Arthur came over. He did not speak. I thought he was going to pass by in the trench, but he took my hand and gave it a long warm squeeze. Then he went on.

Many times afterwards I talked with him but never once did he refer to that morning.

Tommy told me an officer from one of the other platoons had been wished on us. He had been to France before and was supposed to be a daredevil. A rather strange incident involved this character. Roy Murray, a good man from the 73rd, had chased a Heinie who was carrying a small machine-gun, a queer weapon almost as light as a rifle. The German ducked into a sap leading to a latrine and was shot as he tried to scramble overland. He and the gun fell back into the latrine.

The officer heard about it and wanted to examine the gun. At the same time I was told to go across the road at the head of the trenches to a forward post, where I could watch and listen. I was to take one or two or three men, no more. I chose Tommy, and we went out to a spot about thirty yards in front of the trench. The posts were so spread out that every man was needed to guard against a surprise attack.

Just before midnight we heard a German patrol. It was quiet, and we heard them when they were still quite a distance away. We crawled in to the post and the boys opened fire. There was not much cover for the patrol, but they fired a few shots back at random and were evidently getting away as fast as possible. Their last shots were from much farther away. Our new officer came to see what the shooting was about, and he had with him the weapon he had retrieved from the latrine. It stank dreadfully, but he was well fortified with rum and did not seem to mind. Not satisfied with carrying the thing around, he came to where Tommy and I were making ready to go out again and began pounding the gun, in an effort to fire it. Tommy was so enraged he took a German egg bomb he had salvaged, and threw it at the officer. The bomb exploded quite near the smelly one, who went scuttling down the trench.

Three times during the night there were German patrols in our area. One patrol crawled within shouting distance of a post Earl was on, and a voice called in English:

"Are you the Pats?"

One of the new men shouted back, before Earl could stop him "No. We're the Forty-Twas."

There was silence for a moment and then two stick bombs landed a few yards in front. They exploded without doing any harm, being too far out, and then two more came closer. Earl and another fellow went over the trench bank with Mills bombs, and when the third pair of stick bombs came, they hurled the grenades. There were shouts and commotion. Then silence. No more stick bombs were thrown, and in the morning they saw a dead Heinie lying in the open.

After midnight the moon became bright and bombing planes flew over. When we heard the crashes of their "eggs" back in the village, we were glad of our location. All the next morning we waited for relief. I had nothing to eat since the previous morning and boiled a messtin of tea. In order to keep awake I cleaned my rifle, oiled the various parts and had the magazine lying on the bank beside me. Suddenly I heard German voices. The next instant a German came around the bay and confronted me. I had a stomach-sinking tension of nerves, but acted without thinking, threw up my rifle and pulled the trigger. There was only a dull click. The magazine was not in the rifle. My knees went weak, but the face of the Hun was that of a man under torture.

He had not known there was no shell in the rifle, and I had acted so quickly he could not dodge. A few heartbeats we stared at each other and then I saw he was not armed. At that moment a rough voice demanded: "What the hell is the holdup?"

I looked beyond my chap and saw other Germans huddled by the trench wall, peering at me. Pushing by them came a husky 49th man. He grinned broadly as I told him what had happened. He had twenty prisoners, he said, and it would not have mattered if I had scared one to death.

Word came for me to go to company headquarters. I was sent to guide in a platoon of the 13th Royal Highlanders, our sister outfit, who were relieving us. When I had them in place, I again reported to the headquarters post. It was at the entrance to one of the concrete undergrounds, and cooks, signallers, runners and batmen were seated around with their loads ready. As we waited for the major we heard German voices. Again I had a touch of nerves. The Germans were not coming along the trench. They were approaching overland. Every man jumped up and made ready to fight, but it was only a lost 49er with four German prisoners in tow.

As we went back we passed a number of corpses. Some had ground sheets over their faces, but lying there, uncovered, was big footed Doggy-all through with fighting.

We billeted in some ruined buildings. We could have slept on spikes. An hour after we had fallen into deep slumber, ignoring all bombing planes, a new man, a batman who had come with a new officer, plunged in where Tommy and I were sleeping on straw piled over ancient horse manure, shouting "Germans! On the road!"

His yell woke me, but I was too thick with sleep to realize what he had said. Tommy had been sleeping soundly but he sprang up, groped for his rifle and could not find it. Then he glanced out and saw a file of German prisoners marching in the moonlight. Wham! It was a regular haymaker, and the batman went down heavily. Tommy was highly strung. He had been wakened from a sleep that was sorely needed. We settled down again, but the rest of the night was filled with small alarms, as troops and prisoners and transports kept going past our ruined stable.

We moved next day to Hamon Wood. It was a glorious spot. Tommy and I had a bivvy on a slope shaded by great trees. Rations were plentiful. Brown had come back to the battalion, and he brought us a treat of chocolate. We went to the River Luce and washed away all the sweat and grime of our fighting and marching, then lay and slept hours away in the cool green wood. The new officer lectured me because I did not have a kilt. I had cut off my old trews and manufactured shorts. My steel hat was battered, my shirt was ragged, and I was brown as a berry. "You," he said, "are a poor specimen of a soldier."

Rumour had it that the 85th Nova Scotia Battalion was near Caix Wood, about nine kilometres away, and when Corporal McLeod of the brigade signallers came to see me, we decided to walk over and visit them. The nine kilometres became eleven, and by the time we arrived, the boys we wanted to see were gone to visit a town farther on. Worst of all, the battalion dinner was over. We were very hungry and had no money. The road back seemed endless, until a Y.M.C.A. tent loomed through the night. We had missed seeing it on the way over. It was in darkness, but McLeod said we might be able to find something to eat, and I agreed.

It was not hard to undo the tent fastening, but we had no light of any sort and it was pitch-black inside. We decided it would be better to go on our hands and knees than to knock something over. I crawled left and McLeod went right. Suddenly I heard a gasp, then a struggle. It became furious, and there were many gasps and grunts, with feet striking boxes. I searched my pockets frantically and discovered one lone match. I lit it. McLeod and a Y man were entangled at close grips, rolling on the grassy floor, too evenly matched for either to gain the upper hand. The Y man was quite winded, but he sat up and grinned after their holds were released. He said he had been sure McLeod was a Hun. He had arrived there that day with two helpers and they had put the tent up in the dusk. Then the other two went ten miles away by truck for more stock, and he went to sleep on the grass by himself. McLeod, as he crawled, had placed the palm of his hand on the Y man's mouth.

I fixed a candle on a box but was laughing myself to weakness, for the sounds of the struggle had been frightening. As soon as I was getting control of myself they started laughing, and for five minutes anyone passing the tent would have been convinced the inmates were lunatics. Then we frankly told the Y man our predicament. At once he made us tea and opened tins of this and that, spread almost half a loaf of bread with peanut butter and jam. We ate to fullness, and shook hands warmly as we left. The Y man was a prince of a fellow and said we had given him his biggest thrill since his arrival in France.

Chapter 7: Arras and Cambrai

The "big guns" came to see us, but inspections were easy. There was no cry about spit and polish, and the speech that Clemenceau made was most interesting. Generals were plentiful-such as Haig and Rawlinson-but with us the French "tiger" was tops. The weather continued sunshiny and clear, with enemy bombers at night. None reached our bivouac, however, and we marched away toward Arras, marching nearly all one night. It was much better than in the heat of the day, and the situation made me think of our going up to Ypres, the men marching through the night: there was only the shuffle of army boots and the creak of equipment, our steps echoing as we passed through sleeping villages. The moon was full and everything was bathed in white light. We arrived at Boves Station just before midnight and found there had been the usual army mixup. We were too soon. There was no train ready for us. So we fell out beside the road and were told there was an hour to wait. Tommy and I found a grassy nook, where we curled up to sleep. When the hour was up the officers said it would be two o'clock when the train came, but we didn't hear him. We were sleeping. At two o'clock there was still no train, but the station master was positive one would arrive at three. Tommy and I were still sleeping. Entrainment took place at ten minutes past four, with those who had stayed awake so fed up they shouted angrily at every order given. Officers with flashlights tried to discover the culprits but had no luck. Murray wakened us, and we felt quite rested.

There was one car less than had been ordered, so the train was packed and soon the atmosphere was stifling, for it was a warm night. At times we dragged along at a snail's pace, and it seemed we would never get to Bouquemaison. It took five hours to do about sixty-six miles. Everyone was tired and tempers short, but we were informed we were to march to Ivergny. "What the hell about breakfast?" roared the chorus.

Officers scurried here and there and we stood at ease. There was a flood of rumours started by two battalion runners, then the impossible happened. Our field kitchens arrived and we were served tea and bully, hardtack and jam. Everyone sat down, and the next thing I knew Tommy was beside me with a loaf of French bread. Did it ever taste good! He had invaded an *estaminet* when he saw a man go away from the place with food, and though the price was high we had a wonderful breakfast. Away we marched to Ivergny and had good billets.

Fine weather and plenty of rations made everyone feel better. We marched in moonlight to Manin, the next night to a Y camp near Duisans. There was no hurry and we had good rations. Then it was away to Arras, and the pessimists, plus the runners, said we were for it. Our own entertaining "D" Company runner said we were to take two tough objectives, Monchy and Orange Hill, and the C.M.R.'s were to start the business by taking Monchy. No one quite believed him.

Away we went on a dark night, and a shower lengthened into a soaking downpour as we reached the outskirts of Arras. Thunder and lightning added to the picture. There was still confusion in high places. Twice we were halted and told we would stay there the rest of the night, and twice we went on. When we did stop it was near a cemetery, and many crude remarks began circulating. Tommy and Brown and

Sparky and I got into a cellar that was fairly dry. We were having a fine sleep when someone roared outside that all were to "stand to." We stayed awake where we lay and waited. After some time a barrage opened and added to the noise of the thunder. No one came with orders and we slept until seven in the morning, when off we went in the continuing rain. Everybody else seemed on the move too. Soon we began meeting walking wounded and German prisoners. The Huns were mostly young fellows and not one of them looked down-hearted, making us feel they were happy to get out of the war.

It was not clear what we were to do, but the sergeant-major said that "D" Company would be in support, that the Shino boys-the R.C.R.'s-were making the attack and we were behind them. One hour and another went by, and shells began falling uncomfortably near. Rumours circulated endlessly. It became five and six o'clock and still the company stayed and shells dropped all around. One tale after another added to the confusion. But we stayed where we were for the night. In the morning we moved. Our platoon went along a road and into a collection of shell-smashed houses. Heavy shelling began, and our officer was wounded. Corporal Jimmy Hughes took command as the sergeant was with another platoon. Geordie Thompson was the company-sergeant-major, but we did not see him that day.

Hughes decided, after two near hits, that we had better take shelter until the strafe stopped. We went down into a cellar, saw light at the far end and found a large group of stretcher bearers there. They said they were to carry wounded to ambulances, which would come up a road to the rear of the ruins when the battle began. There were stone ledges around the cellar walls. Hughes sat on one and so did Harvey. Earl Black and I had purchased a tin of salmon by pooling our resources, and he wanted to know if he were to carry it. I said "Yes," and laughed at him. I was sitting on a wall ledge opposite Corporal Hughes.

No one did much talking, and only the three new men with us were restless. They kept walking around. The rest of us were listening to the shelling. Murray asked me how much more time we had and I told him not more than twelve minutes. Suddenly a warm hand rested on mine. I thought it was Murray and glanced around. It was Steve!

I was so astounded I could not utter a word but sprang up. He gripped my hand tighter and pulled me toward the door. "Let's get from here-fast!" he said. The half-grin was on his face exactly as I had seen it the last time.

He let go of my hand as we reached the stair and pulled back the gas curtain. I caught it and found my voice. "Steve, will you. . . ."

"Bill!" It was Hughes shouting at the top of his voice. "Don't go out! The shelling is terrific!"

But Steve was going up the steps and I was so close to him his boot hit my shin. It caused me to stumble and by the time I had caught my balance he was looking back, smiling. Then, in a heartbeat, he vanished. A shell burst in a ruin across the street and pieces of brick whizzed so close past my head that I ducked. And at that split second I heard a tremendous explosion below!

I plunged down the steps. Fumes of high explosive met me as I jerked the gas blanket aside. The place was in utter darkness. Men were groaning and voices were calling excitedly from the end where the stretcher bearers had been waiting. They lit candles just as I got one going and rushed over to help. The light revealed a perfect shambles. Every man was down and some began struggling to their feet. But the majority did not move. Hughes had not moved. He still sat on the ledge, but blood trickled from a great hole in his head. He had died without falling over. Three men beyond him were dead. Hayward was yelling that his back was on fire. Harvey lay with his head in a pool of blood that gushed from his neck - dead. Earl was lying on the floor with an eye on his cheek and terrible wounds in his stomach but, strangely, was partly conscious. Hayward screamed at me, and I tore his equipment and tunic off ripping at his shirt. His whole back was blood, but there was no serious wound. It was as if very fine shot had peppered him. I used a bottle of iodine from one of the dead men on him, and all his own, then sent him over to the stretcher bearers. They were helping us but said they could not take anyone out, as the shelling was too heavy.

Bill Childs, strangely, had not a wound. He said a new man loading his rifle, had discharged it into our bag of Mills bombs. Then he added that if Earl were not taken to a doctor he would not live. There was very little time to do anything for him, but when we spoke to the stretcher bearers they said they would take Earl out when it was quieter.

"You'll take him now!" I said. "I'm giving you orders." Bill Childs seized a rifle and backed me. A new man joined in, and the three of us made them put Earl on a stretcher and carry him up the stairway. We followed close behind them and made them go so far it would be easier to keep on to the waiting ambulances than to return.

Then it was our zero hour. We did a check and found we had lost twelve men in the explosion. Hughes was dead and he was the one who had the orders, who had known where we were to go. However, we ran in single file along the street, and luck was with us as we met a guide coming to find what had delayed us. He led us to the trench he said was ours and there I posted what was left of the platoon. We did not know the orders or where the rest of the company were, but we stayed on post all the same. Finally it was night.

I could not sleep for thinking about Steve. He had literally pulled me to the stairway, with no ghostly touch but the grip of a strong warm hand. His voice had been completely natural and filled with urgency. He had carried no equipment or rifle or gas mask. No one else had seen him, I was sure, and yet he had spoken quite loudly. His legs had been just in front of me up the cellar stair. The more I thought of it, the more certain I became that there is much in the world we do not understand, that the next phase of life to which we pass is in close communication with those left behind. Some day the connection will be discovered.

It was past midnight before I could stop thinking about my escape from death. Then I was uneasy about our position. Why had no one been around? I slept in little cat naps until just after daylight, then stood up and looked around. Every man was sound asleep. I sat down, not trying to sleep, and some time later stood up again. There had been much to make me nervous. After we had reached the trench, one of the new men started to clean his rifle. It was discharged as he fumbled with it, and the bullet shattered the leg of a big man who was an ex-policeman. Sykes dressed the wound as best he could and got four men to carry him back to a dressing station.

And as it grew dark we had heard a low voice somewhere in the field ahead. It seemed to be calling "Otto! Otto!" Tommy went with me, our rifles at the ready, and a considerable distance ahead we found a wounded German in the grass. He had been shot through the leg, roughly bandaged and sent back toward our lines as a prisoner, but had fainted from loss of blood and lost his way. He could speak enough English to make us understand. Sykes did a good job of bandaging, and the same four men carried him back to the station they had just come from.

These happenings did not help the nerves, and now as I stood I was sure I had seen heads appear above thick grass some distance back of our trench. I began watching, and saw more, then made out a row of men coming straight for us. With fixed bayonets! Had the Hun got to our rear?

They would crouch, then run towards our trench, then crouch again. I stepped out in full view and a man rose and aimed at me. I shouted with all my power: "Who are you?"

The man hesitated, lowered his rifle, and shouted back. "Who are you?"

"The Forty-Second," I yelled.

He shouted something and the line of men stood up. Then I saw an officer running in from the left. He came straight to me. The rest of my platoon had been wakened by the shouting and were on their feet.

"How in the devil did you get here?" demanded the officer.

"We came up yesterday afternoon," I said. "Why?" He was from a unit in the 9th Brigade, and his language for a moment was filled with sulphur. "At a conference an hour ago," he said, "we were told this trench was held by the Germans. Where are they?"

"That I wouldn't know," I said, "but I think you will go quite a distance before you locate any."

The men came across the field and he formed them into a column. There were heated comments and much head-shaking. Then they filed up the slope and we watched them vanish in the same order. "If ever they could put all the stupid things done in this war in one book," said Tommy, "nobody would ever believe it."

At nine o'clock, just as we were going to march, a runner came looking for the officer in command of Fourteen Platoon. I told him there was no officer, that we had not seen Williamson in two days, Hughes was dead, and for the time being I was the only authority. He told me to get moving. "D" Company was to attack over a ridge and was being lined up over to our left at least four or five hundred yards away.

We soon saw the other platoons and joined them. Then I saw Geordie Thompson. I went to him at once and reported what had happened to us, the explosion in the cellar, the policeman's getting shot in the leg, our nearly being the victims of a 9th Brigade attack. "It's all in the run of war," he shrugged. "I heard Lieutenant Craig was looking after you and never gave your platoon a second thought."

He was no more than gone when Lieutenant Craig came and asked where we had been. I gave him our report, and he said we were to go up a long slope alongside the wood until we got to the crest of the ridge. He would take half the platoon in nearer the wood, and I was to take the other half about one hundred yards from the wood and make sure no Germans were hiding in a field of grain that stretched over the entire slope.

It was about noon as we walked over the slope and descended to the foot of the ridge he had talked about. Down the slope in front of us I saw the roof of a large shelter. Two Germans were just outside it. Over to our left, an officer and two others had stopped by the entrance to a dugout, and we saw fifteen or twenty Germans file from it with their hands in the air. But the two Jerries we had seen below ducked into the shelter and were five when they reappeared, with rifles. They fired at us. Sparky was running twenty feet ahead of the rest of us. His body rose in the air, fell and rolled over and over. As we reached him he caught at his middle as if suffering from cramps, straightened and was dead.

Three of the Germans had thrown their rifles away. Tommy was shooting and he winged one of the others. Then all of them put their hands high and began chanting "Kamerad." They were signallers, and there were many instruments in the shelter. I went in and took from the wall a picture of the place with three of the men we had captured sitting in front. The rest of the lads searched our catch for souvenirs, then we pointed to the prisoners getting from the dugout and told them to join the party. They ran over in quick time, glancing back now and then as if not trusting us entirely.

We reached the hollow at the foot of the slope, saw the grain ahead of us, and mounds beside the wood that indicated trenches. Three or four shots rang out and we saw that someone was sniping at us from a post by the mounds. We took shelter at once in an old shell hole. I said we would wait until those on our left had cleared the Hun from the edge of the wood. Barlow was sitting just ahead of me in the crater and McPhee was beside him. He looked around and said: "What does it feel like to be hit?"

"You'll know when you get one," said McPhee with one of his grins.

"Well," said Barlow, "nothing hit me but I can't feel in my legs."

Suddenly, without another word, he tipped forward, dead. We pulled him over and found that a bullet had gone through his heart.

A few shells dropped not too far away, and a shower of clods drove Brown from the shell hole he was in. Then came a lull. On our left was a platoon led by the officer who had got the weapon from the latrine. They were advancing toward a trench at the beginning of the wood. A German officer stood up and pointed his pistol at the officer and fired twice. The officer went down, and a big man charged at the German with his bayonet. The German fired again, then dropped his pistol and put up his hands.

"You ____ squarehead!" We could hear the shout plainly. "You needn't put them up now!"

The big man drove his bayonet into the German with such a lunge that they both went down into the trench. But not a man with the German officer fired a shot. They simply stood with their hands up. There were about fifteen or more of them and we were puzzled until we saw that Hansen, one of our good Lewis gun men, had got over with his weapon and was in a position to sweep the trench.

Fifteen Platoon went into the wood as soon as the prisoners were hustled away. Stretcher bearers were working over our smart officer, and we saw the man with the bayonet being helped from the trench with a great bandage around his thigh. The German officer had not missed him.

Jones and Tom Mills had joined us. They had been with Craig's lot but in some manner had ducked away from him. After the platoons had got going in the wood, we went up into the field of wheat. Then came a sudden French shower but we did not mind it. Brown started to get up when the rain stopped as quickly as it had started, and a regular spray of machine-gun bullets cut into the grain a few yards to our left. Jones was on our flank and he risked being spotted, rose enough to shoot three times at the gunner. There was no reply. After a time we raised up and saw the gun abandoned!

There was no hurry in the wood. The platoons moved forward carefully, and we waited until they were a distance beyond us, then rose and went up through the wheat in file. Three men came from the wood and joined us. They were all MacLean Highlanders. Now there was not a shot being fired, not a bomb bursting. In the area just ahead, the wood thinned to a large clearing and 42nd men were walking across it as if out on a morning stroll. We started to hurry so as to go along even with their advance.

As we hit more level ground, Tommy let out a wild yell and pointed. I had a sickening sensation, as if hit in the stomach. Not one hundred yards ahead of us was an enormous spread of camouflage, and on one side a pile of wicker-work cases. By the cases stood a machine-gun on a tripod. At the entrance to the great gun pit was a bank of faces and grey uniforms-Germans. We were in the open without a chance for cover. There was but one thing to do, bluff it. "Come on," I yelled, and put my bayonet level in front of me. We charged in a manner that would have tickled the "canaries" back in the Bull Ring at Le Havre-and not one German moved!

Not until we were a few yards from them. Then they swarmed out with their hands high. Tommy counted them aloud-twenty-four. It was the emplacement of a monster naval gun, the pit big enough to hold a house. A major came out slowly after the men, a rather pompous fellow. I ran to him, and he eyed me sharply but made no protest as I took a most beautiful pearl-handled Luger from his pocket and a beautiful gold watch from his wrist. "Watch them till I come out," I shouted to Bob Jones, and went down into the gun pit.

Beside the big gun was a pile of hasty discards, Lugers, binoculars, three red-and-grey uniform caps, and stick bombs. I had carried a bomb bucket all the morning, as I had six Mills grenades. Now I put in another pistol, selected two of the caps and a pair of binoculars, climbed out of the pit and took over. Jones had the Germans already started away down the slope, going in pairs, with two of the newest men in the platoon as escorts. I told all the lads to go down into the pit and help themselves, and not be too long.

They were emerging, each man with a Luger, when Williamson and one of the men who had started out with Craig came out from the wood. The sergeant looked in my bomb bucket and said he would like to have one of the Lugers. "Then go ahead," I told him. "Take over the lead and go fast. First men into the next German place will get souvenirs."

He gave me an angry look, and we left him standing by the camouflage. There was no more sound from the wood, and as we went on the wheat suddenly ended and we were in grassland. Ahead of us some distance we could see the outlines of two trenches. There was a shelter of some kind toward the left. From somewhere in that distance a machine-gun began firing at us. The man who had come with Williamson went down, shouting he was shot in the leg. Our Lewis gunner was next, also shot in the leg. His helper picked up the gun and ran about ten steps, then went down, the third in a row to receive a leg wound. We ran all the harder.

A machine-gun, unmistakably a Lewis, opened up on our left and the German gun was silenced at once. Sykes had a revolver, although stretcher bearers were not supposed to be armed, and now he ran beside me with his pistol in his hand. Jones and Mills ran abreast of us. Then came three men, Brown, Tulloch and Thompson, and although I could not see McPhee and the six others, I felt they could not be far behind. As we neared the first trench we saw two Germans running from it and carrying a Maxim between them. Then a German officer jumped up from the trench and shot at us three times with his pistol. He did not touch us, but Brown and Jones fired at him and did not touch him either. The officer turned and ran toward the second trench. Jones stopped and took aim. After he fired the German pitched to earth, as if he had caught his feet on a trip wire.

We reached the German trench and scrambled into it, fairly winded. We had run a considerable distance over fairly rough ground and now we sat and huffed and puffed for some time before getting up to explore. The trench was a long, rather shallow affair, with numerous low-roofed shelters. I dived into the one from which the officer had come and found his kit, a rain coat, and blankets. In the kit were an Iron Cross, his razor, coloured thread and needles, a dictionary in German and English, and a pair of folding scissors. I took the scissors and medal. Jones had moved to the left while I was looting and was after a machine-gunner some distance over, who was shooting toward the far left of the wood. Sykes and Tommy and Brown looked in shelters for souvenirs. There were plenty of gas masks lying about, packs and rain capes and blankets. Suddenly the Germans began shooting at us from the second trench, which was not much more than one hundred yards away.

We shot back at them, but it became dangerous to show a head. Jones crawled well over to the left and raised up. He drew a bead on one of the snipers and drilled him, but in a moment two others were shooting at him. Brown always carried rifle grenades. He gave me his rifle and a grenade. I let it go with a short fuse, and it burst directly over the snipers. A German had just raised to shoot. Sykes was well over on the right, watching, and he said the man went down as if hit by a maul. The sniping stopped.

I went over toward the low building that we now saw was a part of the trench. Sykes went with me, and we approached carefully and slowly. I missed Thompson and mentioned him to Sykes. "He got hit just as we reached the trench," Sykes explained. "I tied him up and he's away."

There was no one in the place. It was more roomy than it looked from the outside and had a table and three beds, and a dozen or more chairs. Two German greatcoats were hanging from hooks and some newspapers were piled as if just received. Sykes sat down to try and decipher some of the headlines-his favourite sport-and I went on through the trench. Past a turn some distance beyond, the trench was wider and much deeper. An elaborate latrine had been constructed in the trench bank. There were two shelters similar to those we had found at first, and I looked inside both for souvenirs but had no luck. There was considerable shooting on the left and I could hear rifle grenades. Our men were attacking over there. I felt I should be getting back, as the afternoon was nearly gone, but I wanted to see around the next bay. As usual, I had my rifle cradled under my arm and a finger on the trigger. The next two seconds will stay with me as long as I live. For many a night afterwards I relived the moment in a dream and woke up shaking and sweating. A blond German my own height came around the bay, carrying his rifle as I carried mine. There was one second of complete surprise. I had not heard a sound, and neither had he. Then we both fired!

I felt his bullet go completely through my body. We were no more than twenty yards apart. He pitched down on his face and rolled over. He had let go of his rifle, and his hands opened and closed three or four times. I stood and watched them and for a moment dared not look down at myself. I could not see blood. Then I stiffly raised an arm and began feeling inside my tunic. For a full sixty seconds I could not believe the man had missed me. I put down the Lee Enfield and made another examination. It was incredible, but I was not touched. Where his bullet went I will never know, for I was sure his rifle had been pointed at my chest. I bent over him, opened his tunic and took a postcard photograph from it. It was a picture of himself with his name on the back. I put it in my pocket and hurried back to find Sykes.

Voices sounded from behind the trench as I reached it, and in came Thompson and Williamson, Hansen and Tulloch. Thompson said the place made a fine company headquarters and they would stay there. As I went back to where the others were staying, a shot from the other trench just missed my helmet, kicking dust from the parados. We crouched at once. Then a shot rang out from up ahead and we heard Jones saying, "I got him that time."

Jones said Brown had a very narrow escape from the sniper. The German had cleverly not fired for some time, and then had opened up when they had gone on to explore the trench further..They could not raise up to risk a shot, as the fellow was quick and accurate. So Brown had continued along the trench and begun firing over the top in the general direction of the German. As he did, Jones and Mills returned along the trench and didn't show themselves until they had reached a point opposite the sniper.

When the sniper had fired at me, Jones was just looking over and the German had his head in full view, probably trying to see whether or not I was a victim. Jones drilled him neatly. Now we went along to see where Brown was, since both Mills and Jones thought the trench swung back to the left and petered out. Suddenly there was another shot that nicked the top of the parapet. "Another of those snipers," said Jones. "We'll have to plan how to give him the treatment."

All at once we came to a covered-in part. We had to crawl under it on our hands and knees, for there was not too much room. Then came fifty yards clear and another covered-in part. Jones went through it, then Mills, and as I got down Sykes said, "That sniper is away back. I'm going to skip over."

He waited a moment as I crawled through, then leaped up and ran around and jumped in on the far side of the covered-in part. I had just emerged when he fell at my feet. I heard a queer bubbling sound, and Jones lit a match in the gathering dark. Sykes' jugular had been cut by a sniper's bullet. He was dead before we let him down.

The trench soon swung left, as Jones had said. There was no more shooting. We got Brown and headed back toward the place Thompson had chosen as company quarters. At the spot where I had got the German officer's scissors I stopped. "That's a nice place with the chairs and beds," I said. "But if the Jerries open up they'll shell it." The others agreed, and we stayed put and began to eat our rations.

It was completely dark and we had just finished eating when the German guns began shooting. Over came salvos of "whizz bangs," some very near where we huddled. Jones and Mills selected a place nearby and Brown moved in with me. All at once shells landed so near that earth fell at the entrance to our shelters. Then there was a wild shout from the low building. We went over and found a shell had made a direct hit on the roof. The first man we came across was a dead MacLean Highlander, then we found Tulloch with a leg badly smashed. Williamson had a piece of shrapnel in his shoulder. Thompson was wounded in the hip, a very painful wound. Voices sounded near, and we found some Fifteen Platoon men back of the trench. As luck would have it, they had two stretcher bearers with them and two German prisoners they had flushed from a dugout.

The stretcher bearers set to work on the wounded. Then a runner came and said Arthur wanted me to go back, take a man with me, meet our relieving battalion and guide a company to our position. The runner said Arthur, with Russell, had come along the end of the trench that turned left, and they were there. We put Thompson on a stretcher. Brown and I took one end of it and we had the two German prisoners at the front end. It was about eight p.m. as we started to carry him out, down over the wheat field and along to the far slope. We went as carefully as possible but Thompson suffered a lot. At length we reached battalion headquarters and there saw twenty German prisoners squatting about a dugout entrance. We got men to take care of Thompson, and Tulloch arrived on a stretcher. We went on to find our relieving company. They were sitting by the road a long way from the area, and as we guided them in it seemed miles to the two German trenches.

Then we started back once more. We saw the dark shape of Barlow in a shell crater, and on reaching headquarters again saw Williamson and went to speak to Tulloch-and he was dead.

Daylight came as we dragged one foot after the other on the endless way back to Arras. Brown quit, but I kept on and at last staggered into the barracks we were to occupy. Sergeant Fordham was there and he grinned at me sheepishly. He had been in only two battles, having been left out because he was an "old-timer."

We slept the rest of that day and all that night. Next morning I went out and sold one Luger and one pair of field glasses, getting one hundred and fifty francs for them. The rations were extremely poor, so I decided Tommy and Brown and Jones should join me in a real feast. I fell in line at a Y canteen, and when it came my turn asked for a dozen tins of cherries and the same of peaches. The clerk looked at me pityingly. "Don't you know," he said, "that you can only have one of anything?"

"Why?" I asked. The shelves were piled with canned fruit, and there were cases in piles at the rear.

"Because we never know what the officers will want," he said irritably.

I got "one of each" and went outside. Tommy was there and I told him my luck. He was ready to charge in and take the fruit. "Officers!" he raved. "Eating the best all the time, waited on hand and foot. We short-handed half the time because so many men are batmen. And now when there's one chance in months to have a feed we can't get it-all because the officers want extra to entertain their French girls."

It was difficult to quiet him, for he didn't care who heard him. Then, as we were leaving, I saw a 42nd batman come from the Y carrying a case of cherries. He was a decent sort for a batman, and I spoke to him, asking him where the officers were dining. "Dunno about them," he grinned. "Three or four of us are having a feed ourselves."

Three or four batmen-a case of canned cherries! "How can you get them?" I asked.

"Easy. I go with chits to get things for the officers . All the clerks do is look at the signature. I make one for myself any time I need something."

He showed us his blank chits, and we went back and bought some paper and made up a few. I had noticed that the signature of one officer was something like a snake with two tails. So I did my best imitation of his hand and boldly walked into the canteen. I came out with a case of tinned peaches. Tommy came out with a case of cherries. We bought fruit and biscuits and cigars for Old Bill. And what a night that was. We had to go four miles to find an *estaminet,* but it was worth it. Madame made us chicory coffee and eggs and chips, and the party didn't end until the military police came and reminded Madame that it was getting very late.

It made me think of one of the nights on our way to Ypres, a dark night threatening rain, with one of the lads flush after a game of poker with the A.S.C. There were Royal Engineers and artillerymen mingled with Forty-Twas, a motley crew, all friendly. In a corner an artilleryman was trying desperately to win San Fairy Ann's appreciation. She was better looking than the average, and many another lad had tried his luck with her. Beside our table were two old sweats whose conversation was as entertaining as a music hall number. One filled his conversation with rhymes, the other employed hyperbole. With him, anything better than ordinary was described *as eucalyptus.*

The artilleryman sang the "Salvation Army Song":

The bells of hell go ting-a-ling-ling, for you but not for me,
O Death where is thy sting-a-ling-a-ling, O grave thy victor-ee?
It had about ten verses. Another cheerful ditty was:

I want to go home, I want to go home,
The bullets they whistle, the cannons they roar,
I don't want to go to the front anymore.
Take me over the sea, where the Alleyman can't get at me,
Oh, my, I'm too young to die, I want to go home.

During a lull when throats were being oiled, a forlorn figure entered in khaki much too large for him and decorated with beer stains. "I'll give yer a song, mytes," he said, obviously wanting a tip. He began at once in a terrible voice.

She was poor but she was honest, victim of a rich man's whim ,
For he wooed her and seduced her, and she was done wrong by him.
It's the syme the whole world over, it's the poor gits all the blyme,
And the rich gits all the pleasure, ain't it a bleedin' shyme!

At the sixth verse someone offered him a drink and that saved us.

Our Old Bill felt quite a dramatic fellow when he'd had a few, so he proceeded to go into his act. He rose, looked around solemnly, and orated: "Today's my daughter's wedding day. Ten thousand pounds I'll give away."

There were cheers and much hand-clapping. "That's the stuff, Bill. Good old

Bill."

Then another pose as Bill, after acknowledging the cheers, shook his head. "On second thoughts I think it best, to leave it in my old oak chest."

Groans on all sides. "You old blighter, Bill."

Then in stepped a sergeant of the military police. Groans. Sighs. Shouts for a last beer. "Allay, Madame. Toot sweet, and the tooter the sweeter." But Madame, looking at the sergeant, said, "No bon. Fini kapoot. Napoo. Buckoo bier. Vous zigzag."

A voice at the back: "Some say, 'good old sergeant,' but I say. . " Some quick shouting drowned him out. The door was opened and the patter of rain on the cobbles made more groans. "Send her down, Davey," some shouted. "Roll on duration".

But there was no real move to go. "Can we have one more song, sergeant?" The voice was pleading. The sergeant took a look out and nodded agreement. Then the voices rolled out more or less in harmony.

Oh, we pushed the damper in, yes we pushed the damper in,
And the smoke went up the chimney just the same.
So we pulled the damper out, yes we pulled the damper out,
And the smoke went up the chimney just the same.

After the fifth stanza the M.P. got wise that it would not change, and out we all had to go. The lad with San Fairy Ann tried to muster some French for parting, twisting uneasily in his chair until she asked: "You hitchey-koo?" And everyone roared. Then we were all outside in the wet darkness. Boots thumped and slipped on wet cobbles and a voice drifted back, Oh, kiss me, sar'gint before I go."

Our party was a real one, too, and there was another San Fairy Ann helping Madame. And the police lad was just as set in his ways.

Everyone was glad when word came to move again. We did not like Arras, as there were too many enemy bombers over at night. On September 1 we moved to Hermaville, not a long march, no more than eight or nine miles. The night of our party the bombers had been over, and Brown and I decided to stay in the local cemetery until daylight. It was warm and we bedded together in a grassy hollow between two graves. In minutes we were sound asleep. Over came the bombers, and we were wakened by crashes either at or near Arras. Some laggard in the lot evidently did not get rid of his load on the target and decided to ditch what was left. There was the roar of his approach and then the grand-daddy of all explosions shook the ground. Sods showered around us, intermingled with heavier pieces that thudded down. It was useless to try and run, so we lay and held our breath, fearing the lad might not be rid of all he had. But our fears were groundless. We heard him far in the distance. The night was quiet again, and we went to sleep.

In the morning Brown stirred first. He gave me a nudge. "It's the same as in the army," he said. "Here's a guy didn't shave, and they've got him up for office."

About one hundred yards from us, a bomb had torn several graves wide open and strewn bits of shattered caskets around.

Nearer, another bomb had apparently gone very deep before exploding and had literally hoisted a casket from its resting place without destroying it. It was almost upright, lodged against a monument that was tilted from its base. The top of the casket had fallen off, and its occupant was still inside, as if standing. He had a long black beard and some decoration on a morning coat. It was easy to guess the burial was quite recent.

Cookhouse rumours at Hermaville said we were there for a week's rest. The next morning we were told to make ready for parade, and some of the lads groaned. No one wanted the parade ground routine. Lieutenant Craig was particularly regimental, and Fourteen Platoon creaked at the joints with every shouted order. Suddenly it ended. A runner had come to the parade ground. There was much scurrying around and then abrupt dismissal. The battalion was to make ready to move on a moment's notice. The groaners who loathed the parade ground were moaning again. We had a cosy billet and the prospect of easy days, and away we were going to continue the war. It was, to Brown and me, sheer irony that when we marched out in the afternoon, too late to reach a regular destination, we had to bivouac in the cemetery again. However, we found a fine dry space between fairly high mounds and slept like babies. The next night tents and tarpaulins arrived, but Brown and I did not want the bother of looking after them, and since the weather was kind we stayed out in our crib between the mounds.

The 42nd moved up to relieve the 58th Battalion in support trenches near Vis-en-Artois. A shout the next day caused me to look around, and I saw Lieutenant Jim Cave and gave a smart salute. He had been gone for so long that I had thought he was wounded. A Sam Browne had not changed him in the least and we had quite a chat. It was quiet where we were. Our platoon was in the cellar of a ruined chateau and did several carrying parties. Back a distance was a pond and the wreckage of a German training school. Beyond the chateau lay a one-street village, badly battered by shell fire. Tommy and I decided to visit it.

We made our way over in the mist of a showery morning and reached the place without difficulty. We had no blankets and had slept cold, as there was a decided chill to the nights, and we wanted to find something to use as a sheet or blanket. We entered three houses and for the first time saw what the Germans could do when forced from an area. They had entered with axes and smashed every stick of furniture, even to pictures on the wall, knocking doors from hinges and breaking every window-wanton, hellish destruction.

The priest's house was not damaged, save at the front where windows and doors had received the treatment. The front room was a mess of broken chairs and tables and a crucifix had been yanked from the wall. But the bedroom was intact. We made a bundle for carrying a beautiful eiderdown puff, two pillows and four fine sheets. Then we went into the cellar and found nothing. There was a cupboard in a corner but it was empty and the door had been left open. The Huns had been ahead of us. Tommy, however, was keen of mind that morning. He said the cellar was not as large as the house. Something was peculiar about the place. Heavy masonry stared at us from four walls, so he seized a corner of the cupboard and suggested I lend a hand. To my amazement it moved easily and there was a square opening in the wall behind it!

We held our candles high and peered in, expecting skeletons. But the secret cupboard was ringed with shelves, and on the shelves were hundreds of bottles. Tommy slid inside and passed out a dozen or so for examination. Wine. We got another sheet and Tommy made a backload of fifteen bottles. We were just back to our chateau cellar when the Hun shelled the village ruins. We handed out half our bottles to the others and said they were to be equally shared. Some lads did not want any, however, and three men got exhilarated enough to start singing that ribald ballad known as "Hoch Der Kaiser." Later a perplexed sergeant-major spent an hour trying to figure out the cause of their hilarity. That night Tommy and I slept warm, and wine with our dinner had allowed us to imagine we were officers.

Unfortunately we did not long enjoy the priest's bedding. We moved into the line and relieved the good old 49th. We were their bosom pals, in the line or out. The Pats were an acquaintance and no more. We did not associate with them, although we held nothing against them. But the Shino boys had our sympathy.

Our front was nothing to brag about. We took over in pitch black darkness on a rainy night, and were thankful to be in reserve. The front consisted of isolated posts, with the Huns on the banks of the Canal du Nord, where they had excellent observation and could make life miserable for us. The only thing to do was lie low in the daytime and be extremely alert at night.

All of us were nervous when word came that the Hun had taken a post from "A" Company, since we figured it would have to be retaken before we left the scene. Nothing came of it, however. Mustard gas was put over that night and we had to wear our gas masks for a time, but it was nothing serious. Some lads sleeping in low ground got some of it and the M.O. looked after them. To us, the rain and chill were the worst part of the trip, and although our friends in "A" Company told some fearsome tales of a post they called The Kiln, casualties were too light to back up their stories.

For some unknown reason our relief was held up two hours, and we had a hard trip out in the dark to a big cave near Vis-en-Artois. It was an enormous place. Rumours ran like wildfire about booby traps connected with rail ropes down the stairways. We were hungry and astounded to learn that no rations had arrived. It was past midnight by the time we were in and every man was grousing. We had no sergeant, so I had to look after the platoon.

Rough hands roused me and I looked up to see a battalion runner. "Come up to the top," he said. "An officer wants to see you."

I felt I had not been sleeping an hour, but if Lieutenant Craig wanted something I had better get there quickly. He was decent enough, but always kept me at arm's length and would not be friendly. However, when I reached daylight the officer standing there was an ex-sergeant from another company, who had been so long getting his commission that I had forgotten him. I started to say "Hi" in the usual manner, but he stopped me short. "You're speaking with an officer," he snapped. "Are you in charge of Fourteen Platoon?"

"Just temporarily," I returned. "Lieutenant Craig is in command but he is not here."

"Very well. Get the men up here at once."

I looked at my watch. It was a quarter to seven. "Sir," I said. "Something is wrong. We only got in here after midnight, and the men have had nothing to eat as the rations haven't arrived. Did Major Arthur give you the order?"

"Don't you dare ask me questions," fumed the mighty one. "I'm giving you an order. Get your men up here in ten minutes or I'll have you before the colonel for disobedience."

Phew! It seemed there was something most important and maybe I had better find out later. So down I went and woke every man. Their language was blue in the ghastly cave-light, but they put on their boots and made ready and up we went to the grey morning. Orders were snapped as if we were prisoners and we were marched off down the road. It was just seven as we came to where a labour battalion was camped. Their breakfast call was blown as we arrived, and men were carrying off bacon and porridge and tea from the cook wagon. The pleasant perfume of warm food was wafted to us, making our mouths water. Then we stopped by a heap of picks and shovels at the entrance to the camp.

We were halted. "Take shovels," came the order. "Every third man will take a pick."

I ran forward from the rear where I had marched. "Sir," I said. "There is some mistake. The 42nd never do road repairs. And there is a labour battalion in this area, as you saw."

The officer wheeled on me. "Get back to your place," he shouted. "Don't try to argue with me. I'll have you crimed."

We were barely out of the camp area when we were halted. There were no shell craters in the road, only a few six-inch places as with every pock-marked highway in the war zone. The officer blared orders and threatened every man who did not jump to it. He set half the platoon to work in that strip and went around a turn with the rest. As he talked I had gone up the road bank and at the top saw, a short distance to the right, a Y.M.C.A. canteen with smoke coming from the pipe, ready for business. I returned quickly and pulled out a handful of francs, told the men where to go, and crossed the road to a log, where I sat down. I pretended to be asleep when the officer returned. He shouted to wake the dead. Where were the men? I stared at him stupidly, then said I hoped they had gone back to the cave. He whipped out a note book. "You will answer to the colonel for this," he roared, and wrote hurriedly.

"One of us will, that is sure," I said. "Want to bet which one?"

He wrote more, his hand trembling with rage. "While you are at it," I went on, losing all control, "put down I said this is the most stupid thing I have ever seen an officer do."

"You," he said, his voice shaking so he could hardly speak, "will be court-martialed."

Then he ran up the road toward the cave.

I immediately went around the corner and handed out francs to the other men, telling them also where the canteen was. They needed no second telling, and I went with them. We had a grand time with toast and jam, biscuits and tinned fruit and good hot tea in abundance. There was no hurry and by the time all were full the sun was warm on the reverse of the slope. One by one we went over and stretched out where the rays were warmest.

At twelve I roused, sat up, then wakened the others and we marched back to the cave, leaving the picks and shovels where they lay. A runner said I was to report to Major Arthur at once. He also told me the rations had come up and a good dinner was in the making.

Not knowing what might lie in store, I visited the major. He sat back in his chair and trouble was written over his face in capital letters. "What are the boys saying?" he asked, then added, "Sit down and tell me everything."

I did, in detail, and could see his worry lift. "You are the most unpredictable man in `D' Company," he grinned, "and I am glad we do not have another. But, as usual, all has ended well. I want you to do me a favour."

"Yes, sir. You can depend on me."

"Please go to every man, individually, and apologize for me. Tell them how truly sorry I am for what happened. It was sheer ignorance such as one would not think possible. I needn't tell you that officer will not be in this company."

There was much more. He said one could never judge what rank would do to an individual, discussed the amount of intelligence possessed by the average person, and again pleaded that I make it all right with "his boys." With me, Arthur was by all odds the best officer in the battalion. No one had more sheer guts than he in a tight spot or anywhere. No officer was as sincere with his men, or had anything like the whole-souled respect that reigned for him in "D" Company.

We were near Cherisy, and the men said that a fine canteen was there and the 85th was in the area. I went over looking for my brother, Hubert, intending to give him the pearl-handled Luger. He was not around, but the men told me that my fiancee's brother had been killed in the fighting at Dury. As I walked back to the cave a German plane came darting from the clouds and opened fire on a sausage balloon, which exploded in a great burst of fire. Smoke enveloped the black-winged Gotha, but it emerged apparently undamaged and soared away. The balloon had been arranged as a trap. The objects in the basket were dummies, but the trick hadn't worked.

As I reached the cave a small crowd had collected and I saw the body of the sour cook being carried away on a stretcher. He had been a very brooding, sullen person, and one wondered what history lay behind his attitude. It was he who had tried to deny us our share of tea at Vimy, and now he had been killed by the one stray shell to fall in the area all that day; even his death seemed an irony of fate.

We moved back to Dainville. I had an opportunity to visit the trenches we had occupied on the sunken road and to see the place where I had fallen into the German trench and gashed my eyelid. It was strange I had not been captured that night, as there had been a Hun post on either side, only yards from where I fell. There was the gap in the wire at that point, and it was easy to go from it and find the crater into which Ross Young and I had fallen and so escaped the machine-guns.

Another draft reached us, and rumours were our entertainment. Most of them said we were blocked in by the Canal. It was flooded in places, the stories said, and completely mined where it was dry. Troops were to be taken over it by plane. Our days were pleasant enough. What training we did was easy, and twice I had a day off and hitch-hiked around back of the front, eating at various places and trading cap badges with men of other units. I now had a belt completely filled with them.

Suddenly we had orders to move by train at eight the next night, and everything was made ready. The most persistent rumour was that we were to make an attack on Cambrai. In the afternoon, as final checks were being made, word was received that a train wreck had cancelled all arrangements and we would be moved by bus. We were to eat and be ready to leave at five p.m. Everyone watched up the road, but no bus appeared. At six it was decided we could shed our marching order. We had left our billets in apple-pie order so could not return there. Finally it was seven o'clock and it began to rain. The old army routine: if ever a move had gone off as announced, with no change of orders, we would probably have felt all was not well with the Canadian Expeditionary Force.

At nine, after we were well soaked with rain, the buses arrived, too few in number. We were crowded unmercifully, as equipment and rifles took up too much space. The comments were lurid. Then after about an hour on the road the buses halted. Drivers got out and there was a discussion. Our driver stuck his head back in and asked where we were supposed to go. He got a full-throated answer: "Boulogne!"

Twenty minutes of going back and forth, and off we went again, only to stop in half an hour. We turned around twice and it was three in the morning before we arrived at Bullecourt, every man so cramped and fed up that I expected to see a window or two smashed out. But nothing so drastic happened. The buses departed, leaving the Royal Highlanders of Canada in the dark, damp and depressed. Officers scurried about with flashlights. There were consultations. We stood and waited and waited. Then a runner we knew was captured and fetched to a huddle with our platoon. What was wrong? "There ain't no guides to take us in," he said. "They was to meet us at the railway station in Queant."

Sweet Mother Machree! We were wet and bone-weary from our ride, and lost. After much going back and forth and reading maps with flashlights, we straggled away in the dark and two hours later arrived at Queant, fed up to the back teeth. As we stood there waiting for the next move, the roar of a mighty artillery barrage shook the morning and kept on. In minutes every man had forgotten his grousing. The big question was the whereabouts of the action, and who were engaged. The main rumour said it was the 4th Division. A little later Sergeant Fordham, who was with us again, said it was two divisions, the lst and the 4th, that they were crossing the Canal du Nord, and we would be for it in the next few days. We stood around an hour and then had breakfast.

Then there was another long wait and finally, at ten o'clock, we moved off and after some marching reached the Canal and crossed by a bridge the engineers had thrown up. We kept on, with occasional delays and consultations, but by two in the afternoon were in trenches west of Bourlon Wood. There were some dugouts in the vicinity and our noses told us they had been occupied by the Germans. They might be more comfortable than the trench, Brown argued, and we investigated two of them. In the first one we found eight dead Jerries, all wrapped in bandages. They were stretcher cases and had been awaiting removal. It was evident they had been abandoned. In one bunk, seated so that his back was against the wall, was an elderly looking Hun with a scraggly beard, probably a flare man. Sims, who had been with us all summer and was always up to tricks, leaned over beside the bearded one and beckoned to a young fellow who had come in the last draft.

"Have a look at this grandpa," he said. "He's not dead. Just making believe."

Ferris, the youngster, said, "You can't fool me. They're all dead." He was very nervous.

"Then watch him," said Sims. He pretended to address the oldster. "Listen, old man. Don't try to pull a sham. If you're not dead, open your eyes."

The German's eyes sagged open, and Ferris stormed from the dugout on the verge of hysteria. Sims had worked his fingers into the whiskers and when he tugged downward the skin of the cheeks pulled the eyes open. It was a rotten thing to do, and

Tommy booted Sims out of the place.

The second dugout was like the first, with five dead men in it, all badly wounded cases who had been left to die. Two German dress helmets were on the wall and there was a quarrel over who saw them first. The matter was solved by placing all the names of the party in a steel hat and having a runner pull out two names. The lucky pair got the souvenirs.

We started making ourselves comfortable in the trench, as there were indications that it would be a cold night. By the time we had supper about a dozen fairly good bivvies had been constructed. Then came word we were not to stay there. Again there was a flow of red-hot adjectives, but out we filed and moved ahead to a sunken road. We stopped there and were told this was it for the night. It was no great distance from where we had been and there was no shelter of any kind. What on earth had we moved for? The grousing was stopped by the arrival of gas shells. They lasted for an hour and by that time our box respirators had become a misery. We took them off and twenty minutes later over came the gas again. Another session with the masks. Another brief respite, and more gas. It went on all night and served to take some attention from the fact that we were nearly frozen in the bitter cold.

No one complained when we were roused early and told to be ready to march off. There was a hasty breakfast without tea and off we went in file until we reached a railway embankment east of Bourlon Wood. There we remained for the day. At first, however, we were told we would move in an hour. At nine we were to move at noon. At noon it would be four o'clock. The waiting was an ordeal and the occasional heavy shell in the vicinity did nothing to ease the situation. About one o'clock we heard one of the Hun's "freight trains" arriving, the huge "coal box" type that went deep before exploding. An anxious five minutes ensued, but there was not another.

After a time I told Tommy I was going to crawl over and see how big a crater the shell had made. We were on the left of the battalion, and a rise of ground would screen me from observation. He said it was a foolish thing to do. But it would be something to kill time, so off I went. Ten yards of crawling put me where I could stand up, and soon I was over to where the huge crater had been made. It would accommodate a bungalow and was shaped like a vast bowl. Bits of metal glinted in the sun. Then, at the very centre, at least ten feet below earth level, I saw a glitter different from the others.

Curiosity got the better of me. I edged over the crater lip and carefully felt my way down, watching for any hot metal. It was slow going, as the chalky soil was powdery, and I did much sliding. At last I was at the spot and used a boot toe to knock away earth from the metal thing. In a moment I became excited. The shell burst had revealed the very tip of a sword blade, buried perpendicular in the earth. I had to crawl from the crater and explore until I found a sharp stick like a tent peg. I used it to excavate and after a long session I had the sword loosened and pulled it forth. It was a Roman sword, with an embossed pattern on the hilt, the finest souvenir I had yet found.

It would never do to let the lads see it. Some others might go over and dig. There would be tales of all kinds, leading to an investigation. Finally I tried to fix it under my tunic, but it would not stay there. And what could I do with it going into action? I stood and debated a dozen ideas and in the end went over to where a post of some sort had been broken off close to the ground. After a long effort I managed to sink the sword beside the post, covering over all sight of the hilt with tramped-down earth, and then I went back to the platoon.

We stayed there until ten o'clock, expecting to move at any time. There was one false alarm, after which we settled in for the night. Tommy and I lay together and had a couple of hours' sleep before we were wakened and told the battalion was really going to move.

Everything was draggingly slow. We began moving soon after three in the morning, and it took us four hours to get to what they called the jumping-off position. There was quite a bit of shelling but nothing dropped close to "D" Company. Lieutenant Craig took charge of the company. We went ahead slowly and it was very cold, but when we passed a limber with a dead gunner lying on it, I saw a fine British warm lying near him. I took it and put it on, and a dozen voices told me it was a bad move, which would bring me bad luck.

I didn't mind what they said in the least, as we had to lie in long wet grass and wait for zero hour. We had no definite word as to the time of the assault, and nobody asked. We had been told wrongly too many times. There was a heavy ground mist, so that we could not see beyond a hundred yards of grassy field. At long last the sun began to break through. I looked around to see where the platoon was lying. Near me were Tommy and Brown and Morris -a chap from our old unit who had been wounded at Vimy-,Walton, an "original" lately come back, Rees, Russell, Sellars, lately returned, Linder, a new man and likeable, Millar, McPhee and Waldvogel. Others were further over.

The sun took on new strength and the curtain of mist vanished, revealing a broad field sloping down to a hollow containing a railway. There was an embankment on the far side and what seemed to be small sheds on the left. On our immediate front we were much farther from the hollow than the rest of the unit, who were on our left on lower ground and nearer to the railway. Suddenly the barrage opened. It was not what we had expected. Lieutenant Craig shouted and we rose and started for the hollow, soon seeing that there was barbed wire near it. "Run," shouted Craig, and everybody started going in high gear.

For about fifty yards there was not a shot fired, but all at once machine-guns were shooting like mad. "Spread out," Craig shouted, and we did. I turned up the collar of the British warm and waved to Brown and away we went. Soon we saw a lumber yard on the right, more mounds, a German soldier running like mad. There was another shot and I glanced back to see Craig go down. It was impossible to tell whether he was killed or wounded. Machine-gun bullets were snapping around our ears and there was another shout. I turned and saw Millar down, evidently hit in the leg, and struggling to rise.

"Stay down!" I yelled. "Or you'll get hit again!"

Straight ahead of us I saw Germans frantically setting up a machine-gun on a tripod, and with the downgrade I really put on speed. Someone nudged me on my right side. "Get over!" I yelled. "Keep away from me!"

I veered left and reached the wire, went over it without looking at it, my eyes on the Germans, and was conscious of Waterbottle beside me, a great Russian giant in kilts who seemed to leap the whole barrier of wire, and Tommy, shooting as he ran. Brown and Linder were right behind and both of them were shooting. One German scuttled away with his head down. His three mates were lying on the ground, brought down by the rifle bullets. Things happened so fast in the next few minutes it was hard to keep track of them. We saw a German machine-gun shooting at us from the left part of the embankment, saw Sellars and two men reach one of the small buildings and vanish into it. McPhee set up his Lewis gun and opened fire on the German gun. There was a German post on our left close to the wire. About six Germans were standing there, shooting at us. The din and confusion were terrific and the snapping and crackling of bullets seemed all around us. McPhee won his duel in short order and only one Hun of the crew got away. Waldvogel and Tommy and Brown and I were shooting at the Hun post and we saw four of its occupants go down. The others fled on the far side and vanished around one of the sheds.

At that moment we became aware of a battle on our right. I had not seen any Germans there, but they had been in an underground and were now shooting like mad. Two men of our last draft fired at the Germans in a half-hearted manner, as if they had no hope of hitting anyone, and both went down, were dead when we reached them. Walton and Morris had got over the wire and they opened fire, hitting two of the Germans and making the rest scatter, but both of them were hit, Morris quite badly. Brown and Tommy and I kept shooting and the Germans started running desperately to get over to the left. They veered toward the embankment. We got five of them, but the rest would have escaped had not McPhee spotted them. His Lewis gun ended the matter.

Brown investigated the mound we had reached and found an entrance to a dugout. We went in and found it was a flare store, but no one was there. We came out again and were fired on by still another party of Germans on the right who had appeared from nowhere. McPhee joined us in returning the fire and the Germans took to cover. We kept them down as stretcher bearers got Walton and Morris. Sellars and his men were in a shelter, from which they could shoot at any German on the left. Our dugout had no such advantage, and though we hated staying in an exposed position, there did not seem anything else we could do. On the left the other companies were in a welter of fighting.

Waldvogel said it would be bad if the Huns on our left were not dislodged before dark. So we spread out with Tommy on the right, Brown next him, then myself and Waldvogel on the left. As we started to crawl my equipment fell away from me. I looked to see what the matter was, and Waldvogel told me I had a near one. When I had thought someone was pressing against me as we sprinted and had veered away to escape him, a German machine gunner had cut away all the ammunition on my right, my water bottle as well, and had almost severed the belt, which now gave way.

"Another thing," said Waldvogel. "Where is your kilt?"

I had not realized it was gone. I could not recall its being torn from me, but blood was running down my leg and I had a deep gash above one knee. It was easy to get a kilt and equipment from one of the new men lying by the wire, and then we crawled on. McPhee would attend to the left with the help of Sellars and his trio. Fortune favoured us, as there was low ground near the wire and the Germans could not see us without exposing themselves, so we arranged that only three would crawl at a time, and in turn, as the other watched with rifle ready for a snap shot. In that manner we kept the Huns down and reached a point where we would be back of their covering ridge.

As we crawled again they broke for our left. There were fourteen of them and they ran spread out, going with remarkable speed for men wearing German boots. We dropped five and then had to take cover as a German gun we could not see began shooting at us. McPhee got five more with his Lewis gun. Two survivors vanished on our left. We crawled back and got into the dugout. A stretcher bearer came and tied up my knee, which I had soaked with iodine.

McPhee had moved over and taken post in another of the small shelters, only a few feet below the surface. Rees and another man appeared and joined us. Gradually it became dark. A runner came from the left and wanted to know our strength and positions. He said four officers had been killed and seven wounded. One of the wounded was the gentleman who had taken us out to repair roads, and Tommy said someone would be happy. The runner said the Jerries had been decent in one regard. They had not fired on the stretcher bearers who had gone out all the time, one of them with a wheel barrow, and taken care of the wounded. As it grew darker Tommy went out with me and we moved around our part with care, located six more of our men in the post from which we had driven the Germans on our left. Russell was acting as a company runner and had Rees helping him. They told us about the many casualties, saying there would be another attack. This did not seem possible after all our losses.

The morning confirmed the report, even though we heard that other units of the brigade had also suffered heavy losses. Then we were surprised to see quite a number of 42nd men arriving, Sergeant Fordham among them. They had been left out of the scrap again but now circumstances forced them to join us.

McPhee and his crew got ready to go with us. I checked with the others of the platoon. All were in good spirits except Sellars and his men. They said it was impossible that we had been ordered to attack again, that it was suicide. All I could say to them was ignored, so of£ we went without them. As we reached the embankment and went over it, German shells began landing where we had been, and the next moment one landed exactly on the small shelter Sellars and his men were in. There was a spurt of black earth and debris, sheets of iron rising into the air. Our own batteries opened up, and there was tremendous machine-gun fire on our left where, we learned afterward, the Germans had tried a counter-attack and failed.

An R.C.R. officer was the only one we saw as we reached the higher ground. There was some sniping, but nothing like the previous day. We kept going and reached some high ground, where we began digging in. Beyond us lay a village and in the distance were the outskirts of Cambrai. Five or six R.C.R.s were with us. One carried a real shovel and started digging, but a moment later toppled backwards, shot by a sniper. I took the shovel and started digging where he had begun. I kept at it and by noon had a deep trench.

There was much fighting in front of us and to the left. All at once we saw men coming back, and our colonel went out to meet them, checking with them and sending them to the rear. Then to our amazement a party of us was sent forward. We dug in on high ground nearer to the village. There was some sniping but it was nothing compared to what we had been through. There was no one but an R.C.R. officer. He came at dark and said we should patrol a gap between us and another party that had dug in. As there was no shooting whatever, and word had come that the battalion was being relieved, we did no patrolling.

A runner came and told me a new officer was arriving to take us back, and would be along shortly. We waited and waited and no one came. On our left a German patrol, testing the strength of the line, were routed in a flurry of bombing and shooting. We waited an hour and then I tried to find the officer who was to take us out. Waldvogel went with me. We made a systematic search of all the positions our men had occupied, but he definitely was not there. The machine-gunners and others of our attacking party were relieved, and at last an officer came and hunted me out, saying he was relief for us.

He knew nothing about any 42nd officer. We had been waiting two hours, so once more Waldvogel and I made the rounds. It was useless. No officer had appeared. Off to the right, some distance behind our line, was an old tank. It had been stranded there in the fighting of 1917. We went and looked in it but it was a foul-smelling place, so we returned and waited another hour. Getting desperate, we re-checked, going again to the tank. Waldvogel walked around it, got down and felt with his hands, and found a small opening. He struck a match and peered, seeing army boots. Swearing mightily, he reached in, grabbed a foot and pulled. Out came a batman, a chap over military age, who had been bandied from one officer to another, left out of the lines generally, and was of no use anywhere. The officer came out on his own power, while Waldvogel expressed his frank opinion of persons with yellow streaks down the back. Nothing I could say moderated his language.

The officer was a poor physical specimen. He was new to the front. No one had told him anything definite, and on his way in he had been shocked by the sight of so many dead lying along the way. The batman's dread of the front added to his fear and so he had taken shelter. He was very sorry. It was daylight when we reached shelters near Bourlon Wood. And a message for me said my brother, Hubert, had been severely wounded in action.

For a week we lay about in our shelters and rested, emerging during the first days only to get our tea and rations. A new sergeant tried to get us on parade and was ignored. The officer from under the tank tried to order a rifle inspection-why, we never knew. But he was sent to another company. The third evening I was crossing to a canteen when I heard my name called and presently saw two lads from my home town. They were in uniforms of the R.C.R.'s. They told me they could not leave the immediate area of their hut, and had no supper nor rations. A few questions revealed that they were conscripts, thus the treatment they had received. So I walked over to the canteen, bought what I could in biscuits and canned goods and took it to the men. They were voluble with thanks and ate as if starved.

The next day a draft came to us, most of them conscripts from Quebec. One fine-looking lad told me his name was Lalonde and he was a relative of Newsy Lalonde, the great hockey player.

Then we were shocked to hear that General Lipsett had been killed. He was nearer to us than any other brass hat, being often in the trenches. I had never heard a man speak against him, and I had my own memory of running into him in the trench that night during 1917. His funeral was most impressive, with a special firing party from his old battalion, the Winnipeg Black Devils, attending. At the funeral we saw the Prince of Wales for the first time, and he looked little more than a teenager.

Suddenly I was to some extent in trouble. In the company we had an old

Newfoundlander-at least he seemed old to us, since he was forty-six and looked more. But he was as tough as they come, never groused, and more than did his share in any action. His leave came due, and he was quite excited about it when they called him in and explained he was to go the next day. It was evening when he left, and just as he was going a miserable specimen in a Sam Browne went in and reported old John had not saluted the officer he had met on his way out. He said he had not seen any officer, but they would not accept his story. The upshot of the affair was that they took away his leave. When old John came and told me about it, I could not believe they were serious in the orderly room and went over. I tried hard to keep calm when I discovered who the nincompoop was who had reported him, a pip-squeak who was no good in the line or anywhere else, had probably got his commission through political drag, and was not qualified in any way to be an officer. I was strong in my argument, but the die had been cast. I went out fuming. Suddenly I remembered that one could give another his leave if he wished. It had never been done that I knew of, but was possible. So I went back to the orderly room and asked about my own leave. The orderly sergeant had a big grin. Had somebody spilled the beans? I was due to go the next day!

Their attitude changed when I told them I was giving John my leave, and would take his when it came due again. They argued against it in every way but I stayed pat. Old John was getting a dirty deal and any decent man would admit it. Perhaps some of my comment was a bit strong. At any rate, when John had his papers and was gone, I was told emphatically not to try and pat myself on the back. They would see to it that the war was over before I went anywhere.

Away we went towards Belgium in general pursuit of the fleeing goose-steppers. It was a drastic change from the fighting near Cambrai. There was no hurry, and when we marched through a French village the inhabitants were almost delirious with joy. They lined the road and waved at us, and the children ran alongside crying "Bon Canadaw." The second day we fell out part way through a village, as it was warm and everyone wanted to fill his water bottle. There had been no water supply where we had stayed overnight and here there was a great pump that produced ice-cold Adam's ale. All had to take their turn. We had been over an hour in the place when an old peasant beckoned to Tommy and Brown and me so excitedly that we went to see what he wanted. He led the way to an outbuilding off the main route and worked with a long handled rake until he pulled from under the floor the badly-hacked body of a German officer.

In broken English and with many gestures, he explained the German had been billeted in his house and had treated his wife as if she were a slave, ordering her to shine his shoes and to have a cup of tea ready any time he came in. The old peasant dared not say anything but was enraged to see his wife so afraid of the man. When rumour came of the retreat the officer was eating his supper and shouting displeasure about the meal. The peasant told us he could not stand it anymore. He waited by the door with a club and when the officer came out he cracked him with all his strength. The officer made no outcry, and when the Germans began to go and one enquired about the officer, the peasant told them the man had already gone. It was a happy ending from the peasant's point of view, but his voice was husky with hate and when he stamped on the face of his victim we turned and left him.

That evening as we looked for billets in a small village with only one *estaminet,* we heard shouting in French and went out to see four British soldiers coming across the field. They had lain hidden for two days in a wood and were almost starved. Every man in the platoon wanted to do something for them. They said they had been prisoners since March. They were walking skeletons, with matted hair and beards, rags tied around their feet in lieu of boots, their clothing crawling with vermin. Seeing them so weak-voiced and pitiful made us furious, as all of us had seen German prisoners in England well-fed and well-housed, working on farms in the Midlands. We all chipped in and paid Madame to get them a grand meal. We bought them bread to take with them, and were able to give each man ten francs with which to buy more food.

The next day we met refugees with great sweat-dried Percherons drawing farm carts heaped with mattresses and furniture. Lean cows were tethered to the rear. Men and women, some dressed in their black Sunday best, pushed carts piled with possessions. All of them looked tired and footsore. Some hissed their hatred of the Hun, but the majority were too beaten for conversation, too worn to exhibit any emotion as they realized they were in safe territory at last.

At one place a pig eating at a dead horse by the roadside was driven away with shrill cries by a group of women, who attacked the carcass with knives and stripped every shred of meat for their own consumption. Our rations were bigger and better than they had ever been, and we gave about half our issue to children, and to mothers in whose eyes we read the story of the long paralysis of the Hun. That afternoon we saw, far in the distance, a group of men in grey in full flight over a rise in the ground. Some of our lads wanted to start running after them but were quickly checked by the officer. After the first day we had only one officer in the company and did not see any major.

About five o'clock that afternoon we passed through a scattering of houses that had been vacated. Discipline was lax as the men looked in sheds and alleys and poked along. No one was in a hurry. We were simply keeping the Hun moving back to his fatherland and no one wanted to run into any trouble. I heard someone shouting as I filled my water bottle at a pump and saw a Red Cross sergeant in the doorway of a house. As I went toward him I saw where two shells had dropped that day in the farm lane. There had been casual shelling the previous afternoon as well, since the Hun wanted to keep us from overtaking his troops.

"They shelled here this afternoon," the sergeant said, "and all the people beat it to a highway over there on the left. That is, all but one. They left a woman in this house and she is about to have a baby. The others told us where to find her and there will be an ambulance along presently, but she is not going to wait its coming."

Our platoon was moving on, and I wondered about his story.

"Are you a medical officer?" I asked.

"I had two years at McGill in medicine," he said, "and was in my third when I enlisted. My name is Jim Hallam and I'm from a small town in Ontario."

He sounded sincere, and I shed my equipment and went in. It was not much of a house. The woman was lying on a bed, her hands clenched, staring at the ceiling and muttering. Now and then she shrilled something. "She says her sister left her and so did her neighbour. She is mad as a wet hen. Get a fire going quick as you can. We must have plenty of hot water." He was ripping up a pair of sheets as he talked.

For some days this experience was large in my thoughts. Hallam worked like a professional, or so I thought. The woman yelled invective at times, as if she resented everything in the world. The stove worked well, but the light was only one small oil lamp, so I ran to search two other houses. I did not find any lamps in either. There was not much I could do for Hallam, but I felt he did not want to be there alone and I stayed on. Presently there were four of us. The newcomer was female and Hallam, who could speak French, said the mother was pleased. She didn't want a boy who would have to go to war.

The going was difficult in the dark as I went to catch up with our men, but I found another small village about four kilometres ahead and Brown, Larry Kennedy, Linder and Tommy were in a house that had been abandoned for some time. Furthermore they had carrots and potatoes from the garden in a pot on the stove and had, somehow, acquired a half-tin of margarine. We had a great feast. Kennedy asked us if we had heard the latest news in the battalion. A Dane who had come with the MacLean Highlanders had been awarded the Victoria Cross!

Tommy and I grinned at each other. We had heard two sergeants offering to bet, odds five to one, that it would happen. This for the reason that the Dane was a blue blood, received mail with a family crest, owned a hotel in New York City, and had a private yacht. He was a private in the ranks and yet each night he ate in the officers' mess, and batmen told us they had uproarious times since the Dane was a well-travelled man and filled with witty stories. We had heard he was a good soldier in the line, and Tommy visited the platoon in which he had served to hear what they had to say. He returned chuckling. "It's not safe to go over there with such a question," he grinned.

The next day we reached the fringe of Raismes Forest and entered it in pursuit of a company of Huns we had sighted twice in the distance. There had been no shelling during the day, but it was cold and damp at night and we had to build brush shelters. They were all right for a time, but by midnight many men were up and pacing about, beating with their arms in an effort to get warm. It began to drizzle, adding to the discomfort, and Tommy crawled out, shivering, and tried to thatch our abode and make it rainproof. "Not a drop of rum for us on a night like this," he groused, "and yesterday our transport drivers were so drunk they got lost twice. They have all they want all the time, and so much bread they peddle it for beer."

He quieted and said he was sorry he got worked up so easily, but his nerves were bad. All of us were tense, I told him, but gradually we would recover and be all right. Then we heard Giger complaining bitterly. He had no matches and had lost his charm. Someone asked questions and we heard Giger's high-pitched voice explaining that Binks, a fellow who had gone down the line sick, had given him the charm. It was a wrist-ring of hair that Binks had taken from a Heinie prisoner, who had begged to keep it as it brought certain good luck. Binks had worn it at Parvillers and at Jigsaw Wood and had never had a scratch. Then he had gone out sick. What more proof was needed of the power of the charm? It turned up a little later.

At dawn we were stiff with cold and ate cold rations, then started down a road in the forest. The grass was wet but on the road we escaped the dripping from the trees. Someone said the wood had once been a place where French nobles had bear hunts, and we wondered if any bears remained. At ten o'clock everyone got excited. On a rise ahead two Germans appeared and took hasty shots at us, then ran under the trees. Orders were given for the platoon to spread out on either side of the road at least one hundred yards, to proceed carefully and beware of any cover that might conceal snipers. So we moved slowly, a long extended line well in advance of the main party, but found nothing.

Night found us at a wood-cutter's cabin. There was a lean-to beside it for his horse, and there we crowded together and slept quite warmly, with four men on sentry duty. They were relieved every three hours. Brown was one of the first four and he poked around until he found me, saying he had just seen an officer in "C" Company who had been with us briefly at Lieven. He told me a story about this man. It was one of the experiences that gave humour to the war, and humour was as good as medicine to a frontliner.

The officer had been taking Brown and another chap to a post in some ruined buildings on the outskirts of Lens, and got mixed up in his bearings. No one was in sight. All the wreckage looked alike and there were no trenches in that particular spot, yet he knew the post was nearby. So he led the way around and around, then began shouting at openings in the rubble to ask if a "D" Company post were there. As he got no response his voice kept getting louder. They made a complete circuit of the ruins a second and a third time, and as they started around once more Brown voiced mild protest. "Shut up, Brown," said his mate. "This here's Joshua and we're tramping around Jericho."

The sun shone in the morning and put every man in good spirits. The wood thinned after two hours of tramping, revealing a clearing and a small farm. There was a cottage on a knoll with a shed close by, a fence about the place and three apple trees. Probably everyone else had the same thoughts as I about ripe apples for the taking. At any rate we hurried forward, and all at once a German stepped from the cottage and fired at us. His bullet struck Linder in the head and killed him instantly. Jones and Tommy and I ran back into the trees. We crept around to the other side of the cottage, as the German had ducked back to cover. He did not stay, however, but emerged from a back door and ran like a sprinter. The range was about sixty yards when we fired, and he went down like a log after a queer sideways leap into the air. He was dead when we reached him. We searched the cottage and there was no one in it, had not been for days.

We went along more carefully after that, but there were no more cottages. It was quite warm at noon and we enjoyed a good hour of rest. In the afternoon as we came around a turn in the road we saw a path on the left and walked over to see where it led. To our amazement there was a pile of short logs, recently cut, and a German soldier, a rather slight fellow, was seated on them eating his lunch. His big helmet was beside him on the logs and his rifle leaned against the pile. His back was toward us. Since we were treading on moss and old leaves that were damp in the shade we made no sound whatever, but as Tommy and I stood to whisper to each other we were shoved aside and Giger pushed by us, breathing with short, eager intakes. He was almost running and had reached the logs before the German looked around.

"Kamerad!" The German's arms shot high above his head. But Giger didn't hesitate. He drove his bayonet into the German's middle with all his strength and almost sprawled over him as the man went down. At that split second a second German arrived. He had evidently been answering a call of nature, as he was buttoning his trousers. When he saw Giger's work with the bayonet he leaped to the end of the log pile and seized a woodman's axe lying there, swung it in one motion and, before

Giger could straighten, cut him down with a fearful blow on the neck and shoulder. Then the Hun ran like a deer-and no one fired a shot after him.

There was nothing we could do for Giger. As we reached him he raised the wrist with the hair-ring charm around it, and died with a gaze of startled incredulity.

It was a curious thing, but no one spoke about Giger as we went on. And everyone had talked about Linder getting killed. We were more careful than ever and every man felt relieved when we reached the end of the forest just before dusk. There was a village in the distance with people moving about. A scattering of trees reached part way up the long slope, and two Germans were standing beside the trees, talking. They did not look at the forest and at first I thought they were French labourers. Across the road a short distance from us was a small brick building, and Barron and our officer, who had caught up with us, moved over to inspect it.

I called to them and pointed at the Germans. They looked, then Barron shouted they were Frenchmen, and went on toward the building. They were almost to it when the Germans saw them and started running toward the village. Barron started shooting and the Germans veered to place the trees between us and them, while the officer shouted at Barron that he would hit someone on the village street. Probably the incidents at the woodpile and the clearing where Linder had been killed had made us tense, but something in the way the Germans ran, with Barron shooting so excitedly at them, set Tommy and I laughing. The next minute Brown and Jones joined in and it was a long time before we stopped.

As darkness came we went from the woods to the building. It was larger than it had looked, a warehouse of some sort, with nothing in it except two shovels and a wheelbarrow. The officer said posts must be placed, as it was possible some German force was in the village. So we placed two groups in hollows at the foot of the slope, seven men in each with a Lewis gun, and Barron visited them each hour of the first part of the night. Then I took out two groups and relieved the posts at midnight.

The men relieved were just inside the building with me when machine-gun fire tore tiles from the roof. One of the Lewis guns outside began shooting and then we heard some rifle fire. It sounded as though the Hun were attacking. Then the firing stopped and suddenly both our groups came plunging in to join us.

They had spotted some men crawling towards them from the left and had routed them with machine-gun fire. Then they had seen two other small groups on the right and did not know how many of the enemy were around. Since they had not taken out any extra pans of ammunition, they had to come in.

We waited half an hour and there were no sounds outside, so Barron and I ventured out and crawled over to where our posts had been. There was no one around. We put the posts out again and there was no more shooting. As soon as it was daylight Thirteen Platoon came from the wood and joined us and we deployed and advanced on the village. But the Hun had flown in the night.

It was Thirteen Platoon's turn to lead the advance, but we were now in open ground and not a German was sighted. At noon we ate in a village, getting hot tea from an *estaminet,* and they told us a German party of about thirty had passed through hours before, going at a fast gait. All that afternoon clouds kept gathering, so we felt it would be sensible to stop in a village for the night. There were no Huns, we were sure, for miles. At dusk a cold drizzle began and we halted in low ground with scattered bush growth encircled by a hedge. Orders came that we were to line the hedge and dig in for the night. As soon as he had given them, the officer set off toward a farmhouse about a mile back where he would be comfortable.

Tommy, Brown, and I were at the far reach of the hedge. Just ahead we could see houses that would be warm, and we were sure the French would not want us to lie out in the chilling wet. So off we went. There was no light in the first house, nor the second, and Tommy stole up the street, came back and said there was not a light in the village. It seemed queer, so I went up to the rear door of the first cottage, rapped, and heard nothing. I tried the door and it opened easily. We struck a match and lit a candle, and saw that the place had been vacant for some time. There were two small bedrooms. We took blankets from one of the beds and hung them over the windows, then Tommy and Brown went out into the garden, returning with vegetables which we washed after locating a pump close beside the house. We made a fire in the stove and saw some clusters of beans hung up to dry, took them down, shelled the pods and added them to our dinner.

The room heated so quickly that we had to discard our tunics. It would take a long time for the potful to cook and we were sleepy, so we lay crosswise on the one bed we had not touched and in a moment were sound asleep.

Later I struggled awake, scarcely able to see. The room was filled with steam. The beans had swollen and spilled out onto the top of the stove where they were burning. The fire was down, but a probe with a fork told me our dinner was well done indeed. So we sat down and gorged ourselves, being too tired to bother with tea, and sprawled back on the bed with a blanket over us.

A noise somewhere outside brought me sharply awake. I slipped from the bed and padded to a window. It was morning. And on the street in front two German soldiers were standing, resting from carrying a dixie of some liquid. In an instant I had tried the front door and found it could not be locked. I roused the other two; they needed no urging to get dressed. We took stock and found we had only two bombs with us. We dared not use them, for we could not tell how many Germans there were, and did not know how soon the rest of the platoon would be along. It was a quarter to eight.

We stood by the front door and listened to harsh voices and heavy feet on the cobbles. Then a German came along with heavy tread and entered the next house. He tramped around in a manner that told us the building was empty, came out and walked over to the door where we were standing. He had his hand on the latch and his foot on the step when someone called to him urgently. I had my rifle ready. Had the door moved inward he would have died very suddenly, but he swung about and hurried off as if alarmed.

For two or three minutes we stood and listened, then risked opening the door. Not a German was in sight. Tommy went out and peered around, calling to us softly that the Germans were leaving the far end of the village on the double. Then he looked the other way and told us the platoons were coming up the slope!

We went out the back door and hid around the corner. Fortunately Thirteen Platoon was leading and our officer was with their commander. As Fourteen went by we stole around and fell in at the rear. Bob Jones and Mills had big grins as they saw us but no one shouted anything. After an hour or so we made a halt and the officer strolled over and spoke with Barron. He saw us but did not come near, and we realized he had not arrived in time to see whether or not we had been where we were supposed to.

It was a cloudy day and fairly cool. There were French in three villages we passed through, and they said the Huns had met with some transport and had roared away hours before. It seemed that we might not see another goose-stepper. At nightfall we were at another village, and six posts were put out, as if the officer feared a plane might fetch in attackers. It was drizzling again and cold. Brown and I had an outpost about one hundred yards from a cottage. We shivered until ten o'clock and no officer had appeared, so we figured they were in snug quarters somewhere and went to the cottage. A queer old crone with a blue birth mark on one cheek welcomed us warmly. She looked quite aged. A big, awkward-looking half-wit lolled on a bench in a corner and she told us he was her son. She made us bowls of coffee and we became sleepy in the warmth of her kitchen. In a moment she was unrolling straw paillasses on the floor. We placed our equipment and rifles by the door, lay down and were soon asleep.

Something wakened me toward morning. I glanced around and saw refugees had come in after we were asleep. Seven old women were sleeping on the floor. One, beside Brown, had the appearance of a vulture. Her principal night garment was a man's shirt and she was sitting up scratching herself, her claws making a sound like someone using sandpaper. I got my boots on, wrapped my puttees, and nudged Brown. He opened his eyes and saw that the crone, still scratching, was staring down at him.

"Bill," he said huskily. "Let's drag out of here."

We went out and walked up and down a wet field path for an hour, watching the old women, bundled in shawls and greatcoats, leave the house. Then we went back and had more hot coffee. The old hag could not speak much English but we could understand her. She lifted a trap door and asked us to go down into the cellar. She had lighted a candle and was cackling as if there were some joke on us. There was a good bed in the cellar, a dresser and some chairs. On the floor was the body of a German officer, with the head chopped from it and lying in a corner. It was a horrible sight and we got back up the stairs. "My son did it," cackled the old woman in French. "With his axe. That German was drunk. He was a foul bull. I waited all my life to get my revenge."

She was cackling and raving as if she were mad, and we were glad to get from the place. The sun was beginning to shine. In an hour or so the going was good and the men felt better. It was open country throughout the forenoon, and we were fortunate to stop at noon in a village where everyone could get hot tea, and eggs and chips if he had the money. Farther on the main highway veered to our right, but we had to keep a straight course and were lucky to find a secondary road going our way. Some men were working by the roadside at about two o'clock, and as they saw us one shouted we would find a prisoner-of-war camp about three kilometres ahead.

The information set everyone talking, but the majority thought it was a gag. However, we knew we were on the main travelled way and in places there were trees on both sides. An officer came up from the rear and warned that we should take every precaution in our advance, as there might be German snipers. So we spread out again, covering a wide area, and went slowly.

Eventually we saw four homes ahead on the left of the road. Children were playing in the sunshine and fowl were walking about. Then we saw the prisoners' camp, a low sprawling structure surrounded by three fences of barbed wire, with a barracks on the left to house the guards. Three or four vehicles were disappearing in a cloud of dust. We began to quicken our pace and everyone converged on the road without orders.

Figures appeared from the camp entrance. They rushed out in groups and in seconds we knew they were the prisoners. One group came toward us. A tall prisoner seemed to be their leader, an Australian, and greeted us heartily. He told us they had some terrible treatment on account of having a brute of an officer as commandant. He said there were forty-three Australians in the camp, and six New Zealanders. The rest were British. They had never had enough food and there was no heat in their quarters.

"The regular guards were not too bad," he said. "And it was pretty decent of them to unlock the gates before they left."

Our two platoons were in a group and the released men mingled with us, asking questions about the progress of the war. They had not had any information in weeks, had not received any mail.

All at once there was a great shout from some of the men nearer the camp. We stopped talking and looked about to see a man running at top speed. He was bareheaded and without a tunic, but his grey trousers and boots told us he was a German officer. The prisoners who had tried to catch him could not match his speed, and he was running in a direction that would take him by the four French houses.

Suddenly one of the prisoners talking with us sprang at Mills, and before a move could be made had snatched his Lee Enfield from his grasp. The prisoner wheeled about and took aim at the running man. But the tall Australian leaped toward the fellow. As the shot was fired the Australian knocked the rifle barrel up, so that the bullet went skyward, and then wrested the rifle away.

"Are you crazy?" he demanded.

The frustrated man was raging. "You're the one who's crazy," he yelled. "I could have had him easily."

"Sure," came the retort. "You would likely have drilled him neatly and that would be it. All over in a second. You wanted to save him from what's going to happen."

The sarcasm in his voice was heavy, and as we watched we understood. We saw two women running from yards near the houses. Their screams roused others, and each carried a club. Three men came running from somewhere back of the houses. Then there were more women, one carrying a pitchfork. The runner stopped and looked back, whirled about and sprinted again, swinging to the left. About a dozen released prisoners were jogging along after him and each carried a club of some kind. The screams of the women increased. A swarm of children added their voices to the clamour. Then three more men appeared on our left, coming from fields, each with a club of some nature. The German glanced back again and saw his only chance was sheer speed. He put his elbows down by his sides like a trained sprinter and for a few yards maintained an amazing pace. But he was a middle-aged man and could not keep up the effort. He slowed, seemed to stagger, glanced around wildly, started off again, and suddenly was surrounded. At our distance it was impossible to see what happened. We could see clubs being used, but the German was down and every inhabitant of the place crowded in so that the whole was a jumble of bodies.

The tall Australian smiled. "You wanted to save him from that , eh Jack?"

The man who had seized the rifle looked ashamed. "You're right," he owned. "I wasn't thinking."

"That German," the Australian went on, "was the biggest devil in human form ever let loose. Twice their rations trucks did not get through in time and he went to those houses and took every scrap of food. Threatened to burn the buildings over their heads. Gave the women one hour to cook twenty loaves of bread from their limited stock of flour. One family had a dog and it barked at him. He shot it with his revolver, then shot their pig in the yard, a pet cat, and three or four fowl. Well, this was his finish and he had it coming to him."

We were there more than an hour before our officers broke up the party. It was most interesting to listen to accounts of the daily routine in the prison camp, and the various experiences of the men at the time of their capture. But we had to go on and the next day passed through Valenciennes, a town about twelve kilometres from the Belgian border. We were halted at the outskirts for more than an hour, and a few of us who went to the military latrine erected in a nearby field in usual army style-a long pole across a ditch for a seat, and a screen of rough burlap about five feet high around it-had an unusual experience. We were chatting in comradely fashion, spaced along the pole, when in came a bevy of farm women going to market. They deposited their baskets of produce by the screen, heaved up skirts and petticoats with much grunting, and filled up the spaces on the pole, talking volubly all the while as if we did not exist. No man lingered longer than necessary.

On we went to Quivrechain, across the Belgian border, and there at an *estaminet* were told of a German major killed in the street by infuriated women. He had been captured by Canadians of the 4th Division on our left and was being escorted through the village where he had been commandant. He was the arrogant type who elbowed old women from his path and kicked dogs and children. When he was seen, the villagers snatched up clubs and charged in on the escort, who immediately got out of the way.

Then it was Thulin, after which we dragged wearily into Jemappes, a few kilometres from Mons. It was Saturday night and we were footsore and hungry. There were no more Germans in the country, we felt. But in late afternoon we were amazed to hear shelling again.

A dozen rumours had circulated to the effect that an armistice was to be signed that day. It was said that the Germans had quit, that the war was over. The new men grabbed at every report, and Jones resented their eagerness. "Can't you hear guns?" he demanded. "Does that say the war is over? He'll go back to the border and dig in for the winter. Don't be silly."

To our dismay no rations had come up, so we fell out in the street and were told to find quarters for the night. Those who could not would be taken to the town hall. Brown, Tommy, Jones and I found an old couple who fed us hot coffee, fried potatoes and bread. They had no eggs or chips. The old man kept chattering at us in French, trying to tell us what the shells had done to his town. Mills came in and brought his brother with him. The brother had been in France since 1914 with a veterinary unit and had transferred to us. His name was Jim and he was a quiet type, unlike Tom who was talkative.

We asked where we could find accommodation but the old people were no help, so we went out and wandered along the street. A sergeant came along and said there was a house just along a bit where we could sleep on the top floor. There were no beds but it would be warm. The rations would be up at midnight. Jones asked the reason for the delay, when there were no bridges out and no enemy to hold the rations up. "Because," the sergeant said, "they are bringing our kit bags."

Kit bags! Yes, our kit bags. Those for our platoon were to be stored in a large room at the rear of our billet.

Jones kept asking questions, and we hung on every word the sergeant said. It did not make sense, he said finally, to hold back the news, but he had orders and didn't want to get into trouble.

"How would you feel if you were in our shoes?" demanded Jones.

The sergeant grinned. "All right," he said. "I'll risk my stripes. The battalion is going to stay here and rest up. On Monday morning the armistice is going to be signed. As far as we're concerned the war is over. But keep it to yourselves. There will probably be an announcement some time tomorrow."

He went out and the Mills brothers shook hands. Tommy shook hands with me and Brown shook hands with Jones. Then we did a circling Indian dance, with Brown patting his mouth to make a war cry and shouting "How" at the finish. We didn't want to go to bed but it was cold, so we climbed the stairs and were elated to find that some kind soul had brought in a roll of army blankets.

Chapter 8: Mons

Church bells roused us in the morning and sunshine streamed in the window. We dressed in leisurely fashion, took our rations and discovered the folks in charge of the place had coffee and eggs for us. We ate breakfast in style. The sun was flooding the yard at the back. We went and looked in the rear room and there were our kit bags. Only five or six had locks on them. The rest were simply tied at the top. All had the names and regimental numbers of the owners printed in large letters. I had wangled one of the new bags of good, strong material and had it fastened with the best lock I could buy, for in it were precious souvenirs, the pearl handled Luger, binoculars, badges, a German dress helmet, my German rain cape, and a very fine kilt I had managed to get from stores. I was saving it to wear on leave, and so far the only person who had worn it was Jones. He had borrowed it to go on leave, and tried to tease me by saying that when he went into the red-light district he always informed the females that his name was Bird, and let them read my name on the inside.

It seemed a good time to gloat over my treasures, but the sun was too nice for me to stay in the building. Jones was seated on a bench outside. He had two little girls on his knee and was trying to talk with them. Tommy and Brown were seated by a wall, getting a regular sun bath. The Mills brothers were lying full length on a blanket with their eyes closed."If I could get a loan from the army," said Tommy, "I'd buy this place. I'd stay right here and make it into a tourist tavern. This country will be flooded with tourists next summer. I'll wear this uniform and tell them that this is where I was when the war ended. You want to go on shares with me, Bob?"

"No," grinned Jones. "In a couple of years the Heinies will be coming as tourists and I just couldn't be nice to them."

"I'm going to set up in the Salient," said Brown, "and I'll use one of them long pillboxes as headquarters. The tourist cabins will be sandbagged and have corrugated iron roofs. Rats will run free and there will be a gas alarm by the door. Each afternoon I'll read speeches of the brass hats that have been in the Daily Mail, and serve beer. I'll bet I'll get more business than I can handle. . . ."

"Bird!" It was the voice of the company-sergeant-major, harsh as a whip saw. "Get your section ready at once. Battle order. Leave your other stuff in your billet."

The Mills brothers sat up. Jones pushed the little girls from his lap. I managed to speak. "What's up?" I demanded.

"We re going to take Mons. No use to argue about it. Get our men ready."

"Just a minute." Tom Mills was on his feet. "The war's over tomorrow and everybody knows it. What kind of rot is this?"

"Watch what you say." The sergeant-major's face was pale and set. He was not speaking in his normal voice at all. "Orders are orders. Get your gear on."

Every man argued bitterly and it was difficult to get them ready. We formed up with the platoon while the men swore over trivial matters, hitched around and changed positions. Two cursed steadily, and with frightful emphasis, the ones who had issued the orders.

Away on the left there was the report of shell bursts, and we could see a few long-range crumps leaving black smoke trails. Thirteen Platoon came along and joined us.

Five or six of their men were shouting at us to turn around and attack our headquarters. The officers were worse enemies than any German. No one tried to quiet them, and presently we marched down a street along a road and into a field.

The Hun began to shell with shrapnel and tear gas. No one was hurt, as nothing came very near, and we crossed a deep ditch by using a stretcher as a bridge. It took a long time before everyone was over. Then we came to a brewery. A shell, or the soldiers, had started vats leaking, and there were varied comments as some of the men sampled the beverage. We stayed a time in the building after some German high explosive landed very near the entrance.

The shelling let up. The Princess Pats were in the area, and we were to relieve a company of them and work our way into the city of Mons by way of the railway station. This I learned from a runner who also told me that "B" Company was staying back at billets while "A" Company was to try to effect an entrance somewhere, with "C" Company in support.

It was one o'clock when we left the brewery. Our every forward movement was slow, and finally we reached an open area three or four hundred yards long and about one hundred yards wide, bordered by a bank lined with houses and an abutting street at the far end. Machine-gun fire became a real hazard. We had a new officer who had not been in any action. Studholme was sticking at his elbow and talking to him all the time. They paused by the beginning of the open space and said that they would go along the other side of the bank and we could proceed on the inner side, which was fully exposed. Neither the officer nor Studholme said anything about a division of our forces, but the majority of the men were suddenly on the outside of the bank. They disappeared from sight, and I found I had with me only the two Mills brothers, Bill Childs, Jones and Dick Johnson. Even Tommy and Brown went with the others.

On the right of the opening we saw the 42nd men advancing carefully from one door to another, then spotted three Germans with a machine-gun. We fired at them at once and they vanished. A machine-gun began shooting at us from a distance ahead, shooting along the front of the houses, but a Lewis gun of our "A" Company opened on it and the gunners fired. We saw at once we could greatly help "A" Company by shooting across the open, and they in turn could help us. In this manner we were two-thirds up the length of the open when shells began arriving, air bursts. The first ones dropped around the open ground, but somewhere a Hun must have been in touch by phone, for the next shells came very near us.

Just ahead was a brick building about the size of a garage. I led a rush to it to take cover. The door was locked, but a long plank lay nearby and Jones and I used it to break in the door. The brick walls would resist everything except a direct hit. Once inside, Jones sat on a small keg in the middle of the small building. Tom Mills stood directly behind me and I stood in the doorway. Dick Johnson was close to the building but did not want to go in. He said we ought not to have broken in the door.

Wheeee-crash! A slamming explosion. A shell had burst just beyond the building, about fifteen feet in the air. Johnson was bowled over by the concussion. I was driven back with such force that both Old Bill and I went down heavily. We scrambled up, almost choked with fumes. "That was too close for comfort," I said.

No one answered me. I looked at Jones. He was seated where he had been, his chin in his hands, but blood was pouring from a great hole in his temple. He had been killed instantly. There was a despairing cry behind me. I swung around to see Tom

Mills falling. His brother caught him but had to let him down. "I'm hit " Tom said, and held out his arm. His wrist was almost severed. But as he sank back on the floor I saw he had a fearful wound in the stomach. He died as we looked at him.

His brother went wild. He could not believe Tom was dead and got out his field dressing, begging me to get a stretcher bearer. We had seen the "A" Company bearer across the way. Jim had such agony in his voice that I could not argue with him. I ran across the open in spite of Childs' pleading with me, and not a shell came. The stretcher bearer refused to go over to our building. There was no protection from shells, he said. He could not do much for a bad stomach wound anyway, and all I needed to do to quiet Jim was hold a steel mirror in front of Tom's face. If there were any breath it would show.

I went back. There had not been a shell since the one at our shed. Jim was sobbing, but I got out my steel shaving mirror, explaining what I was doing. "If there's a sign of a breath on the mirror," I said, "he's alive. If there isn't, he's dead".

Not a sign of breath showed. I said "A" Company was going ahead and we had better move up to the end of the opening while there were no shells. There was no protest and away we went. "A" Company men had reached the end on their side and had gone across the end street. But the Germans had set up a machine gun where a through track ran, and not a man could cross to the low side going towards the centre of Mons. Two men had been killed, they told us, and just as we arrived a man who tried to sprint across the road had his eyes shot out.

Bill Childs was carrying two rifle grenades. I took his rifle and a grenade, and worked into a garden of one of the front-facing houses. A small movement caught my eye as I peered through shrubbery. It was the top of a German helmet. I set the rifle at what I felt was the correct angle and shot a four-second fused grenade. Luck rode with me. It dropped exactly where I had intended. There was a faint yell. I dashed back and we ran across the road, and not a shot was fired at us.

On the lower ground were gardens of the houses facing the way we had crossed. To my surprise I found Brown, Gallagher and Kennedy of our platoon. They said the officer had been wounded and was gone, and they did not know where Studholme or the rest of the platoon were. An "A" Company sergeant came up to us, saying that we had better keep low because Germans were probably hiding in the houses, that he had word there was to be no further advance until dark.

We went into the cellar of the nearest house facing the roadway. It was filled with frightened Belgians, all in their best array. A wedding had been in progress and the bride was sitting on the groom's knee. Often some tiny incident will lodge in the memory and remain there when the main features are gone: my only remembrance of the wedding party is seeing the groom make his way to a side door, where he stood on the sill and urinated, the bride hanging to his arm.

We went out and into the gardens. A Belgian saw us, beckoned to us and told us the Germans in the road had come back and set up their gun just outside his gate, on the roadway. But he could not let us go into his house to fire on them, as the Germans would kill him afterwards. It was useless to try and tell him there would be no "afterwards" for them.

We talked things over, and then Brown moved well out into a garden from where he could watch the alleys between the houses. Kennedy joined him. I shed my equipment and helmet, crawled under a gate and up the rise of ground beside a house wall, peered around the corner near the street and saw two Germans. They were watching along the road intently, and glancing now and then at the house fronts and especially at upper windows. Once more I set the rifle as carefully as possible and fired. When the grenade exploded I heard a shout. I looked over and saw one German lying on the cobbles, his heels digging as if he was trying to push himself along. Then I heard voices and heavy boots and cowered low. The other German, with a mate, retreated up the street, dragging the gun mounted on a tripod. They were looking at house windows as if sure the grenade had came from one of them.

It was easy to get back down the grade and under the gate. Brown told me I had been lucky not to bump into a German who had been exploring the next garden. Either he or Kennedy could have shot the fellow easily, but they had been in an exposed position and were afraid there were more. Then Brown gave me the best news of the afternoon: he said he had two rifle grenades.

We sat and talked a time. Stretching away from us was a long garden, in which very large cabbages were the main item. On the far side of the garden was a lot without a building on it, through which we could see the street. I crawled around the back of a small house and entered the cabbage patch. It was easy to get along on knees and elbows, keeping the rifle down. By now there was no shooting anywhere in our vicinity, no shells. The area was ominously quiet.

It was about fifty yards to where I could have a good view of the street, and the last stretch took some time, as I kept as low as possible. At last I lay on my side and peered. Had I known exactly where the Germans were I could not have done better. Their gun was set up in the middle of the street. One German had his helmet off as if adjusting the strap. The other two watched him idly. Their backs were toward me and they were both big men. In a moment I had the rifle adjusted. It was not a long reach, but I did not know the time of the fuse and had to take a chance. The luck of the day stayed with me. Just as I shot, a large tin can or barrel crashed down nearby, in a backyard or possibly on a street. The next instant the grenade exploded at shoulder height over the German gun. The gun crashed over, and I jumped up and ran back the way I had come.

There was no more sound. The three of us went forward, through a board gate and up to the street, our rifles ready. Two of the Germans lay as they had fallen. The third had crawled across the sidewalk and was lying there. The way was clear.

We went back to the cellar where the wedding party waited and found more of Fourteen Platoon there. As we talked with them, Studholme appeared from nowhere and said we would have to "leave our shelter," as the company was to go into Mons. We were to report to an offlcer in the third house ahead. Tommy, Brown, Kennedy, Old Bill, Jim Mills and Gallagher went with me.

By now it was quite dark. When we went into the house we saw the officer was "Bonnie Mary of Argyle." At the Vimy area, when out of the lines, it had seemed to us that the main entertainment of the officers was to have this lad sing "Bonnie Mary of Argyle." He had a good tenor voice, and one night when we were billetted close by the officers' mess we heard him sing it three times in the evening. This so angered one of our boys that he purchased a wheezy old phonograph back in Bruay, somehow secured a record of the song, and managed to get a long rope somewhere. He attached the rope to the machine and by the help of a ladder put it through a pulley at the peak of the barn. "Lights Out" was 9:30. Twice the orderly officer came to our barn to tell us there must be no noise-and this while the officers next door could be heard all over the village. That night as the third rendering of "Bonnie Mary of Argyle" ended with great applause, another voice singing the song opened up in the barn where the "other ranks" were supposed to be asleep. Over came the orderly officer with his flashlight. There were three tiers of bunks and he looked in all of them, seeing only men asleep. He was scarcely gone when again the reedy tenor broke the night's stillness. One of the boys had simply shut off the phonograph and hoisted it to the roof and, as he was in a top bunk, hitched the rope to a spike in the wall. The third time this happened the officer explored every stall and corner in the barn, rending the night with vows of vengeance. All he could hear was snoring in considerable volume. When he was gone our boy lowered the machine, slipped off the rope, wound up the phonograph and shoved it under a lower bunk. The officer came like a wild man and it took him minutes to locate the machine. It had been poked to the far corner and was hard to reach. A long stick was finally found, and out came the machine with its last dying squeal. We laughed until we were weak.

Now, lying on a couch in the house, drunk as a lord, we found "Bonnie Mary of Argyle." He was too drunk to stand.

So away we went, as we saw men on the move, and joined "D" Company led by Major Arthur. When we reached the railway station in Mons, a spray of machine-gun bullets hummed and sang down the wide way, a last salute of fleeing German gunners. By 11:30 p.m. we were in the heart of the city. Fifteen Platoon took a section to clear, with Ross Young in charge. Sixteen Platoon had an area too, and as the will-o-the-wisp, Studholme, was not around, I took our lads plus Geordie Dunbar and away we went.

There was not a light anywhere, but suddenly we were confronted by an elderly Belgian in tall hat, striped trousers and swallow-tail coat. He was surely dressed for the occasion, and said that further along the street was an *estaminet* run by a lady who was hand-in-glove with the Germans. He said German soldiers slept in the basement and German officers were upstairs. We reached the place. It was in darkness, but the door was not locked. The Belgian had a flashlight and he led us down the stairs into the basement. We were too late. There were eight beds on the floor and a window at the far end was open. All the beds had been well occupied, and half the occupants remained, mostly blond, not one of them wearing a stitch of nightwear. They blinked in the glare of the flashlight as they sat up and viewed us, then lay down again. Our guide said they were imports.

We started to go back upstairs. As we did a blond lady in a nightdress came down from above in a perfect fury. She almost spat at me and ordered me out of her establishment. I reached over with my rifle and swept about a dozen bottles of her stock to the floor. She sprang at me, but Brown inserted a half inch of steel in her fat rear. She screamed and screamed, tearing back up the stairs with blood running down her leg. The Belgian was disappointed, we thought, that we did not shoot her. He and Tommy went up the way she had gone and looked in every room. Four German officers had evidently slept there but they were gone. Two packs had been abandoned in one room.

Back in the street the guide said we would not find any Germans along that way, but we tested doors to see if they were locked and did several streets until about three o'clock, when two women who operated a tea room invited us in. They wore jackets over nightgowns and made us hot coffee, but served no food. They could speak excellent English and we were with them for some time.

Finally we left, and at the next corner there was a tea garden. As we went past it lights were turned on. The garden was set up with a very elaborate front and much coloured glass. By this time R.C.R.'s and Pats had begun to filter into the city. It was just breaking day, November 11. We were served tiny glasses of wine, and as we sipped saw a German officer come from the window of a big house across the way. Our hostess assured us he had been living there for some time. Brown grabbed his rifle, asking if he should shoot the fellow or take him prisoner.

"Don't do anything," said our hostess. "Just watch."

We saw what she meant. A Belgian in rough clothing had in his hands a maul used for driving fence posts. There was a large backyard to the house that the German was leaving, and the gate opened outward from it to the street. The Belgian slipped along the sidewalk, hiding behind the opened gate. Along came the German. We saw where he was headed; two of our officers with some men had appeared at the street corner, and he was going to surrender to them. But as he walked out the gate, the Belgian struck from behind with the maul, crushing his skull. He was the last German I saw killed. And the body was lying there till after noon.

It had become full day when Old Bill came around the corner with Jim Mills. He beckoned me to him. Jim was wild-eyed, white as if he had been ill. "He says he's going to shoot whoever arranged to have his brother killed for nothing," whispered Bill. "He really means it. He's hoping Currie comes here today. If he doesn't, he's going to shoot the next higher-up. He says his brother was murdered."

One of the 42nd officers was walking toward us and I went up to him. He was not the one I would have chosen, but something had to be done. I saluted him and told him about Jim. He was startled, for he had not known Jones and Tom Mills were dead. But he said there was no need to worry about Jim. Take him and get him drunk, so drunk he wouldn't know anything for twenty-four hours. When he came out of it he would be all right. He told me to say my piece to Bill and come back to him. Bill agreed to get Jim plastered, and I gave him the money. Then the officer took me up the street to where the adjutant was standing. He said there was to be a parade shortly, but the two deaths must be reported. They asked me many questions, which ended in my having to show a party where to go for the bodies.

The parade was over when we returned, and only five or six of Fourteen Platoon had been in it. The streets were so crowded you could scarcely move. Every citizen in Mons seemed to be out. Tommy and Brown were where I had left them, and both had been treated with hot coffee and cognac until I knew they would shortly be incapable of navigation. What to do about them was a problem. Finally I suggested we go into a restaurant and get something to eat, as it was noon. But the place, though open, was out of action. A waiter, who seemed half-seas-over himself, told us that the cooks had not shown up, that no one was around except himself and he couldn't cook anything. Brown and Tommy sank into chairs and in no time were snoring. I gave the waiter five francs to let them sleep. He insisted I look at their rifles. They were still loaded. I took out the clips and gave them to him for souvenirs.

The next thing I knew Geordie Dunbar was shaking me awake. I was lying in a fine bed in a fine room, on the third floor of a quite imposing residence four streets away from the square. He told me I had entered the house and gone up the stairs, telling Madame that I would shoot anyone who disturbed me. Her husband was out and so she had run along the street until she saw someone with a Black Watch kilt. Dunbar had assured her I was simply tired. I apologized to her the best I knew how, then unloaded my own rifle.

When we were back near the square, a sergeant-major from another of our companies was staggering among the crowd and shouting "Fall in the Forty-Second!" Someone bumped against him and he went down on a small space of ground before a building. He made one or two attempts to rise, then turned on his side and slept.

The crowd was tremendous. Every "safety-first" from the back areas was there. There were R.C.R.'s and Pats everywhere one looked. Belgian women were kissing soldiers in emotional manner, throwing arms around their necks and kissing them on both cheeks, and Belgian men were shaking hands with our men. Some of them were bringing glasses of wine from some source and passing them recklessly to soldiers passing by. It was amazing to see that nine out of ten drank the wine and took care to return the glass safely to the donor. Tommy emerged from nowhere, three parts drunk. He told me Jim Mills was safely in a cellar and "drunk as a boiled owl," whatever that might be, that he was going to the first hotel he could find, take the best room they had, and sleep there until next Sunday. And he was going to charge the bill to the Canadian Government. I assured him it would be paid without a question and gently escaped him.

It would have been better had I too tried to get into a hotel with him, for I was grabbed by two officers of the 42nd and taken to the City Hall. They were both half-drunk, but I could not escape them. Three Belgian dignitaries in top hats gravely offered me a chair, and stood to listen as the officers asked question after question about the manner in which I had lost two men of my section. It was as if I were in a prisoner's box and the officers were lawyers questioning me. They haggled over the smallest query. The Belgians were bored stiff by the proceedings, but too polite to make an excuse and escape. How long the officers would have persisted in their cross-examination I do not know, but luckily for me they were summoned by their company commander who appeared in the building, and as they talked with him the Belgians very kindly showed me a side door by which I made my escape.

I did not know how long I had been grilled, but was stunned when I looked at my watch and saw it was 4:30. Then I realized how weak from hunger I was. There should be some place, I felt, away from the main square, where food was being served. I tried to make my way through the crowd. Belgian and French flags had appeared as if by magic and were still appearing, so that the square was a mass of colour. A Belgian with ribbons in the lapel of his coat caught my arm and tried to get me to drink cognac. He had a bottle in one hand and a glass in the other, and could speak good English. I told him I did not drink. But he insisted it was a special occasion, and I had a difficult time escaping him. Then a band began to play the national anthem. Everyone stood to attention in a sort of way, some singing the words. The noise was deafening. When the music stopped I began pushing my way through the crowd. It was a slow process, and time and again I lost as much ground as I had gained. There were many more drunk than before. A dozen groups of singers had formed, some of them having members from five or six different units, as well as

Belgians.

Gradually, buffeted right and left, I wormed and thrust my way from the square. I turned right, as the traffic seemed least in that direction, but in a moment was caught by a tidal flow of marchers, all carrying flags and singing. I got swept ahead of them to a corner of the square and was a long time getting out again. I had no idea where to go but kept tramping, sometimes being pushed from the sidewalk by shouting paraders. Finally I reached a street beyond the celebrations and wandered along it, practically at the end of my endurance.

Then a voice called "Canada!" I looked, and an old man and woman were standing at the door of a small cottage. They beckoned to me. I went up the walk, and the old lady kissed me. Her husband said I looked exhausted. I told them I had been going since Sunday morning, all the night, and had eaten nothing all the day. They took me in, saying they had been preparing supper and wanted to share it with a Canadian. The heat of the kitchen made my head swim. I found myself seated at the table, eating ravenously. There was good bread and butter, cheese, and bowls of vegetables. Then they put a big plate of soup before me. It was a treat I had not had in a long time. But the food and heat were overwhelming. Suddenly I bumped my head on the table, tried to sit up again and felt dizzy.

"You must sleep," said the old lady. "We have a bed ready."

I mumbled that I couldn't get into their bed as I was too dirty. We had not had a bath for some time. Then my head hit the table again.

When next consciousness came to me, I found myself standing in a tin tub, the old man supporting me. My clothing and equipment were piled in a corner by the stove and the old woman was washing me with a big cloth.

My head was swimming and I was beyond any argument, did not try to say anything. They led me into a little room where they helped me between clean sheets. The old woman kissed me and then they went out and closed the door. Although the cottage was away from the crowds and noise, I could hear the clamour faintly and knew bands were playing. Moonlight was coming in the window. It had been dusk when I went in, so I knew the dinner and bath must have been a long process. In spite of deadening fatigue, I felt something was wrong. I opened my eyes and saw the closet door move ever so slightly. Springing to the floor, I threw the door open. There, crouched among a pile of clothing, was a young German soldier!

He came out and cringed abjectly. He was no more than eighteen years old, a boy with a cloth cap on his head. His face was twisted with apprehension. Perhaps he had been trying to escape the town later than his fellows. He might have been sleeping somewhere, unaware the others had gone, and then, terrified, he had seen the cottage door open and had slipped in, hiding in the closet to wait for the night.

The moonlight showed a postman's rig on hooks in the closet, and I recalled the old couple telling me that they had lost their son and he had been a postman. I took the postman's cap and handed it to the German. He slipped it on, putting his own in his pocket. Then I handed him the postman's cloak and he threw it over his shoulders. I opened the door into the hall softly and let him out the front door. He squeezed my hand warmly, and was gone. I got back quietly into my room, closed the closet door, and when the old woman woke me it was twelve noon the next day.

She had a fine dinner awaiting me. She had washed my shirt and socks and dried them. The old man had shined my equipment. They hovered over me as if I were their own, and begged me to come and sleep there each night. Their kindness was overwhelming. I assured them I would come if we were staying in Mons. Then I put on my equipment and went into the square, saw no soldiers about but finally located the big barracks that had been used by the Germans. About half the battalion was there, and men were arriving every hour, many of them bleary-eyed after the celebrations. "Farmer" was going around with a stern expression, berating every man as he arrived. About four in the afternoon our sergeant-major arrived and by five most of the company was there. And I was notified I was orderly sergeant.

The cook wagon came and set up in the cobbled barrack yard. There was soup in the big container left by the Germans. Some of the boys tried it, but it was a grey-looking mixture and was emptied down the sewer. The men were called into the barracks square and berated anew by Farmer. We were told there could be no relaxation. No man could be absent without leave, there would be drill and marching, and every man must be in at 9:30. Discipline would be maintained as before. His voice and manner indicated we were in for a very stiff time indeed.

There was strong talk up in our area. "D" Company had been assigned the far side of the upper floor, furthest away from everything. The men said if the officers could go out all night to parties and only one or two show up each day, then they, the men, were not going to be kept in prison. My sympathy was with them one hundred percent. I knew if Farmer had his way there would be all sorts of crime reported, every little infraction of the rules. On our floor, against the wall, was a long wide plank. I looked out the windows of the far side and saw a wall not ten feet away. The November night set in early and there were no outside lights, so we opened a window and pushed out the plank until it rested on the wall. A lad went out to the wall, looked down and saw a short plank lying on the ground. He dropped down to it, turned it over and found cleats nailed along the length of it, evidence that it had been used by previous occupants of our quarters. About twelve lads went out that first night and then came the 9:30 call to report to Farmer.

"A" Company reported ten men absent. "Have them up in the morning," said Farmer. "B" Company reported twelve men absent, and the sergeant received the same orders. "C" Company had fourteen men absent. They, too, were to be on the mat in the morning. Then Farmer called "D" Company. "All present and correct, sir," I reported. "Excellent," said Farmer. "I want the same report from the other companies tomorrow night."

The boys came in by midnight, and the last in tipped down the ladder plank so that it fell with the cleats down side. Every night I reported the same, and always at least a third of the company was out having fun, being entertained at little parties and dances. When another unit started the strict regime, a full-sized revolution was escaped only by the quick interference of some wiser higher-ups. The war was over. The men were not going to be treated like dogs while the officers had a gay old time.

The second day in barracks I began thinking about our kit bags and asked if they might be brought in. It ended with two of us going out with some of our transport to collect "D" Company's lot. We knew the big room where they were stored. When we went in and looked around, we saw that every kit bag without a lock had been ransacked. Only underwear and sweaters and such items were left, either on the floor or stuffed back in the bag. Five kit bags that had locks on them had been slit with a knife and there was not much left in them. My kit bag and another that had a good lock were gone.

We stormed into the house and asked who had been at the kit bags. It was some of your men, the old man said. They wore your caps and badges but had riding breeches. The transport men! The lads who stayed in the back areas and had good rations every day of the year! They had moved all the kit bags up and knew where they were. They knew the war was over, and so they had seized the chance to loot. When we went back I reported the thefts to everyone from the sergeant to Arthur. It did no good. Nobody was going to worry over a kit bag. And so went my rain cape, and the pearl-handled Luger, the binoculars and all the rest.

Eventually a parcel came from home, and I took some fudge to the old couple. They were pleased beyond words. Every night after reporting to Farmer I simply walked out the barracks gate. There was always someone on guard who knew me and they looked the other way. In the morning I returned early and got thick slices of bread, climbing up on the hub of the big wheel of the cook wagon to soak them in bacon grease. Wright and Donnelly were the cooks, and Donnelly had a big boil on the back of his neck. As he stood talking to me one morning, my foot slipped from the wheel hub. I put out a hand to save myself but went down, and the heel of my hand descended on Donnelly's boil, literally scooping it from place. He let out an agonized yell and started after me with the bacon knife. We ran the length of the barracks yard before he suddenly stopped, felt gingerly with a hand and began to grin. "It's all right, Bird," he said. "The damn thing's gone and there's no more hurt. You're good as a doctor.

On November 16 I was called to the orderly room and told my leave was ready. The fellow avoided looking at me. He knew perfectly well the dirty deal I had received regarding old John. John had been pathetically happy about his leave, as he had spent it with two cousins who had met him in London. Nottinghamshire had looked good but fat, he said, but contented German prisoners loafing about farm stables had not seemed right; there had been too much in the papers about the condition of our prisoners returned from German camps. Up in Glasgow the crowds had been after Ramsay MacDonald, with barbed wire barricades on some streets and a nine o'clock curfew.

It is strange that I met the officer who had crawled under the tank at Cambrai. He was on the leave boat. He had been over two months in France, so naturally was due to go on leave. We talked practically all the way across the Channel and his case was, no doubt, similar to that of many. He had never been robust, but was a scholar; he was greatly interested in languages and his desire was to be a professor in a university; but his father was a candy manufacturer and had made a barrel of money-he wanted to be able to say that his son had been in the war. He had enough pull to get the lad commissioned in spite of bad eyesight. But now the youngster had survived a rough experience and was going home to tell his father he was going to live his own life, no matter if he were cut off without a cent. We shook hands warmly as we parted in London.

My days passed on wings, but I made my money serve me another three days and was stony broke as I stood on the deck of a boat bound for Calais. It was a nice afternoon and a fellow about my age came over to pass the time of day. I got chatting with him and suddenly he told me he had been just four days in England and was going back to his unit-with two hundred dollars in his pocket!

He said he did not know anyone in England and was the type who simply had to have company. His name was Melvin Kidd. He was from Ontario, serving with a unit that looked after transport, and knew all about horses. We talked steadily. When we got off the boat we looked for a train that would take us to the south of France, and in an hour we were on our way to where American troops were located. We visited three days with them, had wonderful beefsteak dinners, better than our officers would get, and saw poker games in which ten-dollar bills were tossed around as our lads might do with a French franc. One unit was from Pennsylvania and did not mind in the least that it had been eight months in France without being in action. Another was from Massachusetts and had reached the front on October 25.

We left the Americans and started a leisurely Cook's Tour of parts of France that we had not reached during the war. Three times we stopped in cities and saw good shows, but felt out of place, as the audience was civilian. Two-thirds of the time the French trainmen would not take money for a passage. One afternoon we left our train simply because some French cavalry were riding through and Mel wanted to look at the horses. The cavalry were in no hurry to get going again, as they were being served free drinks, and Mel talked with several of the riders. Then we learned that there would not be another train that night, that the village was in a war zone and had suffered much damage, and there were no hotels or accommodation of any sort in operation. After making enquiries at a small shop we located a woman who grudgingly gave us a supper of dark bread and fried eggs. She told us curtly we would not find any place to stay, and seemed to get some pleasure from our predicament.

It was dark and we were tired. But several unoccupied houses were not in bad condition, and at one place not a window was broken. This house was larger than the others, with three stories and closed shutters on all the first-floor windows. Some impulse turned us in the gate and we tried the front door. It was locked. A path ran around to the rear, and to our surprise the back door opened easily. We struck matches and looked around. The place had not been occupied in months, maybe years, and smelled musty. We went up the stairs into a large bedroom, where there were curtains at the windows and an oil lamp on the bureau. We lighted it and saw there was dust on everything. But when we took the bedspread off the bed, the sheets looked clean, and we undressed and were asleep in no time.

Sometime during the night I struggled out of deep sleep like a swimmer in a current. Right over me a beautiful face glowed for an instant, then vanished. I came fully awake at last, reached out to the bed stand, got a match and struck it. There was no one in the room, and Mel was snoring softly.

When we woke in the morning I remembered the face and told Mel about it. He said he did not dream and kidded me about dreaming of fair ladies. But the more he talked the more certain I became that something was not according to Hoyle. He was impatient to get going, but I drew back all the curtains of three windows and let the sunlight in. Then I got down and looked at the coat of dust on the carpet. In a moment I had found footprints. Mel could not believe it until he too had a look. They were a woman's footprints, and they led to the bed, then out of the room again. In the hall we had some difficulty seeing them, as there were no big windows to let in light. But we had matches, and by their light found that the footprints went to a door that opened to a stairway going to the third floor. Up we went and into a hall with doors opening into four bedrooms. It was dark, but we used matches and found a man's imprint as well as a woman's. I had brought my rifle along. Though it was not loaded, I felt safe with it in my hands. We saw that the tracks led into the first room on the left. The door was open. We stepped in, and a woman in bed gave a little cry of fear!

There was a man in bed with her. One glance told me she was the woman who had peered at me in the night. She looked terrified, and the man was sullen. He was swarth and of rather slight physique. "Who are you?" the woman asked fearfully, in good English.

We told her and asked why she had come to our bed, and whether this was her home. She said it was not, but that her home was in the village and had been destroyed by shelling. The people who owned the house were in Paris. She had tried many keys until she found one that fitted the back door. And she had been sleeping in the house for two months. When she seemed finished with her explaining, we asked her if the man were her husband. No, she shrugged. They were not married. He was a deserter from the Italian Army. She had a long tale of his escaping to France by way of Nice and how she had met him, and about his having a considerable sum of money. They bought food and cooked it in the kitchen at night, had been astounded to see the marks of our army boots on the carpet. She had stolen over to the bed and used her flashlight. Her lips quivered as she asked what we were going to do about them. Not a thing, we assured her. She could stay there the rest of her life as far as we were concerned. All we wanted was to get a train out. She talked swiftly to the man in French and they both sat up to wave us good-bye.

The weather was kinder than we had hoped. We decided to hitch-hike in all directions around the old battlefields. So long as we could get meals and a place to sleep, we were in no hurry. So it happened we had a week of travelling in such fashion, not knowing the date or exactly where we were until we saw army signs. Always we headed for the local *estaminet* and our uniforms made us welcome, although Mel insisted on paying for food and a bed at night. We were in Vis-en-Artois again, bringing back memories, then rode into Cherisy with its duck puddles and manure drainage, and had lunch at a cafe in which there was an Army Service Corps man on leave. He knew his lot were not looked on with particular favour by frontliners, but was a pleasant chap. He told us of being in a hut back of the lines, crowded around the one stove with his chums, discussing dreams. A mud-weary frontliner stumbled in from the wet and cold, bound for Blighty on leave. He had come to get thawed out. No one made a move to let him near the stove and when there was a lull in the talk he spoke up. "I had a dream last night," he said. "I dreamt I got mine and went to hell."

He paused and several voices asked curiously, "What was it like, Mac?"

"Just like here," came the answer. "I couldn't get near the fire for A.S.C. chaps."

A French lorry took us to Gentelles Wood and we wandered into the forest where we had stayed the Sunday before August 8, when the great attack began. There were countless bully-beef tins under the trees, some messtin covers and a rusting bayonet. Another ride took us into Amiens, where we found an *estaminet* to our liking. There were two Australians there on leave, and they told us about two American deserters who had hidden in a barn for two weeks. A Frenchman in uniform talked to us about the Germans, with hate in every word. He talked about a barn at Lewarde that the

Germans had used as a concert hall. On its wall were three pictures expressing the German mind. He had been there and seen them, had tried to get the people to destroy them, but no one would take him seriously. A motto above the pictures read: "As Ye Sow So Shall We Reap." The first picture represented an ox drawing a huge wooden plow. A young woman, broken by labour, was guiding the plow and finding it hard work. The second picture was of an old peasant sowing a field, beside him a little boy and behind him the village church and a windmill. Both pictures depicted the despair of the workers. The third picture was of a giant Prussian soldier. It was he who had put fear into the hearts of the workers. And the French lad told us that the Germans had looted Lewarde of every stick of furniture. The Canadians of the lst Division had captured a trainload of it, finding it labelled: "By Order of the Army Command."

Parvillers was a must for me, and I took Mel into the maze of trenches where we had been lost for a whole afternoon. It took me an hour but I finally found the dugout with the spring of cold water. We had purchased a flashlight and with it we looked at the massive dugout, with its rough bunks that would sleep a platoon. An entrance to another trench went up sixteen steps. We went out and found the trench where Doggy had wandered, looking for me. Then we came to the place where the young officer had shaken hands, said "good-bye" and walked into the range of the German machine-gun. As we passed through Folies a funeral was in progress. Boys dressed in white gowns carried crosses and banners and there were many mourners.

We headed for Bourecq, staying at the little *estaminet* where I had eaten countless eggs and chips. Madame was glad to see me and spoke about the bully beef I had taken her one night to help pay for my dinner. Another time it had been those army issue sacks of Old Chum tobacco. The boys preferred cigarettes and would not bother with pipes, and often there would be ten or twenty Old Chum sacks abandoned in a barn billet. Madame's husband was an inveterate smoker and liked Old Chum, so there were many swaps. The name of the *estaminet* always appealed to me-The Fighting Cocks- but neither Madame nor her husband knew why the name had been chosen.

Once we had been billetted in a barn in Bourecq, and there was a huge farm midden enclosed, deeper than average, about two feet of rain water and manure ringed by a stone walk two feet wide. One of the dandies of the platoon had been on leave and returned in beautiful tunic and breeches. As we went to our quarters, someone noticed the buxom farmer's wife was undressing and had not pulled down the blind. In a moment there was a crowd of sightseers. The dandy, trying eagerly to get a good view, slipped off the walk and went backward into the midden. He sank from sight for an instant. When he rose and waded ashore, he looked like nothing on earth. Everyone fled him and he skinned both knees getting back onto the walk. Doors were fastened against him, and he had to walk half a mile to the quarter bloke and spend his last franc inducing that worthy to provide fresh raiment.

We visited Ferfay. I told Mel about the night the guard fixed bayonets as a General was passing. We visited the old huts, but they had been vacated and some men had started to fill in the practice trenches at what had been the Divisional School. It took us another day to find the buried Roman sword and take it to Divion. The old French couple greeted me warmly, assuring me that all my souvenirs would stay there until I returned some day on my way home. We saw our old parade ground, where Sir Robert Borden had inspected the battalion. His first words after the inspection were:

"Boys, I'm going back to Canada." Men in billets could imitate him to perfection. I showed Mel the stable that Sixteen Platoon set on fire, and the little house around the corner where some of the company were ousted to make room for officers. The officers slept in beds while the men had to move into a stable occupied by cows the previous night. It was so cold the men couldn't sleep, so they got a ladder from somewhere and a nimble footed lad went up on the roof and stuffed the flue with sandbags. It wasn't ten minutes before the alarm was given. All the officers rushed out, spitting, choking, gasping. Madame was almost sick from fumes. They couldn't find the ladder because it was down an old well, so a batman was hoisted to the eaves. He got up a bit higher, then slipped and shot down, knocking over those below like ninepins and landing on the hard-frozen ground. Snores were loud in the cow stable when a suspicious Sam Browne looked in. There were no tracks on the frozen mud, so the culprit was never caught. And the officers were smoked out until four in the morning when their fire died down.

Mel said they had no fun of that sort in his outfit. The officers were aloof and the men worked too hard to take part in any tricks. I showed him the old barn with the guard room in the loft, where Earl and I had nearly frozen and had quit at midnight and gone to billets. The sentry was supposed to stand guard at the foot of the ladder going up to the loft, right at the spot where customers of the nearby *estaminet* used to come when too much beer made bladders troublesome. One of the boys was dubbed "The Preacher," as he was shocked by any talk of loose morals. He was on guard one night when the boys invited three old girls in for a beerdrinking contest. They were hefty old farm women of great capacity and went out often by the ladder to relieve themselves. The Preacher had a very bad night of it.

There was so much fun revisiting old billets that we went next day to Hersin-Coupigny, where, along with many of the other lads, I had bought a silk handkerchief to send home. Madame ran a little shop that sold aprons and silk handkerchiefs, assuring us they were made by women of the place who were on the verge of starvation. It was a long time before we found she imported them from Paris and made a tidy profit. She looked just as fat and moist as the last time I had seen her, wore the same black dress and shoes, although both were coming apart at the seams. She was genial until she saw I did not intend buying anything, then suddenly became busy. We stayed at the *Estaminet de la Place,* where one could always trade socks, army underwear or blankets for both food and beer, and where we bought cartwheel loaves of dark bread to carry into the trenches, in spite of army orders posted around the village forbidding such purchases. Madame was in high spirits when Mel paid her in advance for our room, and she prepared us an excellent dinner. She introduced a visiting cousin, a French soldier who had lost an arm at Verdun. He reminded me of a joke that was told and retold while we were there. Some of the British outfits had very distinctive signs on their divisional transport, and we often remarked about one that had a stork standing on one leg. One such truck was stopped outside the *estaminet* one miserable wet day, while the driver had one or two for the road. Brown, always a wag, thought to have a dig at the fellow and said: "When do you think the war will be over?"

The Cockney shrugged, and pointed at his vehicle. "When that ruddy bird puts 'is foot dahn," he said and climbed to his seat.

Being back at Mont St. Eloi was like a visit home. The huts we had slept in so many cold nights were deserted, and it didn't seem half as far when we walked into

Neuville St. Vaast in daytime. But those dugouts we had occupied had become a ghoulish underground, rat-ridden, clammy and foul. We went along the crater line and I showed Mel where we had our post at Vernon Crater, then found the old sniper's plate still where Pearce had placed it. It was much too big for a souvenir. We had a look in Grange Tunnel but it smelled of dampness and was forbidding.

It took us two days to look all around Ypres and Passchendaele. Mel had been in the area with his outfit and showed me where they had stayed. My main interest was in the horrible area where we had made the futile night attack, but it was hard to find. We could count over forty pillboxes when we stood there and the smells assured us many dead were lying around. The bit of road up which we had crawled was dried out to a certain extent, but the slope on the left side was excellent cover for any defending party. It was suicide to try to go up as we had done. Of all the places we saw, we hated the Salient the most. You could smell it clear back to Ypres and far beyond.

Away we went to Lille, then Tournai, then heard that an outdoor song festival at Namur was worth attending. The weather was as mild as August when we arrived at one of the most beautiful places in Belgium, and luck was with us, as there were New Zealanders in a big barrack at the top of the hill. They were unusually friendly and we sat until one in the morning chatting with them. We had a room to ourselves and found that the New Zealanders were fed better than our 3rd Division.

The festival was on Sunday afternoon. Namur is a city along the Meuse River, situated at the foot of a hill, and there was a great open space where market was held. We sat in the sunshine on the slope high above the singers. Their voices seemed to linger in the air, and a two-hour performance seemed to last no time at all. It was the best entertainment I had seen in Europe. We moved down after it was over and went into a large tea room for hot chocolate, talking with many of the citizens. On Monday we simply could not tear ourselves away from the shops and people. Then in the late afternoon the finest barge we had ever seen drew alongside the wharf. The prow was of carved wood painted a bright yellow. There were curtains at the cabin window. A girl in costume fit for the stage came out and invited us on board. She told us she had been born on the barge, had lived in it her nineteen years. Her mother was dead and she and her father were the crew. She showed us all over and invited us into the cabin. There she served a tiny glass of what I thought was wine. The glass was not much larger than a walnut, and the liquid had a lovely taste. The girl asked how we liked it. "A nice sample," I said.

"Sam-pull? Sam-pull? I do not know that word." She looked perplexed and Mel explained. I laughed and told her I did not mean to be impolite, it was just a joke. But she shook her head, and we had refills. She said it was a bottle of treasure for special guests and asked us endless questions about Canada. Then her father returned from an errand and said they must push off. She kissed us and patted our hands, saying she would love to visit Canada.

We waved to her as long as the barge was in sight, then went up to the barracks, as it was six o'clock. The New Zealanders had eaten but had left plenty of food for us since they had seen us on the barge. There was good meat and gravy, plenty of potatoes and carrots. The salt was down the table out of my reach and I asked Mel to pass it. He stood up to reach down the table, but suddenly fell to the floor. "Watch it when you get up," he warned. "I can't use my legs."

His fall had startled him and soon he said he had enough. Then he had to get down on hands and knees and crawl down the corridor to our room. I laughed and laughed at the spectacle. The patient Belgian waiting to clear our dishes asked what he had, and I told him of our visit to the barge. He smiled. "You had peach brandy," he said, "and likely about thirty years old. All the barges have it as a special treat. It is made in the fall and gets more potent each year it is kept."

Presently it was my turn. I had not felt any effects and was sure I was all right-but down I went. My legs were simply useless. So I crawled the length of the corridor, finding Mel in bed and sleeping like a baby. It was quite a process to undress without getting up, but I managed it and then was in alongside Mel. It was all so funny I began to chuckle. Next thing I knew, a New Zealander was shaking us awake and telling us to get a move on or we would miss breakfast. We got up and dressed in a hurry. Our legs were fine and so were our heads. There was no aftermath whatever, but we would not forget the potent barge brandy.

There were clouds in the sky and it was getting on for Christmas, so Mel and I started back to our units. We said a fond good-bye and vowed each other we would write-but never did. There was no 42nd at Mons. I had quite a search, but eventually located them on December 20 at a fine little village called Genval, on the outskirts of Brussels. It was evening, and as I went up the little street I met Tommy. He stopped and shook his head. "At long last," he said. "You are really for it."

He told me that men three days over leave were getting a week in the clink. I was twenty-four days overdue. Furthermore, there were Pats at the end of the village and every billet was jammed to capacity, including the clink. Probably I would be sent to the city jail. What on earth had I been doing? I told him I had been on a tour of the south of France, the old battlefields, then Belgium. Oh yeah, and what had I used for money? A chap by name of Melvin Kidd. He had had two hundred dollars. Tommy shrugged. "I saw Arthur go into the orderly room," he said. "You had better get it over with."

Then I met Brown and he was really worried about me. He had been in the old platoon with me at Aldershot, Nova Scotia, and right through. Whatever had possessed me? I would be stripped and probably given a month in the clink. "Thank you for being a Job's comforter," I said. "Where is the orderly room?"

He pointed to a lighted window in a building farther up the street. Across from it was a beautiful home with ornamental iron fence and a gate with a swan on top. Huge bay windows extended upward to the second floor. There was a small balcony over the front door, and the walls were newly painted stucco. It was a house one would look at a second time. "Some joint," I remarked.

"You needn't look at it," said Brown. "The colonel tried to locate there and the lady turned him down cold. His batman told us. It's the home of the head electrician of Brussels."

I swung along and went into the orderly room, put my pack and rifle in a corner. Major Arthur was talking with the companysergeant-major, and the orderly sergeant was at a desk. They stopped speaking and stared. I saluted. "Well," said the major. "You did come back. We thought you had gone to Canada."

"It's likely I would have if there had been a chance, sir," I said. The major moved to a corner, where he stood and talked in a low tone with the sergeant-major. Presently he turned, waved a hand at me and went out. "Let's get it over with," I said to the sergeant-major. "Where's the clink?"

"You," he said, shaking his head, "are the luckiest guy in the Forty-Second. Arthur never knew how they had held up your leave. I've heard rumours he gave them a talk they won't forget. The orders are on the desk. You will carry on as from now. You will be our orderly sergeant. But don't start celebrating. There is no accommodation anywhere. You will have to make the best of it on this floor."

He put on his balmoral and walked out. The sergeant followed him and I could see vast disappointment on his leathery visage. I sat and looked at the usual routine orders. There was nothing difficult. Being orderly sergeant was really a cinch. It kept one off parade, and wise to all that was going on. The fire had died in the stove and a glance told me all the rationed fuel for the day had been used. I sat a moment before making my decision. Leaving the light on and the door unlocked, I took my pack and rifle, walked across the road, in through the swan gate and pressed the bell button beside the elaborate front door.

The woman who appeared was a beautiful lady. She had perfect poise and spoke excellent English. I told her my circumstances carefully, explained I had heard she refused lodging to our colonel, and added that only the idea of a night on the orderly room floor gave me courage to ring her bell. She listened courteously. Her eyes twinkled, and she nodded. "You are an interesting talker " she said. "I think we will get on well. Turn out your light and lock up and come back. Leave your pack here."

It was hard to believe. When I found myself in a beautiful bed in one of the front bedrooms, with magnificent furniture and deep rugs on the floor, I had to sit up and gloat over my surroundings. I had not had such accommodation before in my life. Everything spoke of wealth and culture and comfort.

In the morning I tried to go down without making any noise, but Madame was awaiting me, smiling. "I know you must be at your office," she said, "and do not think you would like breakfast in our dining room. So I have it for you in the kitchen."

There was toast and tea, eggs and bacon, and Madame in a soft negligee on the other side of the table. "Please don't think this is entirely pity on you for your predicament," she said. "Partly, it is a bit of selfishness on my side of the situation. My husband is very busy with so many troops in barracks and so many Christmas entertainments in the offing. There is enormous demand for electricity. He comes in late and goes out early. Everyone is busy at this season and I like company. So if you do not mind we will have much conversation and I will learn about Canada. Now I want you to meet Carmen, our only child."

Carmen was ten and gave every promise of being as beautiful as her mother. She had only a word or two of English and was quite shy, but managed to ask if she might visit me in the orderly room after school. I told her she was welcome at any time.

Our ration of fuel arrived as I opened the orderly room and soon I had a fire going. I performed the routine duties. Then mail arrived, and there were four parcels for me. There were also written instructions that, since the battalion might move at any time, the parcels for those recently gone on leave were to be opened, and only personal gifts such as razors or a watch or flashlight were to be carried. All candy and cakes were to be discarded.

After school was out, in came Carmen with two companions her own age, shy little girls who stood in the background. Carmen came over and deliberately climbed on my knee, put her arms around my neck and gave me a warm kiss. Her action had me almost flabbergasted, but I tried to act perfectly natural, opened a drawer of the desk and handed her three candy bars. There was no such candy in Belgium, and her face fairly shone. She had a small battle with herself, then slid down, crossed the floor and presented each watching girl with a bar. Then the three of them were munching with little squeals of pleasure. Each day the procedure was the same, though there were occasionally different playmates. And Carmen was very smart in picking up English, much smarter than I in learning her French.

Now there were Christmas decorations going up everywhere. Madame introduced me to her husband, a fine-looking man with a black moustache, who promptly told me I must have Christmas dinner with them. It would be at noon and they could not take "no" for an answer.

All the men were in extremely high spirits, except Farmer. There were crude characters staying a day or so over the ten allotted them for 1918, and he was hard-pressed to find room for them all in the clink. The officers, however, were more human, and there was no drill or parade to bother anyone. Half the lads in trouble over leave were released. Perhaps someone had nerve enough to remind company commanders that the officers had three times as much leave as the men, and had seen one-third as much action.

The Christmas dinner was a grand affair. There were six guests, one the brother of the host, a younger man with a fine tenor voice who spoke good English and was the life of the party. There was plenty of champagne and plenty of toasts-the first being to Canada, to which I was obliged to respond. Not having had any acquaintance with champagne, I was afraid of it, but Madame assured me it was of the finest quality and would not have much effect if I did not take too much. So I sipped eleven to twelve toasts, then the others got something stronger with the dessert. It was enough to get the brother in good voice and he sang two or three songs. Finally everyone was laughing and shouting, and he jumped up to the table, getting a footing among the silver and china, and commenced a gay song having to do with a penurious bridegroom bargaining with an innkeeper for a room at the beginning of his honeymoon. It would never be sung in English at any dinner in my home town, but everyone laughed uproariously, and at points he called to me in English explanations of each verse.

The dinner ended at three, and our regimental Christmas dinner began at five. Many Belgian dignitaries and their wives were present in finest bib and tucker, and the liquid refreshments flowed generously. By seven I was on the dance floor with awkward feet, unable to release myself from a stout, determined Belgian lady with a slight moustache, who had received scant attention from the lieutenant who was her dinner companion. She was half-drunk and quite determined to make a night of it. Fortunately for me, a garter or something gave way and she had to retire to make repairs. In that moment I was among the missing and had a good long walk in fresh air to help the digestion after two dinners, and to have a chance to think of Christmas in the Canadian town I called home.

Every day Carmen became more affectionate. She began staying at the orderly room after her little friends had to go home, trying to learn more English words. I had taken her mother a fine iced cake that had come in a parcel. Carmen pronounced it excellent, and after that I never opened any of the regimental parcels until she was with me after school. She delighted in investigating them, but was never greedy about candy, putting the bars in the desk drawer without being told.

Then suddenly, our happy days ended. We were to move. There was much packing and changing of orders, but I did not mind it after saying good-bye at the house. There Carmen wept, but I promised to write to her. My reason for feeling good was that I was one of an advance party to go ahead and secure billets in a town the unit would reach that night. We rode in style. The three lads with me headed for an *estaminet* on our arrival, but I made quick visits to various houses. "D" Company fared well that night, and I had a very cosy billet for myself. The next day was a repeat performance, but when the battalion arrived I was summoned by Farmer and told I must take over the guard for the night. Three prisoners had escaped the previous evening, and I would be held strictly to account if any more were missing.

At six o'clock I took over and found four men under guard, three of them from "C" Company and good lads in the line. We were billeted in the big kitchen of a rather ramshackle house on a back street. The guard was from "D" Company and composed of new men from the last draft that had reached us. The orderly officer was also a late arrival, very neat in appearance and fully aware of his importance in the army. I found the prisoners had not had their supper, so went to our cook wagon and slipped Donnelly five francs, telling him I had four friends and we wanted a good meal. I had taken one of the guards with me and we had all we could carry, as the battalion was living well and many were on leave. I also took the opportunity to visit the canteen and purchase a tin of Player's cigarettes. When the prisoners saw the fine hot dinner we had, grins were broad. They cleaned up everything with gusto and then I handed over the cigarettes. They had not had a smoke all day, had no money and had been treated like criminals.

Another trip was made to get more blankets. When we arranged our beds I had mine in the middle, with two of the so-called prisoners on either side. We chatted about Parvillers, exchanging experiences, until 9:30 when the orderly officer appeared. He told us we must be alert every moment, we must not relax, because we were responsible for the prisoners, and he used the word as if they were unrepentant killers.

When he was gone, one of the prisoners wanted to go to the privy we were using. One of the guards sprang up and seized his rifle with mounted bayonet. "Put that down," I ordered, "and get down yourself. Jim, you go along to the privy."

"But-but," stammered the guards in unison, "we'll all be in for it if he don't come back!"

"But he will come back," I said. "Just get it through your skulls that he is no criminal but a Forty-Twa, the same as you and me, and a far better soldier than either of us. Because some pigeon brain has hysterics when a man doesn't come back on the due date, these men are used like dirt. I'll be proud to know them after we are demobilized, but I'll never have a thing to do with those who are responsible for them being called prisoners."

Jim returned and said it was chilly outside. The four of them had another cigarette each, then settled down. I told the guards to get down and sleep. All that was necessary was for someone to wake us before the orderly officer arrived in the morning. So we slept warm with our extra blankets, and in the morning it was Jim who saved me by rousing me fifteen minutes before the orderly officer came. The guards were sleeping.

Our fancy Dan was elated when he saw the desperadoes still in captivity and complimented me on my alertness. Funds were getting low, so when I went for breakfast I told Donnelly the candid truth about whom we were feeding, and he rose to the occasion as I knew he would. It was hard to keep from saying things when Farmer came and praised me for my success with the outlaws, but I succeeded. And as an award for my work, I was given a ride to our next destination and again got the billets for our company. We were to stay there a day or so. I had a room in a clean little house where English was spoken, and was just planning on writing some letters when a call came. I was to be orderly sergeant for the day. At noon a chit came saying that, since six men had arrived from leave, it was time to select six more from "D" Company. Some impulse, one of those I so often obeyed, suggested that for devilment I should send in my own name. I did so and took the names myself over to headquarters. The great chief himself told me to wait while he made up the warrants, and the next day I was on my way back to England!

Arrived in London without any plans, and not much money, I met men from the 4th Division whom I knew and had not seen in years. We had a few days together, during which time I met boys from my home town who had been serving with other units. Suddenly my ten days were up, and I dutifully paraded to Victoria Station to return. The official glanced at my papers and told me I could not go. The 42nd had come back to England, were at Bramshott Camp, but had not enough room. All 42nd men returning from leave were to go to Millbank Street and draw funds, then stay in London and report regularly so as to know when they could rejoin the regiment.

As I turned around in good spirits, who confronted me but Tommy! He had received similar information two days previously, but was hanging around the station in hope of seeing someone he knew. We went and drew our money, and at Millbank Street met a sergeant who told us that very few of his rank took advantage of the place arranged for N.C.O.'s on leave, so that there was ample room there. So off we went and established ourselves at The Maple Leaf Club. We decided we would see every good show in the city. We went to "Going Up," "Yes, Uncle," "A Little Bit of Fluff," "The Better Hole," and all the rest, visiting music halls between times. Then we rode all over London on the upper decks of the buses.

As we ate lunch one day in a good restaurant, a lady approached and asked if she might talk to us. We assured her we were glad of her company and she told us she belonged to a group who were entertaining men from overseas. She wanted to know about our unit, where we were from, etc., then gave us a card we were to present at an address near Regent Street. We went there the next day, winded by the long walk although we had been assured it was "only a step." The address was a large stone house. A butler admitted us and looked after our caps. Then he escorted us into a large room where there were two lads from the Seaforth Highlanders and six ladies. We were served tea in very dainty cups and had a hard time balancing them on our knees while the cakes were passed and devoured. We made our escape when the others moved, and were never caught in such a predicament again.

One evening we were going along Edgeware Road when a sailor and a young man smartly togged in a bowler hat and spats bumped on one of the traffic islands, had words and decided to settle matters with their fists. In a moment a crowd had gathered, and as I moved about trying to get a good view I lost Tommy and was suddenly clutched from behind. A stout woman with wheezy breath loaded with beer, and arms like a stevedore's, had me at such advantage that I could not escape her. She hung on for dear life and kept murmuring: "Nah dearie! Nah then!"

No one gave us a glance amid the cheering over the fight. I ran backward, got the lady on the go and crashed her against a stone wall with such force that I was partly released, enabling me to swing as hard as I could and land one on her chin. It was enough to cause her to lose her hold and I escaped-with a lesson to be ever on your guard when on London streets at night.

We were so enthralled with the city at night that we slept all day, got up at six and had a meal, and then set forth. We visited the wharves where the fishing boats came in around three a.m. and were fascinated with the lurid language of the big-muscled fish wives and the way they used their knives. Each night we took in a different area, spending hours talking with night watchmen. Then we would go to Victoria or some other place and get down on the pavement with the tea-and-roll vendors, who dozed under their push carts until the five o'clock rush began. They told us tall tales of things they had seen in the early hours. Many times afterwards I wished I had taken a notebook along, but then they might not have talked as freely.

One night we saw another great scrap, a real battle with fists. Two van-men, as the English called their truckers, tried to back their vehicles into the same roadway near midnight. Neither could get in, and neither would give way to the other. Presently they tossed off jackets and hats and went at it hammer and tongs. They were of the same build and it was a vicious combat. A crowd gathered from nowhere, and when one of the men slipped and fell, the watchers prevented the other from stamping a heavy heel on his face. Finally they were so exhausted with effort that their blows were not much more than a push with the hand, and in the end they had to call it a draw. Each man had his face cut badly, eyes puffed half-shut, but they amazed us by shaking hands and calling it quits.

The next day Tommy roused me at noon and said he was feeling feverish. He dressed, and the attendant at the place where we stayed mixed him a concoction of some nature but it was no help. At four in the afternoon I began trying to locate a doctor. There was no luck on the telephone. Always a female answered and assured me the doctor had more than he could handle, since a 'flu epidemic was raging. So out I went and after an hour of searching, helped wonderfully by a huge bobby, I contacted a doctor and told him the circumstances. He looked a tired man but he went with me, and in half an hour Tommy was on his way to a hospital.

I followed by taxi to make sure there were no difficulties. I was not sure of the hospital's location, but noticed we went by the Crystal Palace, and with the cabby's help jotted down the general direction. That night I did not go out and the next morning tried in vain to get in touch with the doctor. After two in the afternoon the suspense became too much, and away I went in search of the hospital. It took me until four o'clock to find it, and then I had quite a battle to gain admission. When another doctor came to my rescue I went with him. I had to put on a mask before we went into a long ward. Tommy looked wretched but managed a grin at my appearance, then urged me to get out before I caught influenza too.

It was dark by the time I got back and I had no heart to go out for any entertainment. The next forenoon seemed an eternity and then I followed the route again, but in a shorter time since I had learned to watch for various landmarks. Again there was the refusal of admission and again I stayed in the waiting room. Eventually a doctor appeared. Although he was obviously annoyed by my persistence, he went to see if I could visit the ward. He was back quickly and his message stunned me. Tommy had died that morning!

The world crashed around me. It was dark when I found myself back at the quarters we had shared, and midnight before I stopped pacing the room. But there was simply nothing I could do.

In the morning I went to Millbank Street and was informed I should have gone to Bramshott the week before. Having had enough money on hand, since we had been frugal, I had not troubled to go on time for our weekly allowance.

When I reached Bramshott everyone had their medical examination. Most of the officers were absent, but Major Arthur was there. I paraded before him and told him I wanted to revert to ranks. He asked me what was wrong. Twice he had wanted to make me a sergeant and twice I had refused. But each step seemed to me to be a step farther from the comradeship of the ranks. I told him about Tommy, about our nights in London, and at the finish he nodded assent. "You have been unusual-I can't think of another word that suits-but I realize how you feel. You can take down your stripes. Here's a copy of battalion orders that I don't think you've seen. Take it with you." I opened it in our barracks and was amazed. I had been awarded the Military Medal. The citation read:

"Operations at Mons 10/11th November, 1918.

For Courage and Devotion to Duty.

This N.C.O. was in command of a section during the attack on Mons on the night of November 10/11th. When the advance was held up by two enemy machine-gun posts he worked his way forward, and by bringing heavy rifle grenade fire on the posts forced them to withdraw.

He showed great gallantry and initiative throughout."

The award was so unexpected that my emotion was too great for me to go and thank the major. I knew he would not wish it anyway. But how had he known? That was the burning question, and as I thought of it I remembered that Brown had been the only person with me throughout the action. So I hunted him up. He tried to evade me at first, but finally owned that when the major had interviewed several of the platoon at Mons, he had told about my using the rifle grenades.

Two days after I was back with the unit, we set out for Liverpool. The evening before I had been over to Witley Camp to look at the old places, and on the way back, at a bus stop, had heard some shouting. There was a crowd gathered, shouting about the "glass house." I knew what that meant. On the staffs of the Canadian Corps were several with the same mentality and regard for their fellow men as their counterparts in the Prussian divisions; in their view, some poor devil crossing a parade ground at dusk and failing to make a salute to an officer was a criminal, and should be treated like one. It made no difference to them if the soldier, just reading some mail from home, had been too wrapped in thought to notice His Highness. Swift and harsh punishment must be doled out for the good of the army-and was. And if an individual failed a second time to salute his superior, more drastic measures were needed. He was sent to Aldershot, England, for from five to ten days in the "glass house." This place was operated by the British Army and staffed by very large ruffians who lacked all qualities of decency.

One day I met a lad of the 5th C.M.R.s from our Maritimes. I knew him well. He had been a key man on a raid that had cleaned out a German machine-gun post, and he had brought back the gun to prove his case. He was not given any award. There had not been an officer involved, so medals were not considered necessary. He was two days over his leave when he returned to the unit, having served twelve months to get that leave, and was sent to the "glass house" for punishment. He was five feet, seven inches in height and weighed 142 pounds. After his admission, without a word being spoken, a man six feet tall and weighing over two hundred pounds knocked him almost senseless, booting him as he lay on the floor and laughing uproariously. He was knocked down eleven times in one day, knocked unconscious five times during his five days, and had seven teeth knocked out, three by a kick in the mouth as he lay on the floor. Everything was on the double, and no man had more than three minutes in which to wash and shave. As this was impossible, some tried getting up a few minutes early, and were booted back to bed. At least a dozen persons in England promised faithfully to have the "glass house" fully investigated after the war, but evidently the higher-ups thought it a good thing.

This night at the bus stop outside Witley, one of those "glass house" guards got off the bus in civvies, evidently hoping no one would recognize him. Unfortunately for him there were three of his victims on the bus, and all the crowd of soldiers on their way back to Canada knew about the place of torture. There was a great shout. I saw the man start to run. He was calling wildly for the police. A man got alongside and tripped him. He went down with wild yells, but they soon ceased. I could not and did not try to get near. But I saw the shapeless, featureless hulk left on the pavement.

The boys were singing and laughing as the train started for Liverpool, and after a time we pulled into Manchester and stopped. We were told we would be there for over an hour, so we got off. Some women's organization was at the station with cups of tea and small cakes. The boys milled around and a few explored beyond, but the great majority enjoyed the tea and cakes. Manchester folks were there en masse, it seemed, and I had chats with several men in business suits who asked a thousand and one questions about Canada.

We were off again, but for a long time the train simply crawled, as we had to wait at three places to let another train go by. Then the boys began to be uneasy. There were no washrooms on the train, and the cups of tea became a regret. Each passing hour made the lads more desperate. No one could sit still. Then windows were dropped and the boys called from one section to another. There was no passageway on the train-all were in the same predicament. Something had to be done. After much calling back and forth, it was agreed that whereas an individual might get into serious trouble, nothing would be done if the whole battalion committed the same offense. So, at a shout, one half were to find relief at windows on the north side, one half on the south side. The signal came, and a moment later we arrived at Liverpool station!

The situation was beyond description. Organizations of women were awaiting us with tea and buns, and the amazing spectacle that swept into view must be still talked about in the circles of old ladies. We on the south side faced the railway yards and were all right, but those on the north, after bitter moments of indecision, flooded the interior of the cars, both seats and floors, their only care being not to contact a fellow traveller. Our packs were in the racks.

There were many red faces and much laughter. Many boys were only intent on escaping the scene. Then away we went to the dock. We were to return on the *Adriatic*, a very fine boat, and the R.C.R.s were already on board. Filing up the gang plank was a slow process, but to my delight my brother was on the wharf, walking with crutches. He was in hospital in Liverpool and had got leave to see me. There was so much to talk about that the whole battalion was on board, and they were shouting that the gang plank was going up, before I noticed. I just made it, and on deck there was only the faithful Brown. The rest were all below.

"You have surely messed it this time," he said. "There is not one, get it, not one single hammock or cabin or anything left below. I don't know where you can put your pack and rifle. And we've all been issued our meal tickets."

Just then the dinner gong went and away he rushed. I moved over to the rail and waved to my brother, watching a member of the ship's staff who was writing in chalk on the first-class cabin doors: "Two officers," "One officer," etc. He stopped, scanned his list carefully, put the chalk down on a ledge and went below deck. I looked around and saw two doors on my right, opened the first and entered a beautiful stateroom with bath. In seconds I had deposited my rifle and pack, taken the key and locked the door from outside. Then I got the chalk and marked OCCUPIED in large letters, and went down to get a meal ticket.

A dozen fellows asked me curiously what I was going to do for a sleeping place. Each time I shrugged and said I would wait till I was sleepy. There was much hilarity in some of the cabins and we carried on until late. It was a quarter of twelve when I went up on deck, not a person in sight. I unlocked the door and went in, and had a wonderful night's rest.

Not one person knew where I was staying. Everyone was in great spirits and at first the officers did not bother us at all. However, as we went around the deck we saw some of the lieutenants, wonder boys who had arrived in the last five minutes, flirting with a number of nurses who were on board. We saw one bright boy who had joined the regiment in October exhibiting a German helmet and Iron Cross he had purchased from some frontliner, and we wondered what fiction he was circulating. Then, the third morning out, these lads wanted to shine before their admirers, and made a great show of rounding up all the lowly ranks for "exercise."

The lack of desire, sheer stupidity, and awkwardness of the men were so discouraging that the officers decided something really simple would have to be devised. From some quarter they produced three long ropes. We were to have a tug-of-war tourney. Men were simply numbered off with no regard to size, and so it happened I was thrown the end of the rope and told I would be the anchor man. At five feet nine and 170 pounds, I was anything but. However, we lined up, and I suddenly noticed an iron upright just behind me. I tossed a coil of the rope around it and held on to the end. When our team gained a few inches, the gain was held, as the loop around the upright was firm. But when the other team tugged with might and main they could not gain an inch. So they were declared losers. We pulled the third team in the same way. This caused the officer in charge of the other team to come and investigate our prowess. His team out-weighed us by at least three hundred pounds. What he saw filled him with disgust. "I'm through," he roared. "We can't do anything with this type of fellow."

So we were freed from their attentions and enjoyed the rest of the trip. On the evening of our last night out, our emotions ruled us, turning us to a riot of horseplay. We wrestled and made mock speeches. Then we gradually quieted, each man with his own thoughts. Everyone watched for a chance to leave without having to say farewells.

In my fine sheets I could not sleep and began to forget where I was. I seemed to be in an atmosphere rancid with stale sweat and breathing, the hot grease of candles, the dampness of the underground. I saw cheeks resting on tunics, mud-streaked, unshaven faces. . . men shivering on chicken-wire bunks. Then, from overhead, the machine-gun's note louder, higher, sharper as it swept bullets over the shell crater in which I hugged the earth. . . the rumble of guttural voices and heavy steps in an unseen trench just the other side of the black mass of tangled wire beside which I lay. . the long-drawn whine of a coming shell. . . its heart-shaking explosion. . the seconds of heavy silence after, then the first low wail of the man down with a blood-spurting wound. . . It was too much. I got up and dressed, although it was only four o'clock in the morning.

It was cold but I wore my greatcoat, and to my amazement there were other dark figures near the rail. We stood, hunched together, gazing ahead into the darkness. Presently another figure joined us, then another. In an hour there were fourteen of us, and no one had spoken, although we were touching shoulders. The way we stood made me think of a simile. Ah-we were like prisoners. I had seen them standing together, staring over the wire to the field beyond, never speaking. And we were more or less prisoners of our thoughts. Those at home would never understand us, because something inexplicable would make us unable to put our feelings into words. We could only talk with one another.

All at once the watchers stirred, tensed, craned forward. It was the moment for which we had lived, which we had envisioned a thousand times, that held us so full of feeling we could not find utterance. Far ahead, faint, but growing brighter, we had glimpsed the first lights of home!

Epilogue

My diary is sketchy and has many omissions, but it still gives me thrills to read it. How different things might have been, had there been no Simms or Fordley at the beginning, I will never know. The sergeant-major, like many of his kind, dodged going to France; but some lads, angered beyond caring by his treatment, left him lying unconscious on a station platform when their draft left for the front.

In the years since 1918, the pain of war memories has been eased by many contacts with old wartime friends. Brigadier E. A. Anderson, who was present the morning they found me in the ruins of Petit Vimy and heard the story of Steve pulling me from the bivvy in the railway embankment, became City Clerk of Moncton, New Brunswick. He drove to Amherst, Nova Scotia, to visit me on two different occasions and was immensely interesting to talk with. In an Ontario town I was thrilled to see our old platoon sergeant, Turner, in an audience, and had a great visit with him.

The gas I absorbed the night I gave Harry Hayward my gas mask gave me a bad time in the early twenties. Finally I had to sit for a week with my arm in a strong solution, as it was greatly swollen. The doctor said he might have to amputate. During the time I read everything I could get my hands on. So it happened that a copy of the Halifax *Sunday Leader* came into my possession. The front page carried an offer of twenty-five dollars cash for the best fish story. I had never written anything but got some stiff cardboard and a pencil, and with my left hand composed a story. Mrs. Bird corrected the grammar, typed it and sent it in. Back came the first-prize money and an urgent invitation for me to go to Halifax at the expense of the *Leader* for an interview with the editor. Down I went and was delighted to discover the editor was Perry Giffen, afterwards with the Peterborough *Examiner,* a grand gentleman whom I had last seen on a stretcher at Vimy. Thus began my writing career.

In 1931 the late H. Napier Moore, then editor of *Maclean*'s , asked me to revisit the battlefields and write a series of stories on them as they were "thirteen years after." The depression was in full swing, so I jumped at the chance. When my articles appeared I was flooded with letters, over five thousand of them, far too many to try and answer. Then the Canadian Legion branches of many towns and cities asked me to visit them and tell the story of what the old front lines now looked like. In all, I visited 106 branches of the Legion and met old wartime friends in many places. At Stratford, Ontario, there were four hundred in the audience. A strike was on at a furniture factory and there had been so many threats of violence that a unit of the military was called to the scene. And in command was Lieutenant-Colonel Fordley! When I heard his name I promptly said I hoped he would be at the meeting, so that I could have him explain when an order posted in front of a colonel's office is not an order. Unfortunately, someone at the Legion branch I visited in the morning heard the story, and took the trouble to hunt up Fordley and inform him he was in for a surprise. Naturally he did not attend the meeting.

In 1932 I had a long letter from Wilson, who had been with me in the house ruin when Lieutenant Crood so nearly got us killed by shell fire. Wilson was living in Sudbury, and full of kind words regarding the experiences we had together.

There was a large crowd when I spoke at Kingston, Ontario and after the meeting

I was told that a gentleman in a car by the curb wanted to speak to me. It was some distance from a light. The gentleman shook my hand, put his head back and gave a military order as if on parade. "Who am I?" he asked. To be candid or not to be? I took my courage in hand. "Batty Mac, sir," I said. He grabbed my hand again and roared with delight. It was Macdonell, who had commanded our 7th Brigade before going to take over the lst Division. I simply had to get into the car with him and he took me to his home. There we talked until after two in the morning, and his knowledge of the abilities and idiosyncrasies of the officers of the 42nd was simply amazing.

In the 1940's, *Blue Book* offered a large cash prize for the "Best True Experience of World War I." I wrote a complete account of the night I had to go into the German trench and grabbed the sentry's rain cape as it caught on my revolver, thus getting something with which to disguise my Canadian helmet when the three members of the German listening post came pushing past me. It won me the prize over many entries from both Canada and the U.S.A.

One night in the twenties as I sat at the dinner table, something seemed to crackle in my ear. All at once I was hearing the words of the shepherd boy from Hawes as he counted the shells dropping near where we huddled in the mud of Passchendaele. I suddenly recited them to my surprised family. And in 1952 when at Cupar, Fife, in Scotland, I met a fine old gentleman who was one of the heads of the sugar beet industry in that area. He invited us to his house for dinner, a great stone edifice over two hundred years old. During conversation at the table he informed me he had a hobby. He had attended sheep dog trials in both England and Scotland and was collecting the unique terms used by the shepherds in counting sheep. They were largely in dialect, and very interesting. His one disappointment, he said, was the dialect spoken by the shepherds from Hawes. They were extremely reticent, and their speech too difficult to distinguish.

"Get your pencil and paper, sir," I said, "and I will give you the count in Hawes." He stared at a Canadian talking about Hawes, but got the pencil, and I gave him: "Yan, tean, tether, mether, pip, cesar, azar, castra, horna, dick, yan-a-dick, tean-a-dick, tether-a-dick, mether-a-dick, bumfit, yan-a-bum, tean-a-bum, tether-a-bum, mether-a-bum, jigget." So I had to explain when and where I had learned to count to twenty in Hawes.

One of the many letters I received during 1932 was from a lad in Calgary who had served with a Lewis gun crew in "C" Company of the 42nd. He was an excellent soldier and a better than average type of man. It was a long letter. He said he had wanted for years to talk with someone from the unit who would understand him. One night "C" Company was responsible for losing the only man the Germans ever got by raiding our trenches. The Lewis gunner was on a post used to defend our flying patrols on that particular front. It was a dark, raw night, and he and his crew had a good trench and a fine field of fire. Suddenly they saw a German patrol of from ten to twelve men just in front and going toward the left. At such short range it would have been comparatively easy to eradicate the Germans with one sweep of machine-gun fire, as there was no cover at that point. But one of those inexplicable things happened. A sudden inertia, or some other thing impossible to explain, seized them. Not a man in the post made a move. They simply stood and watched until the Germans had passed by and were lost in the darkness. Then, a few minutes later, they heard the sounds of fighting and knew the Germans were a raiding party. It would have been easy for them to slip out from their post and get between the raiders and their line of retreat, but again the incredible happened. They simply stayed where they were and made no move whatever. And it was twenty minutes later, he wrote, before they shook themselves from the sort of coma that had held them. Now he wanted to make amends.

I wrote him that many, probably dozens of men, had acted similarly under like conditions; that I had lain in a part of our no man's land and watched a German officer crawl away when I could have shot him simply by pulling the trigger; and that he was not to let such thoughts bother him. The war was history and belonged to the past. No one had been killed through his lapse, and there was no need of any remorse. He wrote again and thanked me for my letter, saying it had helped him greatly.

One night a week later the doorbell rang, and there stood Major Ralph Willcock, one of the greatest soldiers and gentlemen in the 3rd Division. We had a wonderful session that night, recounting experiences and unit episodes, and he said he was satisfied with his record except for one night: the night the Germans took a prisoner on "C" Company's front. He had been over the area personally and had been reasonably sure the enemy could not get an opportunity to raid a post. He could not explain how the Germans had got so near without being seen. I listened attentively as he went over the circumstances, then handed him the letter from the lad in Calgary. He read it, reread it, jumped up and paced the floor, finally took his seat again and asked if he could have the letter. Most certainly, I said, and he told me he would make a trip to Calgary to see the Lewis gunner, that he admired his courage in writing me as he had done, and would now have a real peace of mind regarding that particular night.

After I returned from the war, there began to seem no way in the world to get my souvenirs back. Orders had been that nothing was to be carried in our packs but army issues. The story ran that all packs would be searched. So I had to be content with getting no more than my diaries out of France. Then came the trip for *Maclean's* and again fortune smiled her brightest. At Vimy Ridge was a gentleman of the engineers, Major Simpson, and he was kindness itself. When I mentioned my problem, he told me he could ship anything from France to any organization, but not to an individual. So he made a large strong box that would hold everything, and I became at that moment the President of the Frontliners' Association of Nova Scotia. The box was shipped to me at Amherst. The contents went on display in many towns and cities on Remembrance Day, and are now in the Military Museum on Citadel Hill, Halifax.

One of the letters I received was from an R.C.R. who had been drafted into that unit against his will. He told me of a day I well remembered. The 42nd had come out of the line after a miserable four days of rain and cold and mud. We had a decent billet on a hill, and in the morning the sun shone in full warmth as if repenting for previous weather. We all sprawled out on the hillside, unshaven, most of us scraping mud from our puttees and boots, some with our shirts off chasing seam squirrels. On our left a road ran down to a flat area in front. On the far side of the road the Royal Canadian Regiment was drawn up in order, belts white with blanco, bayonets glistening from sandpaper applications, all brass aglitter. In the frontal area the engineers had dug something that looked like a cellar. A neat wooden stairway led down into it, and there was a tangle of barbed wire across the far side from the steps.

Our camp was on a sort of peninsula. On our right another road came down and joined the one on the left. As we lolled in the sunshine a cavalcade of motor cars came into view on the road at our right. There was a pennant on the first car. The boys stared, and one made the announcement: "That there is George Vee."

There was no question but that he was right. And no question either regarding the fact that the driver had made a mistake in the roads, and instead of taking the royal party past the glittering R.C.R.'s, had taken it past a horde of dirty, unkempt, unshaven, louse-hunting Forty-Twas. We watched with interest as the party reached the place the engineers had excavated. His Majesty stepped from his car, walked to the wooden stairway and descended into the phony shell crater. There he stood while an attending officer removed the royal headgear and replaced it with a steel helmet. A carload of photographers swarmed to the place, and the officer gently posed the King so that he was apparently looking over the top where the barbed wire dominated. Next week one of the boys who had relatives in London received a copy of the Daily Mirror. Its front page featured a picture showing the King at the front. He was actually looking, the caption said, over no man's land.

In my series "Thirteen Years After," I told about the tall Australian prisoner who had prevented a fellow from shooting the fleeing German commandant, so that French civilians could get at the Hun with clubs and pitchforks. In some manner a copy of that issue *of Maclean s* was placed among a pile of reading matter going on a ship to Sydney, Australia. A women's organization in Sydney collected reading material and sent it to isolated areas. So I was much surprised to receive a long letter from that tall Australian who had been a prisoner. He said he had received a dog-eared copy of Maclean's with the story in it while leading an anthropological expedition along a remote coast in Tasmania. It was a most interesting letter, telling much of what had happened at the prison camp. He signed himself as a "Peripatetic Anthropologist."

When I had begun writing for a living, I remembered the grim old French woman who had showed us the German officer in her cellar, decapitated by her half-wit son. She had made much of the fact that at long last she had her revenge on the Germans. The more I thought about her, the more I became convinced that when the Hun had invaded France in 1870, she had been one of the fine young French girls who were raped by German soldiers. The French version of the invasion stresses such happenings, and the old woman was of the age to make it a possibility. The half-wit could very well have been the product of the outrage. And what greater revenge than to have him kill a German invader of his generation? Re-creating the setting in accurate detail and describing the old woman and her son exactly as they had been, I wrote a story that was purchased by American, Canadian and British magazines, and starred in *O'Brien's Best Stories.*

One last story will round out this personal account of the war. A party of old crocks used as Pioneers was sent to an isolated area in Belgium during the last weeks of the fighting. No newspapers reached them and they knew nothing of the war until the morning after the signing of the Armistice, when a dapper British officer arrived, fell in the party, adjusted his monocle and read a copy of the all-important cease-fire message in grave and impressive tone. After he had finished there was a heavy silence, then an old Cockney stepped forward and saluted. "Beg pardon, sir," he said, "but 'oo's won?"

William Richard Bird
1891-1984.

Will Bird was born in Mapleton, Nova Scotia, May 11, 1891. He was the first son of Stephen Bird, by his second wife, Augusta (nee Bird), of Amherst, Nova Scotia. He was preceded by his two half-brothers, Harry (1885) and Hubert (1886), from his father's first wife. In 1893 a fourth Bird brother, Lew, was born.

In December 1895, with Augusta 4 months pregnant, tragedy struck the family when their father, Stephen died suddenly. Five months after Stephen Bird's death, Augusta gave birth to another son, a namesake for her late husband, Stephen Carmen.

Later that year Augusta Bird moved back to her hometown of Amherst bringing with her the 5 year old Will, Lew, the baby Stephen and the two sons from the late Stephen's previous marriage, Hubert and Harry.

The younger boys were educated in Amherst, at the High School and later Stephen went to work for the Canada Car Company. Both Will and Stephen competed in athletics, were keen baseball players and "red-hot" fans of both baseball and hockey. The two were very close, shared mutual likes and dislikes and "could read each other's minds".

With the outbreak of war in 1914, Stephen enlisted as a Corporal in the 25th Nova Scotia Battalion. Will also rushed to join the Colours but Stephen, using his influence, had Will turned down. Disheartened Will went to the Prairies to farm. In May 1915 the 25th Battalion sailed for England.

The 25th Battalion went to France in mid-September 1915 and occupied trenches at Kemmel, just south of Ypres, Belgium. On September 25th the inexperienced men of the 25th suffered their first fatality. Just before 5 pm on October 8, 1915 the Germans blew a large, underground explosive charge beneath the 25th's frontline trenches. The explosion created a hole 65 feet by 35 feet and 25 feet deep. It had killed 2 men outright, wounded 20, and 10 men were listed as "missing".

That same October found Will bringing in the harvest on a small farm in Saskatchewan, pitching sheaves into a wagon, when Stephen walked out from behind a farmcart ! They did not speak and soon Stephen vanished. Three days later Will received official notification that Stephen Bird, was missing, presumed dead in the mine explosion. His body was never found.

The well-liked Stephen had been popular amongst his comrades and one wrote to the Bird family after his death; "He had splendid courage and when urged to fall back a little further a few minutes before the explosion his reply was 'I am staying right here' ".

Another wrote "He was a friend at all times and under all circumstances, no one need wish a better friend, we all loved him and we all mourn his loss". No one mourned his loss more than Will.

Will returned to Amherst and in April 1916 enlisted in the 193rd Battalion, Nova Scotia Highlanders. The 193rd Battalion was a locally-raised battalion and the men who comprised its ranks were all from the area and included Hubert Bird, Will's half brother. (The number block allocated to the 193rd Nova Scotia Highlanders was 901001 to 904000, Will Bird's service number was 901552).

In October 1916 the 193rd sailed for England. Upon arrival it was broken up for reinforcements and Will Bird and a number of his friends were shipped to France to reinforce the 42nd Battalion, The Black Watch of Canada, in the frontline. On January 5, 1917 the men from Nova Scotia joined the kilted Montrealers in the trenches in front of the infamous Vimy Ridge.

The 42nd had served in France since 1915 and had fought in the major battles of Mount Sorrel and the Somme when Will joined them in late 1916. Throughout the war the Black Watch fought with exceptional ferocity and success. By the end of the war 800 men had been killed and 2000 wounded of the 6000 men who passed through the ranks of the battalion. Shortages of reinforcements from Montreal brought many men from across Canada into their ranks and this is how Will Bird ended up with the Montrealers.

Will Bird served with the 42nd Battalion throughout the war until demobilized back in Canada in March 1919. He was awarded a Military Medal for bravery in the capture of Mons, on the night of 10-11 November 1918, the last night of the war.

Will returned to Southampton, Nova Scotia and in 1919, married Ethel Sutton, his childhood sweetheart and had 2 children, Stephen Stanley in 1920 and Betty in 1923. The family moved to Amherst in 1923 and later to Halifax.

Like many veterans Will did not know which way to go after the war but through some good fortune and good writing found a career in journalism. During the 1930's his First World War memoir "And We Go On" was published, followed by a series of articles on visiting the old battlefields for Macleans magazine. The two publications brought Will into prominence in the burgeoning remembrance movement brought about by the aging veterans in the 1930's.

Will Bird was a prolific writer on many topics: fiction, non-fiction, books, magazines, articles, newspapers, columns and short stories. Over the years he became a literary presence in his native Nova Scotia.

The years took a toll on the many who survived the war. In 1939, Will's half brother Hubert, who had lost a leg at the Drocourt-Queant line, died. But the hardest blow came in 1944 when his son, Stephen was killed in Normandy. He was 24. Captain Stephen Stanley Bird of the North Nova Scotia Highlanders was killed in action July 8, 1944. He is buried in Beny-sur-Mer Canadian War Cemetery, France. Will often blamed his writing about his war experiences as a factor in his son's rush to enlist.

The road continued to take its toll and in 1977 his half brother, Harry died and in 1982, his beloved Ethel passed away. Will followed her in 1984.

Will Bird is survived by his daughter, Betty Murray, of Amherst and 4 grandchildren. Stephen McKay Murray carries on the name and will never have to suffer the fate of his namesakes.

GLOSSARY OF NAMES

ALWAY Lance Corporal Arthur Alway, of Gloucester, England. Killed in action 31 October 1917.

Captain ARTHUR Major William Arthur Grafftey, MC, of Westmount, Montreal, Quebec, wounded.

BABER Lieutenant Walter Crosbie Baber, of Montreal, wounded. Died at Montreal, 1959.

Mel BAILLIE Private Melville McKay Bailey, of Nokomis, Saskatchewan. Killed in action 2 November 1917.

BARRON Sergeant Wilton Havelock Barron, MM, of Hantsport, Nova Scotia, born in Canada, wounded twice. Died at Hamilton, Ontario, 1957.

Roy BAXTER Private Roy Raymond Baxter, of Truemanville, Nova Scotia, born in Canada.

BELLIVEAU Private Frederic Joseph Belliveau, of Joggin Mines, Nova Scotia. Killed in action 9 April 1917.

BINKS Lance Corporal Norman Binks, of Yorkshire, England, wounded. Drowned 1924.

Hubert BIRD Private Hubert Craige Bird, of Athol, Nova Scotia, wounded. Died Amherst, N.S., 1939.

Steve BIRD Corporal Stephen Carman Bird, of Amherst, Nova Scotia. Killed in action 8 October 1915. Age 19.

Earl BLACK Private Earl William Black, of Amherst, Nova Scotia, wounded twice.

Herman BLACK Private N. Herman Black, of Oxford, Nova Scotia. Killed in action 9 April 1917.

Ira BLACK Private Ira Garnet Black, of Valley Road, Nova Scotia. Killed in action 2 November 1917. Age 25.

BOLAND Private Bert Young Boland, of Eganville, Ontario. Killed in action 12 August 1918. Age 21.

Bill BROWN Private William Henry Brown, of Nortonville, Nova Scotia.

BUNTY Private Francis Alvin Bunt, of Collingwood, Ontario, wounded.

Arthur BURKE Private Arthur Silas Burke, of Sackville, New Brunswick. Died of wounds 24 March 1917.

Sam BURNET Private Samuel Burnet, of River Hebert, Nova Scotia. Died at Halifax, 1952.

BURNETT Private Joseph Burnett. Killed in action 3 November 1917.

Leon CASEY Private Leon Melville Casey., of Amherst, N.S. Killed in action 29 September 1918.

Sergeant Jim CAVE Lieutenant Jordayne Wymarus Cave, MC, of Cork, Ireland.

Bill CHILDS Private William Henry Childs, of Toronto, Ontario. Born 1881.

CHRISTENSON Private Robert Christenson, of Hillerod, Denmark. Killed in action 8 August 1918.

Nobby CLARK Sergeant Harry James Clark, MM, of Montreal, Quebec. Killed in action 2 November 1917.

COCKBURN Private William Brown Cockburn, of Killinliloch, Scotland. Killed in action 8 August 1918. Age 25.

CRAIG Lieutenant Mathew Kerr Craig, of Kilmarnock, Scotland, wounded twice.

CROOD Lieutenant Meyer Tutzer Cohen, MC, of Toronto, Ontario. Killed in action 3 November 1917.

Eddie CUVILLIER Sergeant Edward Leo Cuvillier, MM, of Amherst, N.S. Killed in action 8 August 1918. Age 22.

Sgt Jimmy DAVIES Company Sergeant Major James Lancaster Davies, DCM, MM, of London, England. Died in New Zealand, 1949.

DINESEN, VC Private Thomas Dinesen, VC, of Copenhagen, Denmark. Died at Copenhagen, 1974.

DYKES Private James Dykes, of Bonny Bridge, Scotland. Killed in action 15 November 1917. Age 26.

EGGLESTONE Private Charles Alfred Egglestone, of Leeds, England. Killed in action 4 November 1917. Age 19.

FARMER Private Allan Sidney Farmer, of Kirks Ferry, Quebec. Killed in action 3 November 1917. Age 21.

FERNLEY Private Egerton Fernley, of Saskatoon, Saskatchewan. Killed in action 8 February 1917. Age 32.

FERRIS Private Daniel Ferris, of New York City, U.S.A.

FLYNN Private Timothy Flinn, Of Cork, Ireland. Killed in action 5 November 1917. Age 34.

Ab FORDHAM Sergeant Albert George Fordham, MM, of Essex, England, wounded twice.

Gerald GARD Private Gerald Gard, of Amherst, Nova Scotia.

GILROY Private Lloyd Curtis Gilroy, of Spring Hill, Nova Scotia. Killed in action 9 April 1917. Age 19.

Howard GORDON Private Howard Carleton Gordon, of Oxford, Nova Scotia. Killed in action 16 November 1917. Age 22.

GRANT Private H. Grant, wounded, prisoner-of-war.

Barney GUINEY Corporal Burnie Guiney, of Renfrew, Ontario. Died at St. Catharines, 1957.

HALDANE Private James Haldane, of Quinsey, Massachsets. Killed in action 12 August 1918. Age 29.

Captain HALE Captain William Hale, MC, of Gananoque, Ontario, wounded.

Charlie HALE Private Charles William Hale, of Westville, Nova Scotia, wounded.

HANSEN Private Karl Godtfred Hansen, of Denmark.

HARVEY Private John Albert Harvey. Killed in action 26 August 1918. Age 18.

Harry HAYWARD Private Harry Alexander Hayward, of Amherst, Nova Scotia, wounded.

Red HERRON Sergeant J.L. Herron, MM, of Forrester Falls, Ontario.
HICKEY Private David J. Hickey, of St. John's, Newfoundland. Killed in action 31 October 1917. Age 22.
Jimmy HUGHES Corporal James William Hughes. Died of wounds 26 August 1918.
Walter JACKSON Private Walter Tupper Jackson, MM, of Tidnish, Nova Scotia.
Charlie JENKINS Private Charles Wentworth Jenkins, of Joggin Mines, Nova Scotia. Killed in action 9 April 1917. Age 24.
JENNINGS Private Joseph Henry Jennings, of Warwick, England. Killed in action 2 November 1917. Age 37.
JOE Private Alexander L. Sonier, Killed in action 8 June 1917.
Bob JONES Lance Corporal Bernard Robert Jones, of Staffordshire, England. Killed in action 10 November 1918. Age 29.
CSM KENNEDY Company Sergeant Major W. Kennedy, DCM, MM, of Dalbeatie, Scotland. Died of wounds 18 November 1917. Age 35.
Lorne KENNEDY Corporal L. Kennedy, wounded twice.
Melvin KIDD Private Melvin Ralph Kidd, of Merlin, Ontario.
LALONDE Private J.H. Lalonde.
Lieutenant LARSON Lieutenant Kenneth Archibald Campbell. Killed in action 23 January 1917. Age 24.
LAURIE Private Laurie Bedford Bacon, of Nappan Station, Nova Scotia, born in Canada, wounded. Died Amherst, Nova Scotia, 1958.
LEGGE Private William Henry Legge, of Scott's Bay, Nova Scotia. Killed in action 9 April 1917.
Art LESLIE Private Arthur William Leslie, MM, of Apple River, Nova Scotia.
LOCKERBIE Private Douglas William Lockerbie. Killed in action 14 August 1918.
LUGAR Private A.W. Luggar, wounded.
Glenn LUNN Private Glendon Isaac Lunn, of Advocate Harbour, Nova Scotia. Killed in action 2 November 1917. Age 25.
McDONALD Private Alexander McDonald. Killed in action 25 April 1917. Age 19.
Lieutenant MacDONALD Lieutenant S. MacDonald, wounded.
Charlie MacDONALD Private Charles MacDonald, of Montreal, Quebec.
RSM Percy MacFARLANE Regimental Sergeant Major Percy William MacFarlane, DCM, of Montreal, Quebec, wounded twice. Died at Montreal, 1949.
McINTYRE Lieutenant Robert McIntyre, MC, MM, of Montreal, Quebec. Killed in action 3 November 1917, wounded 3 times. Age 33.
Hugh MacKINNON Private John Hugh MacKinnon, of Eureka, Nova Scotia.
Lt Col Bartlett Mc LENNAN, DSO, of Montreal, Quebec. Killed in action 3 August 1918. Age 49.
Capt McLEOD Captain James Duncan McLeod, MC, wounded. Died 1928.

Lance Corporal K.K. MacLEOD Kenneth Keith MacLeod, of Fraser Ridge, Ontario. Died of wounds 5 November 1917.

Roy MacMILLAN Corporal Peter Roy MacMillan. Died of wounds 10 April 1917. Age 24.

McPHEE Lance Corporal W.J. McPhee, MM, wounded.

Joe McPHERSON Private Joseph Alexander McPherson, of Calgary, Alberta. Killed in action 9 April 1917.

MEDICAL SERGEANT Sergeant Charles Albert Owston, DCM, MM, of Liverpool, England. Killed in action 9 April 1917.

MICKEY Private Daniel McGillivary, of Doctor's Bank, Nova Scotia. Died of wounds 17 November 1917. Age 33.

Jim MILLS Private J. Mills, of Montreal, Quebec, wounded.

MILLS Private Thomas Mills, of Montreal, Quebec. Killed in action 10 November 1918. Age 23.

Roy MURRAY Private R. Murray.

NEATH Corporal Ernest Neath, of Westville, Nova Scotia.

NORTON Private Herbert Stanley Norton, of Alliston, Ontario, wounded.

OLD DUNDEE Private Alonzo Crammer Gilbert, of Parrsboro, Nova Scotia. Died of wounds 23 January 1917. Age 26.

ORMANDY Sergeant Glen W. Ormandy, MM, of Brantford, Ontario.

ORR Sergeant Andrew Orr, of Montreal.

H.J.PEARCE Private H.J. Pearce, wounded.

PEEPLES Private Chester Garfield Peeples, of Hartford, Conneticut, wounded.

REES Private Alfred Thomas Rees, of St. John, New Brunswick.

RUSSELL Private William John Russell, DCM, MM, of Victoria Village, Newfoundland.

Gordon SEDGEWICK Private Gordon Sedgewick, of Toronto, Ontario. Killed in action 28 September 1918. Age 21.

Sammy SEDGEWICK Corporal Samuel George Sedgewick, of Toronto, Ontario, wounded twice.

SIDDALL Private Charles Harold Siddall. Killed in action 13 August 1918. Age 29.

SIMMS Private F. Simms, wounded.

SLIM Private William James Good. Killed in action 8 June 1917. Age 18.

Corporal STEVENSON Corporal Alexander Douglas Stevenson. Killed in action 9 April 1917. Age 42.

STEWART Private Robert Alexander Stewart. Killed in action 2 November 1917. Age 34.

Lieutenant STEWART Lieutenant Robert William Stewart. Died of wounds 25 March 1917. Age 26.

STUDHOLME Sergeant F.R. Studholme, MM, wounded.

SYKES Private Sam Sykes. Killed in action 28 August 1918.

Sgt Geordie TAYLOR Company Quarter Master Sergeant G. Taylor, wounded twice.

THORNTON Private John Thomas Thornton. Killed in action 12 August 1918. Age 20.

TULLOCH Private John Sewell Tulloch. Died of wounds 28 August 1918. Age 28.

UPHAM Private Arthur Douglas Upham. Died of wounds 18 November 1917. Age 19.

WALDVOGEL (WATERBOTTLE) Lance Corporal John Waldvogel, MM, of Wisconsin, U.S.A., wounded.

WESTCOTT Lance Corporal Frederick Gilbert Westcott, of Somerset, England. Killed in action 9 April 1917. Age 23.

Ralph WILLCOCK Major Ralph Willcock, DSO, MC, wounded.

WILLIAMS Private J.E. Williams, MM.

Sgt Jim WILLIAMSON Sergeant James Williamson, DCM, of Montreal, Quebec, wounded. Died at Montreal, 1935.

Ross YOUNG Sergeant R.E. Young, DCM, wounded.